JAMSA'S

C/C++

PROGRAMMER'S BIBLE

The Ultimate Guide to C/C++ Programming

By Kris Jamsa, Ph.D.
and Lars Klander

JAMSA
PRESS
...a computer user's best friend®

Published by
Jamsa Press
2975 S. Rainbow Blvd., Suite I
Las Vegas, NV 89102
U.S.A.

http://www.jamsa.com

For information about the translation or distribution of any Jamsa Press book, please write to Jamsa Press at the address listed above.

Jamsa's C/C++ Programmer's Bible

Printed in the United States of America.
98765432

ISBN 1-884133-25-8

Publisher	**Technical Advisor**	**Director of Publishing Operations**
Debbie Jamsa	Phil Schmauder	Janet Lawrie
Content Manager	**Cover Photograph**	**Cover Design**
Todd Peterson	O'Gara/Bissell	Marianne Helm
		James Rehrauer
Composition	**Illustrators**	**Copy Editors**
Eugene Marks	Eugene Marks	Ann Edwards
James Rehrauer	James Rehrauer	Dorothy Oppenheimer
Nelson Yee	Nelson Yee	Renée Wesberry
Proofers	**Indexer**	**Technical Editors**
Rosemary Pasco	John Bianchi	C.J. Bockmann
Jeanne K. Smith		LingYan Tang

This book identifies product names and services known to be trademarks or registered trademarks of their respective companies. They are used throughout this book in an editorial fashion only. In addition, terms suspected of being trademarks or service marks have been appropriately capitalized. Jamsa Press cannot attest to the accuracy of this information. Use of a term in this book should not be regarded as affecting the validity of any trademark or service mark.

The information and material contained in this book are provided "as is," without warranty of any kind, express or implied, including, without limitation, any warranty concerning the accuracy, adequacy, or completeness of such information or material or the results to be obtained from using such information or material. Neither Jamsa Press nor the author shall be responsible for any claims attributable to errors, omissions, or other inaccuracies in the information or material contained in this book, and in no event shall Jamsa Press or the author be liable for direct, indirect, special, incidental, or consequential damages arising out of the use of such information or material.

This publication is designed to provide accurate and authoritative information in regard to the subject matter covered. It is sold with the understanding that the publisher is not engaged in rendering professional service or endorsing particular products or services. If legal advice or other expert assistance is required, the services of a competent professional should be sought.

Jamsa Press is a wholly-owned subsidiary of Gulf Publishing Company:

Gulf Publishing Company
Book Division
P.O. Box 2608
Houston, TX 77252-2608
U.S.A.

http://www.gulfpub.com

Table of Contents

III

MACROS AND CONSTANTS

UNDERSTANDING STRINGS

FUNCTIONS

KEYBOARD OPERATIONS

MATH

FILES, DIRECTORIES, AND DISKS

V

ARRAYS, POINTERS, AND STRUCTURES

DOS and BIOS Services

Memory Management

Date and Time

REDIRECTING I/O AND PROCESSING COMMAND-LINES

PROGRAMMING TOOLS

ADVANCED C

GETTING STARTED WITH C++

OBJECTS

X

INHERITANCE AND POLYMORPHISM

GENERIC FUNCTIONS AND TEMPLATES

EXCEPTION HANDLING AND TYPE PORTABILITY

XIII

XIV

AN INTRODUCTION TO PROGRAMMING · C1

Computer programs, also known as *software*, are made up of a series of instructions that the computer executes. When you create a program, you must specify the instructions that the computer must execute to perform the desired operations. The process of defining the instructions the computer is to execute is known as *programming*. When you create a program, you store the instructions in an ASCII file whose name usually contains the extension C for a C program and CPP for a C++ program. For example, if you create a C program that performs payroll operations, you might name the file containing the program instructions *payroll.c*. When you create programs, you specify the desired instructions using a *programming language*. C and C++ are only two of many programming languages. Many programmers use programming languages such as BASIC, Pascal, and FORTRAN. Different programming languages provide unique features and have their own strengths (and weaknesses). In any case, programming languages exist to let us define the instructions that we want the computer to execute.

The instructions a computer executes are actually sets of 1's and 0's (binary digits) that represent electronic signals that occur inside the computer. To program the earliest computers (in the 1940s and 1950s), programmers had to understand how the computer interpreted different combinations of 1's and 0's because the programmers wrote all their programs using binary digits. As programs became larger, it became very impractical to make programmers work in terms of the computer's 1's and 0's. Instead, researchers created programming languages that let people express the computer instructions in a form more meaningful to humans. After programmers placed their instructions in a file (called a *source file*), a second program (called a *compiler*), converted the programming language instructions into the 1's and 0's (known as *machine code*) the computer understood. The files on your disk with the EXE and COM extensions contain the machine code (1's and 0's) the computer will execute. Figure 1 illustrates the process of compiling a source code file into an executable program.

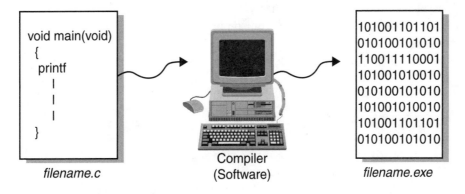

Figure 1 A compiler converts source code instructions into machine code.

After you create a source code file, you run a compiler to convert the instructions into a format the computer can execute. If you are using, for example, Borland's *Turbo C++ Lite™* (included on the companion CD-ROM that accompanies this book), you will use the Compile menu Compile to OBJ option to invoke the compiler (that is, instruct it to compile the source file). The following Tips walk you through the steps required to create and compile a C program.

CREATING AN ASCII SOURCE FILE · C2

When you create a program, you must place the program statements that you want the computer to execute in a file called a *source file*. If you are not using *Turbo C++ Lite* or a full-featured compiler and editor, you should create your program files using an ASCII editor, such as the EDIT program that DOS provides. You should not create programs using a word processor (such as Microsoft *Word*® or Corel's *WordPerfect*®). As you know, word processors let you format documents by aligning margins, italicizing and underlining text, and so on. To perform these operations, word processors embed special characters within your documents. Although these characters are meaningful to your word processor, they will confuse the compiler that converts your source file to machine code, and this confusion will cause errors. When you create your source file, make sure you assign a meaningful name that accurately describes the program's function to the file. For example, you might name the source code for a billing program *billing.c*, and the source file for a game program *football.c*.

If, on the other hand, you are using a compiler that includes a built-in editor, you should create your programs within that editor. For example, if you are using *Turbo C++ Lite*, you will use the File menu New option to create a new program file. To create your first program within *Turbo C++ Lite*, perform the following steps:

1. Select the File menu New option. *Turbo C++ Lite* will create the *noname00.cpp* file.

2. Enter the following code into the *noname00.cpp* window:

```c
#include <stdio.h>
void main(void)
 {
    printf ("Jamsa\'s C/C++ Programmer\'s Bible!");
 }
```

3. Select the File menu Save As option. *Turbo C++ Lite* will display the Save File As dialog box.

4. Within the Save File As dialog box, enter the name *first.c* and press ENTER. *Turbo C++ Lite* will save the *first.c* program file.

Although the *first.c* program contains six lines, only the *printf* statement actually performs any work. When you execute this program, *printf* will display the message *Jamsa's C/C++ Programmer's Bible!* on your screen. Every programming language (just like languages such as English, French, and German) has a set of rules, called *syntax rules*, which you must follow when you use the language. When you create C programs, you must obey the syntax rules of the C programming languages. Examples of syntax rules include the parentheses that follow the name *main* and the semicolon at the end of the *printf* instruction. When you type in your program, you must be very careful that you do not omit any of these elements. Double-check your typing to ensure that you have successfully typed in the C program instructions exactly as they appear earlier. If the instructions are correct, save the contents of the file to your disk. In the next Tip you will learn how to compile your source file and to convert your C programming instructions to the machine language that your computer can understand and execute.

3 COMPILING YOUR C PROGRAM

In the previous Tip you created the C source file, *first.c*, which contains the *printf* statement that will display the message *Jamsa's C/C++ Programmer's Bible!* on your screen when you execute the program. A source file contains instructions in a format you can understand (or at least you will be able to understand after you learn C). An executable program, on the other hand, contains instructions expressed as 1's and 0's that the computer understands. The process of converting your C source file to machine code is known as *compiling*. Depending on the C compiler you are using, the command you must perform to compile your source file will differ. Assuming you are using Borland's *Turbo C++ Lite*, you can compile the program (*first.c*) that you created in Tip 2, using the following command sequence:

1. Select the Compile menu Build All option. *Turbo C++ Lite* will display the Compiling dialog box.

2. If the compiler successfully completes the compilation, it will prompt you to *Press any key*. If the C compiler does not create the file *first.exe*, but instead displays error messages on your screen, you have probably violated a C syntax rule, as the next Tip discusses.

3. If you successfully typed in the C statements as shown in Tip 2, the C compiler will create an executable file named *first.exe*. To execute the *first.exe* program, you can either select the Run menu Run option or press the CTRL+F9 keyboard shortcut.

When you execute the program, your screen will display the following output:

```
Jamsa's C/C++ Programmer's Bible!
C:\>
```

Note: *In some installations,* **Turbo C++ Lite** *will generate the output and return you immediately to the editing window. In such cases, select the File menu DOS Shell option to view the program's output.*

UNDERSTANDING SYNTAX ERRORS

4

As you read in Tip 2, every programming language has a set of rules, called *syntax rules,* which you must obey as you specify your program statements. If you violate a syntax rule, your program will not successfully compile. Instead, the compiler will display error messages on your screen that specify the line of your program that contains the error and a brief description of the error. Using your editor, create the file *syntax.c,* which contains a syntax error. In the following example, the program fails to include an ending quote at the end of the message *Jamsa's C/C++ Programmer's Bible!*:

```
#include <stdio.h>

void main(void)
  {
    printf ("Jamsa\'s C/C++ Programmer\'s Bible!);
  }
```

When you compile this program, your compiler will display a syntax error message when it encounters line five. Depending on your compiler, the actual error message will differ. In the case of *Turbo C++ Lite,* your screen will display the following error messages:

```
Error syntax.c 5: Unterminated string or character constant in function main
Error syntax.c 6: Function call missing ) in function main()
Error syntax.c 6: Statement missing ; in function main()
```

Although the source code *syntax.c* only contains one error, the C compiler will display three error messages. The missing quote caused a series of cascading errors (one error leads to another) within the compiler.

To correct syntax errors within your programs, perform the following steps:

1. Write down the line number of each error and a brief description.

2. Edit your source file, moving your cursor to the first line number the compiler displays.

3. Within the source file, correct the error and move the cursor to the next line number. Most editors will display the current line number to help you locate specific lines within the file.

In the case of the file *syntax.c,* edit the file and add the missing quote. Save the file to disk and use your compiler to compile it. After you correct the syntax error, the compiler will create the file *syntax.exe.* To execute *syntax.exe,* select the Run menu Run option. The program will run and will yield the output shown here:

```
Jamsa's C/C++ Programmer's Bible!
C:\>
```

THE STRUCTURE OF A TYPICAL C PROGRAM

5

In Tip 2 you created the source file *first.c,* which contained the following statements:

```
#include <stdio.h>

void main(void)
  {
    printf ("Jamsa\'s C/C++ Programmer\'s Bible!");
  }
```

These statements are similar to those you will find in most C programs. In many cases, a C source file may begin with one or more *#include* statements. The *#include* statement directs the C compiler to use a specific file's content.

In the case of the file *first.c*, the *#include* statement directs the C compiler to use a file named *stdio.h*. The files an *#include* statement specifies are ASCII files that contain C source code. You can print or display each file's contents by following the steps discussed in Tip 13. Files that you name within an *#include* statement, which usually use the *h* extension, are called *include files* or *header files*. Most header files contain statements your programs commonly use, although you will learn later in this book about other uses for header files. When you direct the C compiler to include the file's contents, you do not have to type the statements into your programs yourself. After the *#include* statements, you will usually find a statement similar to the following:

```
void main(void)
```

Each C program you create will include a line similar to the *void main* statement. As you read in Tip 1, a C program contains a list of instructions you want the computer to execute. As the complexity of your programs increases, you will break them into small pieces that are easier for you (and for others who read your programs) to understand. The group of instructions you want the computer to execute first is called your *main program*. The statement *void main* identifies these statements (the main program) to the C compiler.

Clearly, because the C compiler will determine which statements form the main program and which statements are supplementary, you must have a way to tell the C compiler which instructions correspond to each section of your program. To assign program statements to a specific section of your program, place the statements within an opening brace ({) and a closing brace (}). The braces are part of the C syntax. For every opening brace you must have a brace that closes the group of statements.

6 ADDING STATEMENTS TO YOUR PROGRAM

As you have read, the program *first.c* used the *printf* statement to display a message on your screen. The following C program, *3_msgs.c*, uses three *printf* statements to display the same message. Each statement is contained within the program's opening and closing braces:

```
#include <stdio.h>

void main(void)
 {
   printf("Jamsa\'s ");
   printf("C/C++ Programmer\'s ");
   printf("Bible!");
 }
```

Note the space character within the *printf* statements. The space character is important because it ensures that the program will correctly display the text on your screen (by placing a space between words). As the number of statements in your programs increases, so too does the likelihood of syntax errors. Double-check your program to ensure that you correctly typed each statement, and then save the file to disk. When you compile and execute the *3_msgs* program, your screen will display the following output:

```
Jamsa\'s C/C++ Programmer\'s Bible!
C:\>
```

7 DISPLAYING OUTPUT ON A NEW LINE

Several of the previous programs have displayed the message *Jamsa's C/C++ Programmer's Bible!* on your screen display. As your programs become more complex, you might want the programs to display their output on two or more lines. In Tip 6, you created the program *3_msgs.c*, which used three *printf* statements to display a message on your screen:

```
printf("Jamsa\'s ");
printf("C/C++ Programmer\'s ");
printf("Bible!");
```

Unless you tell *printf* to do otherwise, *printf* will continue its output on the current line. The goal of the following program, *one_line.c*, is to display output on two successive lines:

```
#include <stdio.h>
void main(void)
  {
    printf("This is line one.");
    printf("This is the second line.");
  }
```

When you compile and execute the *one_line.c* program, your screen will display the following output:

```
This is line one.This is the second line.
C:\>
```

When you want *printf* to begin its output on a new line, you must include the special *newline character* (\n) within the text that you direct *printf* to display. When *printf* encounters the \n character, it will advance the cursor to the start of the next line. The following program, *two_line.c*, uses the newline character to display the second line of text on a new line as desired:

```
#include <stdio.h>
void main(void)
  {
    printf("This is line one.\n");
    printf("This is the second line.");
  }
```

When you compile and execute the program *two_line.c*, your screen will display the following output:

```
This is line one.
This is the second line.
C:\>
```

Many of the programs this book presents use the newline character. In fact, almost every program you write will normally use the newline character in one or more places.

C CONSIDERS UPPER- AND LOWERCASE LETTERS AS DIFFERENT 8

As you type your programs, you must keep in mind that C considers upper- and lowercase letters as different. As a rule, most C commands use lowercase, most C constants use all uppercase, and most C variables use mixed case. C programs make extensive use of lowercase letters. Because the following program, *uppererr.c*, uses the uppercase letter M in the name *Main* when C expects the name *main*, the program will not successfully compile:

```
#include <stdio.h>
void Main(void)
  {
    printf("This program does not compile.");
  }
```

When you compile the *uppererr.c* program, the *Turbo C++ Lite* compiler will display the following message:

```
Linker error: Undefined symbol _main in module TURBO_C\C0S.ASM
```

The relatively meaningless message that the *Turbo C++ Lite* compiler returns is the result of your spelling *Main* with a capital *M*. In this case, to correct the error you must simply change *Main* to *main*. After you change *Main* to *main*, re-compile and execute the program.

UNDERSTANDING LOGIC ERRORS (BUGS) 9

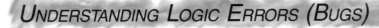

In Tip 4 you learned that if you violate one of the C language rules, the compiler will display a syntax-error message and your program will not successfully compile. As your programs become more complex, there will be many times when the program successfully compiles, but does not correctly perform the task you wanted. For example, assume that you want the following program, *one_line.c*, to display its output on two lines:

```
#include <stdio.h>

void main(void)
 {
    printf("This is line one.");
    printf("This is the second line.");
 }
```

Because the program does not violate any of C's syntax rules, the program will successfully compile. When you execute the program, however, it will not display its output on two lines; instead it will display the output on one line, as shown here:

```
This is line one.This is the second line.
C:\>
```

When your program does not work as you desire, the program contains *logic errors,* or *bugs.* When your programs contain a logic error (and eventually your programs will), you must try to discover and correct the cause of the error. The process of removing logic errors from your program is called *debugging.* Later in this book you will learn several different techniques you can use to locate logic errors within your program. For now, however, the best way to locate such errors is to print a copy of your program and examine the program line-by-line until you locate the error. A line-by-line program examination is called *desk checking.* In the case of the program *one_line.c*, your desk checking should reveal that the first *printf* statement does not contain the newline character (\n).

10 UNDERSTANDING THE PROGRAM DEVELOPMENT PROCESS

When you create programs, you will usually follow the same steps. To begin, you will use an editor to create your source file. Next, you will compile the program. If the program contains syntax errors, you must edit the source file and correct the errors. After the program successfully compiles, you will try to run the program. If the program runs successfully and performs as you expect, you are done creating the program. On the other hand, if the program does not work as you expected, you must desk check the source code to locate the logic error (as discussed in Tip 9). After you correct the error, you must compile the source code to create a new executable file. You can then test the new program to ensure that it performs the task you want. Figure 10 illustrates the program development process.

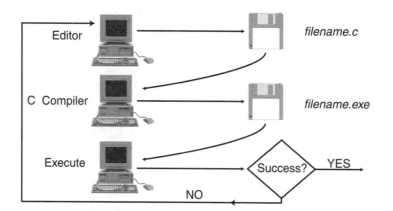

Figure 10 The program development process.

11 UNDERSTANDING THE FILE TYPES

When you create a C program, you place your statements in a source file that uses the C extension. If your program successfully compiles, the compiler will create an executable program file with the EXE extension. As you read in Tip 5, many programs use header files (which use the *h* extension) that contain commonly used statements. If you examine your directory after compiling a program, you will likely find one or more files with the *OBJ* extension.

These files, called *object files*, contain instructions in the form of 1's and 0's that the computer understands. You cannot execute object files, however, because their contents are not quite complete.

The C compiler provides routines (such as *printf*) that perform commonly used operations and reduce the number of statements you must include in your programs. After the compiler examines your program's syntax, it creates an object file. In the case of the program *first.c*, the compiler would create an object file named *first.obj*. Next, a program called a *linker* combines the program statements in your object file with the functions (such as *printf*) the compiler provides to build the executable program. In most cases, when you invoke the compiler to examine your source code, the compiler will automatically invoke the linker for you if your program successfully compiles. Figure 11 illustrates the process of compiling and linking a program.

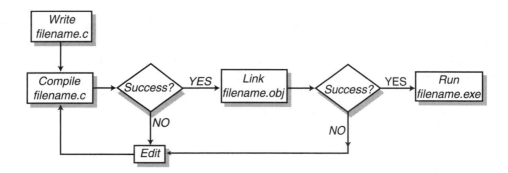

Figure 11 *The process of compiling and linking a program.*

BETTER UNDERSTANDING THE LINKER

C 12

In Tip 11 you learned that when you compile your C program, a second program called a linker combines your program statements with predefined routines (which the compiler provides) to convert an object file to an executable program. As is the case with the compilation process, which can detect syntax errors, the linker process can also encounter errors. Consider, for example, the following program, *no_print.c*, which erroneously uses *print* instead of *printf*:

```
#include <stdio.h>

void main(void)
 {
    print("This program does not link");
 }
```

Because the *no_print.c* program does not violate any C syntax rules, the program will successfully compile, producing an OBJ file. However, the *Turbo C++ Lite* linker will display the following error message because of the undefined *print* statement:

```
Error: Function 'print' should have a prototype in function main()
```

Because the C compiler does not provide a function named *print*, the linker cannot create the executable program *no_print.exe*. Instead the linker will display the error message shown previously. To correct the error edit the file, changing *print* to *printf*, and recompile and link your program.

UNDERSTANDING HEADER FILES

C 13

Each program presented throughout this book uses one or more *#include* statements to direct the C compiler to use the statements a *header file* contains. A header file is an ASCII file whose contents you can print or display on your screen. If you examine the directory that contains your compiler (the directory *tclite* in the case of Borland's *Turbo C++ Lite* compiler), you will find a subdirectory named *include*. The *include* subdirectory contains the compiler's header files. Take time now to locate your compiler's header files. You might even want to print the contents of a commonly used header file, such as *stdio.h*. You will find C programming statements within the *include* file. When the compiler encounters an *#include* statement in your program, the compiler compiles the code the header contains just as if you had typed the header file's contents into your program source code. Header files contain commonly used definitions and provide the compiler with information about compiler-provided functions, such as *printf*. For now, you may find a header file's contents difficult to understand. As you become more conversant in C and C++, however, you should print a copy of and examine each header file you use. The header files contain valuable information and provide you with programming techniques that will make you a better C programmer.

14 ❨ HELPING THE COMPILER LOCATE HEADER FILES

In Tip 13 you learned that when the C compiler encounters an *#include* statement, the compiler adds the header file's contents to your program, just as if you typed the header file's contents into your source file. Depending on your compiler, your environment entries may contain an INCLUDE entry that tells the compiler the name of the subdirectory that contains the header files. If when you compile a program your compiler displays an error message stating that it is unable to open a specific header file, first check the subdirectory that contains your compiler's header files to ensure that the file exists. If you find the file, issue the SET command at the DOS prompt, as shown here:

```
C:\> SET    <ENTER>
COMSPEC=C:\DOS\COMMAND.COM
PATH=C:\DOS;C:\WINDOWS;C:\BORLANDC\BIN
PROMPT=$P$G
TEMP=C:\TEMP
```

If your environment does not contain an INCLUDE entry, check the documentation that accompanied your compiler to determine if your compiler requires such an entry. Usually, the compiler's installation will place within your *autoexec.bat* file a SET command that assigns the INCLUDE entry to the subdirectory that contains the header files, as shown here:

```
SET  INCLUDE=C:\BORLANDC\INCLUDE
```

If your compiler uses the INCLUDE entry and your *autoexec.bat* file does not define the entry, you can create the entry yourself, placing it in your *autoexec.bat* file.

Note: The *Turbo C++ Lite* program will only look for include files within its **include** subdirectory.

15 ❨ SPEEDING UP COMPILATIONS

When you compile a source file, the C compiler might create one or more temporary files that exist only while the compiler and linker are working. Depending on your compiler, you may be able to use the TEMP environment entry to specify where the compiler creates these temporary files. If your computer has multiple hard drives, some of which have more available space than others (especially if your compiler runs within Windows and therefore uses virtual memory and swap files), you might consider assigning the TEMP entry to point to the drive with the most available space. This way, the compiler will create its temporary files on the very fast hard drive, which will speed up the compilation process. Assuming that your *D* drive has that extra space, you can place a SET command within your *autoexec.bat* file to assign the TEMP entry to the *D* drive, as shown here:

```
SET TEMP=D:
```

16 ❨ COMMENTING YOUR PROGRAMS

As a rule, each time you create a program you must ensure that you include in the program *comments* that explain the processing the program performs. In short, a comment is a message that helps you read and understand the program. As your programs increase in length, the programs become more difficult to understand. Because you may eventually create hundreds and possibly thousands of programs, you will not be able to remember the purpose of every statement within every program. If you include comments in your program, you will not have to remember each program's details. Instead, the program's comments will explain the processing.

Most newer C and C++ compilers provide two ways for you to place comments within your source file. First, you place two forward slash (//) characters together, as shown here:

```
// This is a comment
```

When the C compiler encounters the double slashes, it ignores the text that follows to the end of the current line. The following program, *comment.c*, illustrates the use of comments:

```
// Program: comment.c
// Written by: Kris Jamsa and Lars Klander
// Date written: 12-22-97
// Purpose: Illustrates the use of comments in a C program.

#include <stdio.h>

void main(void)
 {
    printf("Jamsa\'s C/C++ Programmer\'s Bible!"); // Display a message
 }
```

In this example, you immediately know by reading these simple comments when, why, and who wrote the program. You should get in the habit of placing similar comments at the start of your programs. Should other programmers who must read or change the program have questions, they will quickly know the program's original author.

When the C compiler encounters the double slashes (//), it ignores the text on the rest of that line. Most newer C source files use the double slashes to designate a comment. If you are reading an older C program, you may encounter comments written in a second form. In the second acceptable comment form, the comment appears between a set of slashes and asterisks, as shown here:

```
/* This is a comment */
```

When the compiler encounters the opening comment symbol (/*) it ignores all text up to and including the closing comment symbol (*/). Using the /* *comment* */ format, a single comment can appear on two or more lines. The following program, *comment2.c*, illustrates the use of the /* *comment* */ format:

```
/* Program: COMMENT.C
   Written by: Kris Jamsa and Lars Klander
   Date written: 12-22-97

   Purpose: Illustrates the use of comments in a C program. */
#include <stdio.h>

void main(void)
 {
    printf("Jamsa\'s C/C++ Programmer\'s Bible!");   /* Display a message */
 }
```

As you can see, the program's first comment contains five lines. When you use the /* *comment* */ format for your comments, make sure that every start comment symbol (/*) has a corresponding end symbol (*/). If the end symbol is missing, the C compiler will ignore much of your program, which will eventually result in syntax errors that will be difficult for you to detect.

Most C compilers will return a syntax error if you try to place one comment within another (nest comments), as shown here:

```
    /* This comment has /* a second */ comment inside */
```

IMPROVING YOUR PROGRAM READABILITY 17

In Tip 16 you learned how to use comments within your programs to improve their readability. Each time you create a program, assume that you or another programmer will eventually have to change the program in some way. Therefore, it is essential that you write your programs so they are easy to read. The following C program, *hardread.c*, will display a message on your screen:

```
#include <stdio.h>
void main(void){printf("Jamsa\'s C/C++ Programmer\'s Bible!");}
```

Although this program will compile and successfully display the desired message, the program is difficult to read, at best. A good program not only works, but is also easy to read and understand. The key to creating readable programs is to include comments that explain the program's processing and to use blank lines to improve the program's format. In later Tips you will learn the important role indentation plays in producing readable program code.

18 PAYING ATTENTION TO COMPILER WARNING MESSAGES

When your program contains one or more syntax errors, the C compiler will display error messages on your screen and will not create an executable program. As you create programs, there may be times when your compiler will display one or more *Warning messages* on your screen, but will still create the executable program file. For example, the following C program, *no_stdio.c*, does not include the header file *stdio.h*:

```
void main(void)
  {
    printf("Jamsa\'s C/C++ Programmer\'s Bible!");
  }
```

When you compile this program, the *Turbo C++ Lite* compiler will display the following warning message:

```
Warning no_stdio.c 3: Function 'printf' should have a prototype in function
main().
```

When the compiler displays a warning message, you should immediately determine the cause of the compiler complaint and correct it. Although the warnings might never cause an error during your program's execution, some warnings create the opportunity for errors that are very difficult to debug later. By taking time to locate and correct the cause of compiler warnings, you will learn much more about the inner workings of C and C++.

19 CONTROLLING COMPILER WARNINGS

In Tip 18, you have learned that you should pay attention to the warning messages that your compiler displays on your screen. To help you make better use of compiler warnings, many compilers let you set the message level you desire. Depending on your compiler, you may use a command-line switch to control the warning level or you may use *pragmas*, which Tip 145 explains. A *pragma* is a directive to the compiler. As you will learn, different compilers support different *pragmas*. For example, to disable the *Identifier is declared but never used* warning within *Turbo C++ Lite* , your code would include the following *pragma*:

```
#pragma warn -use
```

If you are not using *Turbo C++ Lite,* refer to the documentation that accompanies your compiler to determine if you can turn off specific warning messages.

20 USING COMMENTS TO EXCLUDE PROGRAM STATEMENTS

In Tip 16 you learned that you should use comments within your programs to improve your program's readability. As your programs become more complex, you may use comments to help you debug (remove errors) from your programs. When the C compiler encounters the double slashes (//), the compiler ignores all the remaining text on the current line following the double slashes. Likewise, when the compiler encounters the starting comment symbol (/*), the compiler ignores all the text that follows, up to and including the closing comment symbol (*/). As you test your programs, there may be times when you want to eliminate one or more statements from your program. One way to eliminate the program statements is to simply delete the statements from your source file. A second way to eliminate statements is to *comment them out*. The following program, *nooutput.c*, comments out all the *printf* statements:

```
#include <stdio.h>

void main(void)
 {
    // printf("This line does not appear");
    /* This is a comment
       printf("This line does not appear either");
    */
 }
```

Because both *printf* statements appear within comments, the compiler ignores both of them. As a result, no output appears when you execute the program. As your programs become more complex, using comments to disable statements will become very convenient.

As you learned in Tip 16, most C compilers will return one or more syntax errors if you try to place one comment within another (nested comments). When you use comments to disable statements, be careful that you do not inadvertently nest comments.

Understanding the Importance of Names   21

As you examine the Tips presented throughout this book, you will encounter variable names and functions whose names begin with an underscore, such as *_dos_getdrive* or *_chmod*. You usually only use such variables and functions within the DOS environment. If you are writing programs that will execute under DOS, Windows, Macintosh, UNIX, or possibly some other operating system, you should avoid using these functions because they will probably not be available under the other systems. Therefore, to move your program from DOS to another operating system, you will have to perform additional programming. Some functions may have two implementations; one with an underscore (*_chmod*), and one without (*chmod*). As a rule, use the function or variable that does not use the underscore, which is in this case *chmod*.

Understanding the Semicolon   22

As you examine C programs, you will find that the programs make extensive use of semicolons. The semicolon in C has special meaning. As you know, a program is a list of instructions that you want the computer to perform. When you specify those instructions in C, you use the semicolon to separate one statement from another. As your programs become more complex, you may find that a statement does not fit on one line. When the C compiler examines your program, it uses the semicolon to distinguish one statement from the next. The C language syntax defines the use of the semicolon. If you omit the semicolon, a syntax error will occur and the program will not successfully compile.

Introducing Variables   23

To perform useful work, programs must store information, such as a document that you edit over multiple computer sessions, within a file and also internally. As you know, each time you run a program, the operating system loads your program's instructions into the computer's memory. As the program runs, it stores values in memory locations. For example, assume that you have a program that prints a document. Each time you run the program, it will display a message asking you the name of the file, as well as the number of copies you want to print. As you type in this information, the program stores the values you enter in specific memory locations. To help your program track the memory locations in which it has placed data, each memory location has a unique *address*, such as location 0, 1, 2, 3, and so on. Because there can be billions of such addresses, keeping track of individual storage locations can become very difficult. To simplify storing information, programs define *variables*, which are names that the program associates with specific locations in memory. As the word variable implies, the *value* that the program stores in these locations can change or vary throughout the program's lifetime.

Each variable has a specific *type*, which tells the computer how much memory the data the variable stores requires and which operations the program can perform on the data. Given the previous example of a program that prints a document, the program might use a variable named *filename* (which stores the name of the file you want to print) and one named *count* (which stores the number of copies you want to print). Within your program, you reference variables by name. Therefore, you should assign meaningful names to each variable. Within your C programs, you usually declare your variables immediately following *main*, before your program statements, as shown here:

```
void main(void)
{
   // Variables go here

   printf("Jamsa\'s C/C++ Programmer\'s Bible!");
}
```

The following program shows how you would declare three integer variables (variables that store counting numbers, such as 1, 2, and 3):

```
void main(void)
{
   int age;       // The user's age in years
   int weight;    // The user's weight in pounds
   int height;    // The user's height in inches

   // Other program statements go here
}
```

Each variable has a type that defines the amount of memory the variable requires, as well as the operations the program can perform on the data. To declare an integer variable, your C programs use the type *int*. After you declare a variable (that is, tell the program the variable's name and type), you can then assign a value to the variable (that is, store information).

24 ASSIGNING A VALUE TO A VARIABLE

A variable is a name that your program associates with a storage location in memory. After you declare a variable within your program, you can assign it a value. In C, you assign a value to a variable by using the equal sign (called the *assignment operator*). The following program declares three variables of type *int* and then assigns each variable a value:

```
void main(void)
{
   int age;       // The user's age in years
   int weight;    // The user's weight in pounds
   int height;    // The user's height in inches

   age = 41;      // Assign the user's age
   weight = 165;  // Assign the user's weight
   height = 73;   // Assign the user's height

     // Other program statements
}
```

25 UNDERSTANDING VARIABLE TYPES

When you declare variables within your programs, you must tell the C compiler the variable's name and type. A type defines the set of values the variable can store, as well as the set of operations that the program can perform on the data. C supports four basic types, each of which is listed in Table 25.

Type Name	Purpose
char	Stores a single character, such as a letter from A through Z
int	Stores counting numbers (called integers), such as 1, 2, and 3, as well as negative numbers
float	Stores single-precision floating-point numbers (with a decimal point), such as 3.14 or −54.1343
double	Stores a double-precision floating-point number (which is more precise than a single-precision floating-point number). You will use *double* for very large or very small numbers

Table 25 The four basic types C supports.

Many of the Tips presented throughout this book examine each of these types in detail. Most of the Tips in this book will use one or more variables of the basic types.

Declaring Multiple Variables of the Same Type — 26

As you learned in Tip 24, when you declare a variable within your program, you must tell the C compiler the variable's name and type. The following statements declare three variables of type *int*:

```
int age;
int weight;
int height;
```

When you declare variables of the same type, C lets you list the variable names on one or more lines, with commas separating each variable name, as shown here:

```
int age, weight, height;
float salary, taxes;
```

Commenting Your Variables at Declaration — 27

In C programs, comments help someone who is reading your program to better understand it. When you choose variable names, you should select names that meaningfully describe the value the variable will store. For example, consider the following declarations:

```
int age, weight, height;
int x, y, z;
```

Both declarations create three variables of type *int*. In the first declaration, however, you have an idea of how to use the variable simply by examining the variable's name. In addition to using meaningful names, you should also place a comment next to each variable declaration that further explains the variable, as shown here:

```
int age;        // The user's age in years
int weight;     // The user's weight in pounds
int height;     // The user's height in inches
```

Assigning Values to Variables at Declaration — 28

After you declare a variable within your program, you can use the C *assignment operator* (the equal sign) to assign a value to the variable. C lets you assign a value to a variable within the variable's declaration. Programmers refer to the process of assigning a variable's first value as *initializing* the variable. The following statements, for example, declare and initialize three variables of type *int*:

```
int age = 41;        // The user's age in years
int weight = 165;    // The user's weight in pounds
int height = 73;     // The user's height in inches
```

Initializing Multiple Variables During Declaration — 29

In Tip 26 you learned that C lets you declare two or more variables on the same line, as shown here:

```
int age, weight, height;
```

When you declare multiple variables on the same line, C lets you initialize one or more of the variables:

```
int age = 44, weight, height = 73;
```

In this example, C will initialize the variables *age* and *height*, and leave the variable *weight* uninitialized.

30 USING MEANINGFUL VARIABLE NAMES

When you declare variables in your programs, you should choose meaningful variable names that describe the variable's use. You can use a combination of upper- and lowercase letters in your variable names. As discussed in Tip 8, the C compiler distinguishes between upper- and lowercase letters. If you use upper- and lowercase letters in your variable names, you must always specify the same upper- and lowercase letter combinations. As you get started, you should probably stick to lowercase letters, because doing so reduces the possibility of entry errors from mixed cases.

You must give a unique name to each variable you declare within your programs. In general, you can use an unlimited number of characters in a variable name. Your variable names can contain a combination of letters, numbers, and the underscore character—however, the names must start with a letter or underscore. The following statements illustrate some valid variable names:

```
int hours_worked;
float tax_rate;
float _6_month_rate;   // Starting _underscore is valid
```

C predefines several keywords that have special meaning to the C compiler. A *keyword* is a word that has meaning to the compiler without your giving it meaning. For example, *float, int,* and *char* are all keywords. As you create variable names do not use these keywords. Tip 31 lists C keywords.

31 UNDERSTANDING C'S KEYWORDS

The C programming language defines several keywords that have special meaning to the compiler. As you choose variable names (and create your own functions), do not use these keywords. Table 31 lists C keywords:

C Keywords

auto	*default*	*float*	*register*	*struct*	*volatile*
break	*do*	*for*	*return*	*switch*	*while*
case	*double*	*goto*	*short*	*typedef*	
char	*else*	*if*	*signed*	*union*	
const	*enum*	*int*	*sizeof*	*unsigned*	
continue	*extern*	*long*	*static*	*void*	

Table 31 The C keyword list.

32 UNDERSTANDING VARIABLES OF TYPE INT

A *variable* is a name that the C compiler associates with one or more memory locations. When you declare a variable within your program, you must specify the variable's type and name. A variable's *type* specifies the kind of values that variable can store and the set of operations that the program can perform on the data. C uses the type *int* to store integer values (positive and negative counting numbers). The C compiler normally allocates sixteen bits (two bytes) to store values of type *int*. A variable of type *int* can store values in the range –32,768 through 32,767. Figure 32 shows how C represents an integer value:

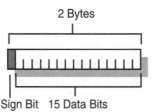

Figure 32 How C represents an integer value.

Values of type *int* are whole numbers; they do not include a fractional portion as do floating-point numbers. If you assign a floating-point value to a variable of type *int*, most C compilers will simply truncate the fractional portion. If you assign a variable of type *int* a value outside the range -32,768 through 32,767, an overflow condition will occur and the assigned value will be in error.

UNDERSTANDING VARIABLES OF TYPE CHAR 33

A *variable* is a name that the C compiler associates with one or more memory locations. When you declare a variable within your program, you must specify the variable's type and name. A variable's *type* specifies the kind of values that variable can store and the set of operations that the program can perform on the data. C uses the type *char* to store character (byte) values. The C compiler normally allocates eight bits (one byte) to store values of type *char*. A variable of type *char* can store whole number values in the range –128 through 127. Figure 33 shows how C represents a value of type *char*.

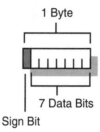

Figure 33 *How C represents a value of type* **char**.

Programs can assign a value to a variable of type *char* in one of two ways. First, the program can assign a character's ASCII value. For example, the letter A has the ASCII value 65:

```
char letter = 65;   // Assign letter the character A
```

Second, your program can use a character constant, which appears within single quotes, as shown here:

```
char letter = 'A';
```

Variables of type *char* only hold one letter at a time. To store multiple characters, you must declare a character string, which is discussed in this book's Strings section.

UNDERSTANDING VARIABLES OF TYPE FLOAT 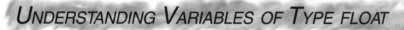 34

A *variable* is a name that the C compiler associates with one or more memory locations. When you declare a variable within your program, you must specify the variable's type and name. A variable's *type* specifies the kind of values that variable can store and the set of operations that the program can perform on the data. C uses the type *float* to store floating-point values (positive and negative numbers that contain fractional portions). The C compiler normally allocates 32 bits (4 bytes) to store values of type *float*. A variable of type *float* can store values with six to seven digits of precision in the range 3.4E–38 through 3.4E+38.

C stores the value as a 23-bit *mantissa*, which contains the fractional number, an 8-bit exponent, which contains the power to which the computer raises the number when resolving its value, and a single sign bit which determines whether the value is positive or negative. In other words, if a variable contained the value 3.4E+38, the sign bit would be 0, which indicates the number is positive; the 23-bit mantissa would include a binary representation of 3.4, and the 8-bit exponent would include a binary representation of the 10^{38} exponent. Figure 34 illustrates how C represents a value of type *float*. Tip 337 explains mantissas and exponents in detail.

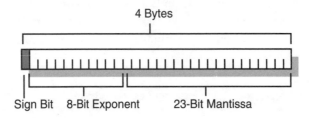

Figure 34 *How C represents a value of type* **float***.*

Note: *This Tip and other, later Tips, represents floating-point numbers in* **scientific notation***. Simply put, scientific notation lets you represent any number as a single digit to the left of the decimal point, and unlimited number of digits to the decimal point's right, and an exponent representing 10 raised to that exponent's value. When you determine the number's actual value, you multiply the number (the* **mantissa***) by the value 10^x (where* **x** *represents the* **exponent***). For example, the number 3.1415967E+7 evaluates as 31415967.0 or $3.1415967 * 10^7$.*

35 UNDERSTANDING VARIABLES OF TYPE DOUBLE

A *variable* is a name that the C compiler associates with one or more memory locations. When you declare a variable within your program, you must specify the variable's type and name. A variable's *type* specifies the kind of values that variables can store and the set of operations that the program can perform on the data. C uses the type *double* to store floating-point values (positive and negative numbers that contain fractional portions). The C compiler normally allocates 64 bits (8 bytes) to store values of type *double*. A variable of type *double* can store values with 14 to 15 digits of precision, in the range −1.7E-308 through 1.7E+308. Figure 35 illustrates how C represents a value of type *double*.

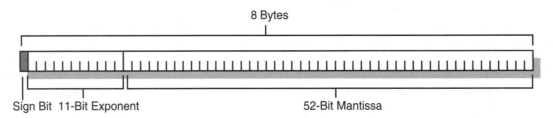

Figure 35 *How C represents a value of type* **double***.*

36 ASSIGNING VALUES TO FLOATING-POINT VALUES

A *floating-point* value is a value that contains a fractional part, such as 123.45. When you work with floating-point values within your programs, you can refer to the values using their decimal format, such as 123.45, or you can use the value's exponential format, 1.2345E2. Therefore, both the following statements assign the variable *radius* the same value:

```
radius = 123.45;
radius = 1.2345E2;
```

In a similar way, both the following statements assign the variable *radius* the same fractional value:

```
radius = 0.12345;
radius = 12.345E-2;
```

37 UNDERSTANDING TYPE MODIFIERS

C provides four basic data types (*int*, *char*, *float*, and *double*). As you learned, each type defines a set of values the variable can store and a set of operations that the program can perform on the data. As you have learned, variables of type *int* can store values in the range −32,768 through 32,767. Likewise, variables of type *char* can store values in the range −128 through 127. To help you change the range of values that variables of type *int* and *char* can store, C provides a set of type modifiers—*unsigned, long, register, signed,* and *short.* A *type modifier* changes (modifies) the range of values a variable can store or the way the compiler stores a variable. To modify a type, place the type modifier in front of the type name in a variable declaration, as shown here:

```
unsigned int inventory_count;
register int counter;
long int very_large_number;
```

Several following Tips discuss these four type modifiers in detail.

UNDERSTANDING THE UNSIGNED TYPE MODIFIER

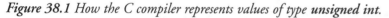

38

A *type modifier* changes (modifies) the range of values a variable can store or the way the compiler stores a variable. As you have learned, variables of type *int* can store positive and negative values in the range –32,768 through 32,767. Within the representation of a value of type *int,* the value's most significant bit indicates the value's sign (positive or negative), as you learned in Tip 32. In some cases, your program may never need to store a negative value within a specific variable. The *unsigned* type modifier tells the compiler not to use the most significant bit as a sign bit, but instead to let the bit represent larger positive values. A variable of type *unsigned int* can store values in the range 0 through 65,535. Figure 38.1 illustrates how the C compiler stores an *unsigned int* variable.

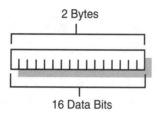

*Figure 38.1 How the C compiler represents values of type **unsigned int**.*

As discussed in Tip 33, variables of type *char* can hold values in the range –128 through 127. When you use the *unsigned* type modifier with variables of type *char,* you can create variables that can store values in the range 0 through 255. Figure 38.2 illustrates how the C compiler represents an *unsigned char* variable.

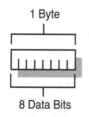

*Figure 38.2 How the C compiler represents variables of type **unsigned char**.*

The following statements illustrate declarations of variables with type *unsigned int* or *unsigned char:*

```
void main(void)
  {
    unsigned int current_seconds;
    unsigned int status_indicator;
    unsigned char menu_border;    // Extended ASCII character
  }
```

UNDERSTANDING THE LONG TYPE MODIFIER

39

A type modifier changes (modifies) the range of values a variable can store or the way the compiler stores a variable. Variables of type *int* can store positive and negative values in the range -32,768 through 32,767. As previously shown in Tip 32, the C compiler represents values of type *int* using 16 bits, with the most significant bit indicating the value's sign. In many cases, your programs must store integer values that are larger (greater than 32,767) or smaller (less than –32,768) than the range of values a variable of type *int* can hold. The *long* type modifier tells the compiler to use 32 bits (four bytes) to represent the integer values. A variable of type *long int* can store values in the range –2,147,483,648 through 2,147,483,647. Figure 39 shows how the C compiler stores a *long int* variable.

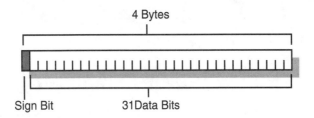

Figure 39 How the C compiler represents values of type **long int**.

Note: *Many C++ compilers also support the type* **long double**, *which your programs can use to represent floating-point numbers with up to 80 digits of precision, rather than the standard 64 digits of precision. Values of type* **long double** *use 10 bytes of memory, with a 60-bit mantissa and a 19-bit exponent. The range for a long double value is 3.4E-4932 to 1.1E+4932. To determine whether your compiler supports* **long double** *declarations, check your compiler's documentation.*

40 COMBINING THE UNSIGNED AND LONG TYPE MODIFIERS

In Tip 38 you learned that the *unsigned* type modifier directs the C compiler not to interpret a value's most significant bit as a sign indicator, but rather, to use that bit to represent a larger value. Likewise, in Tip 39, you learned that the *long* type modifier directs the compiler to double the number of bits it uses to represent an integer value. In some cases, your programs may need to store very large positive values. By combining the *unsigned* and *long* type modifiers, you can direct the C compiler to allocate a 32-bit variable capable of values in the range 0 through 4,292,967,265. Figure 40 illustrates how the C compiler would represent an *unsigned long int* variable.

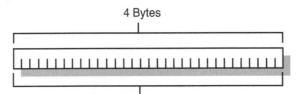

Figure 40 How the C compiler represents values of type **unsigned long int**.

The following statements declare variables of type *unsigned long int*:

```
void main(void)
  {
    unsigned long int very_large_value;
    unsigned long int national_debt;
  }
```

41 WORKING WITH LARGE VALUES

As you have learned, variables of type *int* can store values in the range –32,768 through 32,767. Likewise, variables of type *long int* can store values in the range –2,147,483,648 through 2,147,483,647. When you work with large values in your programs, do not include commas. Instead, work with large numbers as shown here:

```
long int big_number = 1234567;
long int one_million = 1000000;
```

If you include commas within your numbers, the C compiler will generate a syntax error.

Understanding the register Type Modifier   C 42

A variable is the name that your program associates with a memory location. When you declare a variable, the C compiler allocates memory to hold the variable's value. When your program must access the variable, slight overhead occurs (the computer consumes time) while the CPU accesses memory. Depending on the variable's use, you can sometimes direct the compiler to store the variable in a register (which resides within the CPU itself) to increase your program's performance. Because the compiler can access the value much faster when it resides in a register, your program will execute faster. The *register* type modifier directs the compiler to keep the variable in a register as often as possible. Because the CPU has a limited number of registers, the compiler cannot permanently assign the variable to a register. Instead, the compiler will try to keep the variable in a register as often as possible. The following statements show use of the *register* type modifier:

```
void main(void)
  {
    register int counter;
    register unsigned status_flags;
  }
```

You should use the *register* type modifier with variables that your program repeatedly accesses, such as a *loop* variable that the program accesses each time it loops.

Understanding the short Type Modifier   C 43

As discussed in Tip 32, the C compiler usually represents variables of type *int* using 16 bits. Therefore, the variables of type *int* can store values in the range –32,768 through 32,767. If you are using a 32-bit compiler, however, the compiler may represent an integer value using 32 bits, which means a variable of type *int* could store values in the range –2,147,483,648 through 2,147,483,647. If you store a value that is outside the range a variable of type *int* can store, an *overflow condition* occurs, and the assigned value is in error. (Tip 50 explains overflow in detail.) Programmers write some programs knowing that when an overflow occurs, the compiler consistently assigns the errant value (meaning that the errant value is always the same) to the overflowed value. In other words, the programmer writes the program to use overflow. Should you move a program that uses values of type *int* in this way (that is, that counts on the value overflowing) from a 16-bit to 32-bit environment, the overflow would no longer occur because the 32-bit integer can store a larger value. If you write a program based on overflow, which presumes that the compiler represents *int* variables with 16 bits, you can use the *short* type modifier to ensure that the compiler represents a variable using 16 bits. The following statements illustrate declarations of variables of type *short int*:

```
void main(void)
  {
    short int key_value;
    short int small_number;
  }
```

Omitting int from Modified Declarations   C 44

Within this section you have learned about several C type modifiers, including *long*, *short*, and *unsigned*. The following statements illustrate how to use these three modifiers:

```
unsigned int status_flags;
short int small_value;
long int very_big_number;
```

When you use these three type modifiers, most compilers will let you omit the *int*, as shown here:

```
unsigned status_flags;
short small_value;
long very_big_number;
```

45 UNDERSTANDING THE SIGNED TYPE MODIFIER

As you learned in Tip 33, C compilers usually represent variables of type *char* using eight bits, with the most significant bit representing the value's sign. Therefore, variables of type *char* can store values in the range –128 through 127. In Tip 38, you learned you can use the *unsigned* qualifier to direct the C compiler to not interpret the sign bit, but instead to use the bit to represent a larger positive value. Using the *unsigned* type modifier, a variable of type *char* can store values in the range 0 through 255. If you are using a variable of type *char* and you assign the variable a value outside the range of valid values, overflow will occur and the value the computer assigns to the variable will not be the value you desire. In some cases, however, you will write programs with overflow in mind. If you plan to move such a program to a different compiler, which may represent variables of type *char* as unsigned, you can use the *signed* type modifier to ensure that the second compiler represents variables of type *char* using 7 bits for the data and 1 bit for the sign bit. The following statements show declarations of type *signed char*:

```
void main(void)
  {
    signed char byte_value;
    signed char menu_choice;
  }
```

46 MULTIPLE ASSIGNMENT OPERATIONS

As you have learned, C uses the equal sign (=) as its assignment operator. Normally, your C programs will assign values to variables on distinct lines, as shown here:

```
count = 0;
sum = 0;
value = 0;
```

When you want to assign the same value to multiple variables, C lets you perform all the assignments at one time, as shown here:

```
count = sum = value = 0;
```

When C encounters a multiple assignment operation, C assigns values from right to left. As a rule, only use multiple assignments to initialize variables. Using such operations for more complex operations will decrease your program's readability. For example, the following program assigns two variables the uppercase equivalent to the character the user types:

```
ltr_save = letter = toupper(getchar());
```

47 ASSIGNING ONE VARIABLE TYPE'S VALUE TO A DIFFERENT TYPE

A type defines the set of values a variable can store and the set of operations that your programs can perform on the data. C provides four basic data types (*int*, *float*, *char*, and *double*). Some cases may require you to assign the value of a variable of type *int* to a value of type *float*, or vice versa. As a general rule, you can successfully assign a value of type *int* to a variable of type *float*. When you assign the value of a variable of type *float* to a variable of type *int*, however, you must use caution. Most compilers will truncate the floating-point value, discarding the fractional portion. On the other hand, another compiler might round the value rather than truncate it (meaning that, if the fractional portion of the value is greater than .5, the two compilers will convert the value differently). If you want to ensure that your program performs floating-point value to integer value assignments consistently, you might consider using the *ceil* and *floor* functions, which this book's Math section presents.

48 CREATING YOUR OWN TYPES

A type defines the set of values a variable can store and the set of operations that your program can perform on the data. C provides four basic data types (*int*, *float*, *char*, and *double*). As you have learned, you can combine type modifiers to change the range of values a variable can store. As the number of variables your program declares increases, you may find it convenient to create your own variable name that provides a shorthand name for a commonly used type. For example, consider the following declarations of type *unsigned long int*:

```
unsigned long int seconds_since_january;
unsigned long int world_population_in_2000;
```

Using C's *typedef* statement, you can define the type name *ULINT*, which is identical to the type *unsigned long int*, as shown here:

```
typedef unsigned long int ULINT;
```

After you create the type name, you can use the name to define variables, as shown here:

```
ULINT seconds_since_january;
ULINT world_population_in_2000;
```

As your programs use more complex variable declarations, you may find that creating a new type name is very convenient, because type names can save you excess typing time and reduce the possibility of entry errors.

Note: *The code within this Tip defines ULINT in all capital letters because it is easier for another programmer to determine custom types if you represent the types differently than default types. You can make the type all capital letters, all lowercase letters, or a combination of both—it is your choice. However, you should be consistent in how you name custom types across multiple programs or multiple types within the same program.*

ASSIGNING A HEXADECIMAL OR OCTAL VALUE C 49

Depending on your application, there may be times when you must work with *octal* (base 8) or *hexadecimal* (base 16) values. At such times, you tell the compiler you want to work with values that are not decimal values. If you precede a numeric value with a 0 (zero), such as 077, the C compiler treats the value as octal. Likewise, if you precede a value with 0x, such as 0xFF, the compiler treats the value as hexadecimal. The following statements illustrate how to use an octal and hexadecimal constant:

```
int octal_value = 0227;
int hex_value = 0xFF0;
```

UNDERSTANDING OVERFLOW C 50

As you have learned, a variable's type defines the range of values a variable can store and the operations that a program can perform on the variable. Variables of type *int*, for example, can store values in the range –32,768 through 32,767. If you assign a value outside this range to a variable of type *int*, an *overflow* error will occur. As you have already learned, C uses 16 bits to represent variables of type *int*. The C compiler uses the most significant of the 16 bits to determine the variable's sign. If the most significant bit is 0, the value is positive. If the most significant bit is 1, the value is negative. C then uses 15 bits to represent the variable's value. To understand why overflow occurs, you must consider the value's bitwise implementation. Consider the following values:

```
     0     0000 0000 0000 0000
     1     0000 0000 0000 0001
     2     0000 0000 0000 0010
     3     0000 0000 0000 0011
     4     0000 0000 0000 0100

32,765    0111 1111 1111 1101
32,766    0111 1111 1111 1110
32,767    0111 1111 1111 1111
```

If you add 1 to the value 32,767, you would expect the result to be 32,768. However, to C the value becomes –32,768, as shown here:

```
32,767     0111 1111 1111 1111
+    1     0000 0000 0000 0001
-------    --------------------
-32,768    1000 0000 0000 0000
```

The following program, *overflow.c*, illustrates how overflow occurs:

```c
#include <stdio.h>

void main(void)
  {
    int positive = 32767;
    int negative = -32768;

    printf("%d + 1 is %d\n", positive, positive+1);
    printf("%d - 1 is %d\n", negative, negative-1);
  }
```

When you compile and execute this program, your screen will display the following output:

```
32767 + 1 is -32768
-32768 - 1 is 32767
C:\>
```

As you can see, adding a value to 32,767 yields a negative number, while subtracting a value from −32,768 produces a positive number. One problem that makes overflow difficult is that within your programs, you will often not notice the error because the C compiler does not return an error when the overflow occurs. In other words, the program continues to execute, despite the overflow. As a result, when you debug your programs, you may have a difficult time detecting errors that result from overflow.

Note: *If you use the* **Turbo C++** **Lite** *compiler, or most other newer compilers (such as Microsoft's* **Visual C++®** *or Borland's* **C++ 5.02®***), the compiler will warn you of the potential overflow problem. The* **Turbo C++** **Lite** *compiler will return warnings of* **Constant is long in function main** *and* **Conversion may lose significant digits in function main()***, but will nevertheless run the program (and overflow the variables). As a general rule, even if a compiler warning message does not stop the compiler from compiling the program, you should observe such messages closely and respond appropriately.*

51 UNDERSTANDING PRECISION

As you have learned, computers represent numbers internally using combinations of 1's and 0's (binary digits). In previous Tips, you learned that because a type has a fixed number of bits, each type can only hold a specific range of values. If you assign a value outside the type's range, an overflow error occurs. Floating-point values can experience overflow and can suffer from insufficient precision. A value's *precision* defines its degree of accuracy. Values of type *float*, for example, provide six to seven significant digits. Assume, for example, you assign the value 1.234567890 to a variable of type *float*. Because type *float* only provides seven digits of significance, you can only count on values 1.23456 to be accurate. Values of type *double*, on the other hand, provide 14 to 15 significant digits. As a result, a value of type *double* could accurately store 1.234567890.

When you work with floating-point numbers, you must be aware that the computer represents values using a fixed number of bits. Therefore, it is impossible for the computer to always represent values exactly. For example, the computer may represent the value 0.4 as 0.3999999, or the value 0.1 as 0.099999, and so on. The following program, *precise.c*, illustrates the difference between double and single precision:

```c
#include <stdio.h>

void main(void)
  {
    float accurate = 0.123456790987654321;
    double more_accurate = 0.1234567890987654321;

    printf("Value of float\t %21.19f\n", accurate);
    printf("Value of double\t %21.19f\n", more_accurate);
  }
```

When you compile and execute the *precise.c* program, your screen will display the following output:

```
Value of float   0.1234567890432815550
Value of double  0.1234567890987654380
C:\>
```

ASSIGNING QUOTES AND OTHER CHARACTERS 52

As you work with variables of type *char*, or with character strings, there may be times when you must assign a single- or double-quote character to a variable. For example, to write *Jamsa's C/C++ Programmer's Bible*, you must include two single quotes within the string. In such cases, you must place the character within single quotes preceded by a backslash (\), as shown here:

```
char single_quote = '\'';
char double_quote = '\"';
```

In addition to the quote characters, your programs may often require that you assign one of the special characters listed in Table 52. To do so simply place the character's symbol immediately after the backslash character. In all cases, you must use lowercase letters to represent the special character.

Escape Character	Meaning
\a	ASCII bell character
\b	Backspace character
\f	Formfeed character
\n	Newline character
\r	Carriage return (no linefeed)
\t	Horizontal tab
\v	Vertical tab
\\	Backslash character
\'	Single quote
\"	Double quote
\?	Question mark
\nnn	ASCII value in octal
\xnnn	ASCII value in hexadecimal

Table 52 C-defined escape characters.

GETTING STARTED WITH PRINTF 53

Several tips presented throughout this book have used the *printf* function to display messages on the screen. When your program uses *printf*, the information you direct *printf* to print is called *printf's parameters* or *arguments*. The following statement uses *printf* to display the message *Jamsa's C/C++ Programmer's Bible!* on your screen display:

```
printf("Jamsa\'s C/C++ Programmer\'s Bible!");
```

In this case, the character string (the letters that appear within the double quotes) is *printf's* only parameter. When your programs begin to work with variables, you may want to use *printf* to display each variable's values. The *printf* function supports more than one parameter. The first parameter must always be a character string. You can make the parameters following the first character string be numbers, variables, expressions (such as 3 * 15), or even other character strings. When you want *printf* to display a value or variable, you must provide *printf* with information about the variable's type within the first parameter. In addition to specifying characters within the first parameter, you can include *format specifiers*, which tell *printf* how to print the other parameters. Such format specifiers take the form of a percent sign (%) followed by a letter. For example, to display an integer value, you use the %*d* (*d* for decimal value). Likewise, to print a floating-point value, you can use %*f*. The following *printf* statements illustrate how you might use format specifiers with *printf*:

```
printf("The users age is %d\n", age);
printf("The sales tax is %f\n", cost * 0.07);
printf("The user\'s age: %d weight: %d height: %d\n",
  age, weight, height);
```

As you can see, within *printf's* first parameter, you can specify one or more format specifiers. Note that the third statement does not fit on one line and continues to the next. When your statements cannot fit on one line, try to find a good place to wrap the line (such as immediately after a comma), and then indent the line that follows. The purpose of indentation is to improve your program's visual appeal and to make obvious to someone who is reading your program that the line contains a continuation of the previous line. Several tips that follow discuss in detail different *printf* format specifiers.

54 DISPLAYING VALUES OF TYPE INT USING PRINTF

The *printf* function supports format specifiers that provide *printf* with information about its parameter types (such as *int, float, char*, and so on). To display values of type *int* with *printf*, use the *%d* format specifier. The following program, *intout.c*, uses the *%d* format specifier to display values and variables of type *int*:

```
#include <stdio.h>

void main(void)
  {
    int age = 41;
    int height = 73;
    int weight = 165;

    printf("The user\'s age: %d weight: %d height: %d\n", age, weight, height);
    printf("%d plus %d equals %d\n", 1, 2, 1 + 2);
  }
```

When you compile and execute the *intout.c* program, your screen will display the following output:

```
The user's age: 41 weight: 165 height: 73
1 plus 2 equals 3
C:\>
```

Note: *Many C compilers treat the **%i** format specifier as identical to **%d**. If you are creating a new program, however, use the **%d** specifier, because the **%i** specifier is a legacy specifier and future compilers may not support it.*

55 PRINTING AN OCTAL OR HEXADECIMAL INTEGER VALUE

The *printf* function supports format specifiers that provide *printf* with information about its parameter types (such as *int, float, char*, and so on). Depending on your program, there may be times when you want to display an integer value in its octal (base 8) or hexadecimal (base 16) format. The *%o* (letter o, not zero) format specifier directs *printf* to display a value in octal. In a similar way, the *%x* and *%X* specifiers direct *printf* to display a value in hexadecimal format. The difference between *%x* and *%X* is that the latter displays hexadecimal values in uppercase. The following program, *oct_hex.c*, illustrates the use of the *%o, %x*, and *%X* format specifiers:

```
#include <stdio.h>
void main(void)
  {
    int value = 255;

    printf("The decimal value %d in octal is %o\n", value, value);
    printf("The decimal value %d in hexadecimal is %x\n", value, value);
    printf("The decimal value %d in hexadecimal is %X\n", value, value);
  }
```

When you compile and execute the *oct_hex.c* program, your screen will display the following output:

```
The decimal value 255 in octal is 377
The decimal value 255 in hexadecimal is ff
The decimal value 255 in hexadecimal is FF
C:\>
```

DISPLAYING VALUES OF TYPE UNSIGNED INT USING PRINTF C 56

As you have learned, the *printf* function supports format specifiers that provide *printf* with information about its parameter types (such as *int, float, char*, and so on). To display values of type *unsigned int* with *printf*, you should use the *%u* format specifier. If you use *%d* instead of *%u*, *printf* will treat the value specified as type *int*, which will probably display the wrong result. The following program, *u_intout.c*, uses the *%u* format specifier, as well as *%d*, to display the value 42000. The *u_intout.c* program illustrates the type of error that can occur if you use the wrong format specifier:

```
#include <stdio.h>

void main(void)
  {
    unsigned int value = 42000;

    printf("Displaying 42000 as unsigned %u\n", value);
    printf("Displaying 42000 as int %d\n", value);
  }
```

When you compile and execute *u_intout.c* program, your screen will display the following output:

```
Displaying 42000 as unsigned 42000
Displaying 42000 as int -23536
C:\>
```

Note: *When you compile this program under* **Turbo C++ Lite**, *the compiler will display two error messages, because the compiler sees the constant value 42,000 that the program tries to assign to the* **unsigned int** *variable* **value** *as a* **long** *number, rather than an* **int***. In this case, because the program's purpose is to show the mistakes that can arise from* **unsigned int** *declarations, you should ignore the compiler warnings. Other 16-bit compilers will issue similar warnings.*

DISPLAYING VALUES OF TYPE LONG INT USING PRINTF C 57

As you have learned, the *printf* function supports format specifiers that provide *printf* with information about its parameter types (such as *int, float, char*, and so on). To display values of type *long int* with *printf*, you should use the *%ld* format specifier. If you use *%d* instead of *%ld*, *printf* will treat the value specified as type *int*, quite probably displaying the wrong result. The following program, *longout.c*, uses the *%ld* format specifier, as well as *%d* to display the value 1000000. The *longout.c* program illustrates the type of error that can occur should you use the wrong format specifier:

```
#include <stdio.h>
void main(void)
  {
    long int one_million = 1000000;

    printf ("One million is %ld\n", one_million);
    printf ("One million is %d\n", one_million);
  }
```

When you compile and execute *longout.c* program, your screen will display the following output:

```
One million is 1000000
One million is 16960
C:\>
```

DISPLAYING VALUES OF TYPE FLOAT USING PRINTF C 58

As you have learned, the *printf* function supports format specifiers that provide *printf* with information about its parameter types (such as *int, float, char*, and so on). To display values of type *float* with *printf*, you should use the *%f* format specifier. The following program, *floatout.c*, uses the *%f* format specifier to display floating-point values:

```
#include <stdio.h>

void main(void)
  {
    float price = 525.75;
    float sales_tax = 0.06;

    printf("The item cost is %f\n", price);
    printf("Sales tax on the item is %f\n", price * sales_tax);
  }
```

When you compile and execute the *floatout.c* program, your screen will display the following output:

```
The item cost is 525.750000
Sales tax on the item is 31.544999
C:\>
```

As you can see, by default, the *%f* format specifier provides little output formatting. However, several Tips in this section present ways to format output using *printf*.

59 DISPLAYING VALUES OF TYPE CHAR USING PRINTF

As you have learned, the *printf* function supports format specifiers that provide *printf* with information about its parameter types (such as *int, float, char*, and so on). To display values of type *char* with *printf*, you should use the *%c* format specifier. The following program, *char_out.c*, uses the *%c* format specifier to display the letter A on your screen:

```
#include <stdio.h>

void main(void)
  {
    printf("The letter is %c\n", 'A');
    printf("The letter is %c\n", 65);
  }
```

As you can see, the *char_out.c* program will display the letter A using the character constant 'A', as well as the ASCII value 65. When you compile and execute the *char_out.c* program, your screen will display the following output:

```
The letter is A
The letter is A
C:\>
```

60 DISPLAYING FLOATING-POINT VALUES IN AN EXPONENTIAL FORMAT

As you have learned, the *printf* function supports format specifiers that provide *printf* with information about its parameter types (such as *int, float, char*, and so on). In Tip 58, you learned that by using the *%f* format specifier, you can display floating-point values. Depending on your program's requirements, there may be times when you will want to display values using an exponential format. To display a floating-point value in an exponential format, use the *%e* or *%E* format specifier. The difference between *%e* and *%E* is that the *%E* format specifier directs *printf* to use a capital E in the output. The following program, *exp_out.c*, uses the *%e* and *%E* format specifiers to display floating-point values in their exponential format:

```
#include <stdio.h>

void main(void)
  {
    float pi = 3.14159;
    float radius = 2.0031;

    printf("The circle's area is %e\n", 2 * pi * radius);
    printf("The circle's area is %E\n", 2 * pi * radius);
  }
```

When you compile and execute the *exp_out.c* program, your screen will display the following output:

```
The circle's area is 1.258584e+01
The circle's area is 1.258584E+01
C:\>
```

As you can see, by default, the *%e* and *%E* format specifiers provide little output formatting. However, several Tips in this section present ways to format output using *printf*.

DISPLAYING FLOATING-POINT VALUES

61

In Tip 58 you learned that using the *%f* format specifier, you can direct *printf* to display floating-point values using their decimal point format. Likewise, in Tip 60 you learned that you can use the *%e* and *%E* format specifiers to direct *printf* to display a floating-point value using an exponential format. In a similar way, *printf* supports the *%g* and *%G* format specifiers. When you use the *%g* and *%G* format specifiers, *printf* decides whether it should use the *%f* or *%e* format, depending on the technique that will display the output in the format most meaningful to the user. The following program, *flt_pt.c*, illustrates the use of the *%g* format specifier:

```
#include <stdio.h>

void main(void)
 {
   printf("Displaying 0.1234 yields %g\n", 0.1234);
   printf("Displaying 0.00001234 yields %g\n", 0.00001234);
 }
```

When you compile and execute the *flt_pt.c* program, your screen will display the following output:

```
Displaying 0.1234 yields 0.1234
Displaying 0.00001234 yields 1.234e-05
C:\>
```

DISPLAYING A CHARACTER STRING USING PRINTF

62

A *character string* is a sequence of zero or more characters. (The Strings section discusses character strings in more detail.) One of the most common operations your programs will perform is character string output. As you have learned, the *printf* function supports format specifiers that provide *printf* with information about its parameter types (such as *int*, *float*, *char*, and so on). To display a character string using *printf*, you should use the *%s* format specifier. The following program, *str_out.c*, uses the *%s* format specifier to display a character string:

```
#include <stdio.h>

void main(void)
 {
   char title[255] = "Jamsa\'s C/C++ Programmer\'s Bible";

   printf("The name of this book is %s\n", title);
 }
```

When you compile and execute the *str_out.c* program, your screen will display the following output:

```
The name of this book is Jamsa's C/C++ Programmer's Bible
C:\>
```

DISPLAYING A POINTER ADDRESS USING PRINTF

63

As you have learned, the *printf* function supports format specifiers that provide *printf* with information about its parameter types (such as *int*, *float*, *char*, and so on). You have also learned that a variable is a name that your program corresponds with a memory location. As your program's complexity increases, you will eventually work with memory addresses (called *pointers*). When you begin to work with pointers, there may be times when you must display a pointer address. To display a pointer address using *printf*, use the *%p* format specifier. The following program, *ptr_out.c*, uses the *%p* format specifier to display a memory address:

```
#include <stdio.h>

void main(void)
  {
    int value;
    printf("The address of the variable value is %p\n", &value);
  }
```

When you compile and execute the *ptr_out.c* program, your screen will display the following output:

```
The address of the variable value is FFF4
C:\>
```

When you use the *%p* format specifier, the pointer's actual value and the format *printf* uses to display the value will differ from one operating system to another. The Pointers section discusses in detail the use of pointers.

64   PRECEDING A VALUE WITH A PLUS OR MINUS SIGN

As you have learned, *printf* supports various format specifiers that control how *printf* displays output. By default, when you use *printf* to display a negative value, it will precede the value with a minus sign. Depending on your program, there may be times when you want *printf* to display the sign for positive values as well. To direct *printf* to display a value's sign, simply include a plus sign immediately following the % in the format specifier. The following program, *showsign.c*, illustrates the use of the plus sign within the format specifier:

```
#include <stdio.h>

void main(void)
  {
    int neg_int = -5;
    int pos_int = 5;
    float neg_flt = -100.23;
    float pos_flt = 100.23;

    printf("The integer values are %+d and %+d\n", neg_int, pos_int);
    printf("The floating-point values are %+f %+f\n", neg_flt, pos_flt);
  }
```

When you compile and execute the *showsign.c* program, your screen will display the following:

```
The integer values are -5 and +5
The floating-point values are -100.230003 +100.230003
C:\>
```

65   FORMATTING AN INTEGER VALUE USING PRINTF

As you read in Tip 54, the *%d* format specifier directs *printf* to display an integer value. As your programs become more complex, you will want *printf* to format your data better. For example, assume you want to print out a table on you computer screen which is similar to the following output:

```
Salesman  Quantity
Jones     332
Smith     1200
Allen     3311
David     43
```

When you use the *%d* format specifer, you can direct *printf* to display a minimum number of characters. The following program, *int_fmt.c*, illustrates how you might format integer values using *%d*:

```
#include <stdio.h>

void main(void)
  {
    int value = 5;
```

```
    printf ("%1d\n", value);
    printf ("%2d\n", value);
    printf ("%3d\n", value);
    printf ("%4d\n", value);
}
```

When you compile and execute the *int_fmt.c* program, your screen will display the following:

```
5
 5
  5
   5
C:\>
```

The digit you place after the % specifies the minimum number of characters *printf* will use to display an integer value. If, for example, you specify *%5d* and the value you want to display is 10, *printf* will precede the value with three spaces. Note that the value specifies the minimum number of characters the output will consume. If the value you want to display requires more characters than you specified, *printf* will use the number of characters *printf* requires to correctly display the value.

ZERO-PADDING INTEGER OUTPUT C 66

In Tip 65 you learned how to format an integer value by placing the desired number of digits immediately after the % in the *%d* format specifier. If the integer value *printf* displays does not require the number of characters you specified, *printf* will precede the value with the necessary number of spaces. Depending on your program's purpose, there may be times when you want *printf* to precede the value with zeros (called *zero-padding*), as opposed to spaces. To direct *printf* to zero-pad a value, place a 0 (zero) immediately after the % in the format specifier, prior to the desired number of digits. The following program, *zero_pad.c*, illustrates zero-padding:

```
#include <stdio.h>

void main(void)
  {
    int value = 5;

    printf ("%01d\n", value);
    printf ("%02d\n", value);
    printf ("%03d\n", value);
    printf ("%04d\n", value);
}
```

When you compile and execute the *zero_pad.c* program, your screen will display the following:

```
5
05
005
0005
C:\>
```

DISPLAYING A PREFIX BEFORE OCTAL AND HEXADECIMAL VALUES C 67

In Tip 55 you learned how to use the *%o* format specifier to display octal values and the *%x* and *%X* format specifiers to display hexadecimal values. When your programs output such values, there may be times when you want to precede octal values with a zero (for example, *0777*), and hexadecimal values with *0x* (for example, *0xFF*).

To direct *printf* to precede an octal or hexadecimal value with the appropriate prefix, place a pound sign character (#) immediately after the % in the format specifier. The following program, *show_oh.c*, illustrates the use of the pound sign character (#) in the *printf* format specifier:

```
#include <stdio.h>

void main(void)
 {
   int value = 255;

   printf("The decimal value %d in octal is %#o\n", value, value);
   printf("The decimal value %d in hexadecimal is %#x\n", value, value);
   printf("The decimal value %d in hexadecimal is %#X\n", value, value);
 }
```

When you compile and execute the *show_oh.c* program, your screen will display the following output:

```
The decimal value 255 in octal is 0377
The decimal value 255 in hexadecimal is 0xff
The decimal value 255 in hexadecimal is 0xFF
C:\>
```

68 FORMATTING A FLOATING-POINT VALUE USING PRINTF

In Tip 65 you learned how to format an integer value by placing the desired number of digits immediately after the % in the *%d* format specifier. Using a similar technique, *printf* lets you format floating-point output. When you format a floating-point value, you specify two values. The first value tells *printf* the minimum number of characters you want to display. The second value tells *printf* the number of digits you want displayed to the right of the decimal point. The following program, *flt_fmt.c*, illustrates how to format floating-point values using *printf*:

```
#include <stdio.h>

void main(void)
 {
   float value = 1.23456;

   printf ("%8.1f\n", value);
   printf ("%8.3f\n", value);
   printf ("%8.5f\n", value);
 }
```

When you compile and execute the *flt_fmt.c* program, your screen will display the following output:

```
     1.2
   1.235
 1.23456
C:\>
```

69 FORMATTING EXPONENTIAL OUTPUT

In Tip 68 you learned how to use the *%f* format specifier to format floating-point values. Using similar formatting techniques, you can instruct *printf* to display floating-point output in an exponential format. The following program, *exp_fmt.c*, illustrates the formatted exponential output:

```
#include <stdio.h>

void main(void)
 {
   float value = 1.23456;

   printf ("%12.1e\n", value);
   printf ("%12.3e\n", value);
   printf ("%12.5e\n", value);
 }
```

When you compile and execute the *exp_fmt.c* program, your screen will display the following output:

```
     1.2e+00
   1.235e+00
 1.23456e+00
C:\>
```

LEFT-JUSTIFYING PRINTF'S OUTPUT 70

By default, when you output text using *printf*'s formatting characters, *printf* will display the text right-justified. Depending on your program, there may be times when you want *printf* to left-justify your output. To left-justify text, place a minus sign (–) immediately after the % in the format specifier. The following program, *leftjust.c*, illustrates the use of the minus sign to left-justify output:

```c
#include <stdio.h>

void main(void)
  {
    int int_value = 5;
    float flt_value = 3.33;

    printf("Right justified %5d value\n", int_value);
    printf("Left justified %-5d value\n", int_value);
    printf("Right justified %7.2f value\n", flt_value);
    printf("Left justified %-7.2f value\n", flt_value);
  }
```

When you compile and execute the *leftjust.c* program, your screen will display the following output:

```
Right justified     5 value
Left justified 5     value
Right justified    3.33 value
Left justified 3.33     value
C:\>
```

COMBINING PRINTF FORMAT SPECIFIERS 71

Several Tips presented in this section have discussed various *printf* format specifiers. As you use *printf*'s format specifiers, there may be times when you want to take advantage of two or more format specifiers. For example, you may want to display a left-justified hexadecimal value, preceded with the characters *0x*. In such cases, simply place each of the specifiers after the %. The following program, *full_fmt.c*, illustrates the use of multiple format specifiers:

```c
#include <stdio.h>

void main(void)
  {
    int int_value = 5;

    printf("Left justifed with sign %-+3d\n", int_value);
  }
```

When you compile and execute the *full_fmt.c* program, your screen will display the following output:

```
Left justified with sign +5
C:\>
```

WRAPPING A CHARACTER STRING TO THE NEXT LINE 72

When your programs use *printf*, there may be times when a character string within *printf* will not fit on the current line. In such cases, simply place a backslash (\) at the end of the line, which will continue the text at the start of the next line, as shown here:

```c
printf("This line is very long and because it is so very long, it would not \
fit on the same line.");
```

Note: *If you wrap text to the next line, do not include spaces at the start of the new line's text. If spaces are present, the C compiler will include the spaces within the string.*

73 DISPLAYING NEAR AND FAR STRINGS

The Memory section of this book discusses *near* and *far* pointers in detail. Briefly, *near* and *far* pointers represent variable addresses within the program's memory space. Programs that run within older operating systems, such as MS-DOS, use *far* pointers to increase the range of memory addresses the program can use to store information. When your programs work with *far* string pointers, there may be times you will want to display the string's contents using *printf*. As you will learn in the Functions section, however, the compiler will generate an error if you pass a *far* pointer to a function that expects a *near* address. If you want to display the contents of a *far* string (whose start a *far* string pointer indicates) using *printf*, you must tell *printf* that you are using a *far* pointer. To do so, place an uppercase *F* (for *far*) immediately after the % in the format specifier, as shown here:

```
printf("%Fs\n", some_far_string);
```

Because %*Fs* tells *printf* you are using a *far* pointer, the function call is correct. In a similar way, you can tell *printf* that you are passing a *near* string by placing an uppercase *N* in the format specifier. However, because *printf* expects *near* strings by default, the format specifiers %*Ns* and %*s* have the same result. The following C program, *near_far.c*, illustrates the use of %*Fs* and %*Ns* within *printf*:

```
#include <stdio.h>

void main(void)
  {
    char *near_title = "Jamsa\'s C/C++ Programmer\'s Bible";
    char far *far_title = "Jamsa\'s C/C++ Programmer\'s Bible";

    printf("The book\'s title: %Ns\n", near_title);
    printf("The book\'s title: %Fs\n", far_title);
  }
```

Note: *Visual C++ does not distinguish between* **near** *and* **far** *pointers. If you try to compile the* **near_far.c** *program under Visual C++, the compiler will return an error. To automatically update your programs to run under* **Visual C++**, *include the* **windef.h** *header file within your programs.*

74 WORKING WITH PRINTF'S ESCAPE CHARACTERS

When you work with character strings, there will be times when you will want to use special characters, such as the tab, carriage return, or linefeed characters. C defines several *escape characters* (that is, characters you precede with C's escape symbol, the backslash) to make including special characters within a string (such as characters you want *printf* to output) easy for you. For example, several of the programs presented in this book have used the newline character (\n) to advance output to the start of the next line, as shown here:

```
printf("Line 1\nLine 2\Line 3\n");
```

Table 74 lists the escape characters you can use within your character strings (and hence the *printf* output).

Escape Character	Meaning
\a	ASCII bell character
\b	Backspace character
\f	Formfeed character
\n	Newline character
\r	Carriage return (no linefeed)
\t	Horizontal tab
\v	Vertical tab
\\	Backslash character

Table 74 C-defined escape characters. (continued on following page)

Escape Character	Meaning
\'	Single quote
\"	Double quote
\?	Question mark
\nnn	ASCII value in octal
\xnnn	ASCII value in hexadecimal

Table 74 C-defined escape characters. (continued from previous page)

DETERMINING THE NUMBER OF CHARACTERS PRINTF HAS DISPLAYED 75

When your programs perform sophisticated screen formatting, there may be times when you want to know the number of characters *printf* has displayed. When you use the *%n* format specifier, *printf* will assign to a variable (passed by pointer) a count of the number of characters *printf* has displayed. The following program, *prt_cnt.c*, illustrates the use of the *%n* format specifier:

```c
#include <stdio.h>

void main(void)
  {
    int first_count;
    int second_count;

    printf("Jamsa%n\'s C/C++ Programmer\'s Bible%n\n", &first_count, &second_count);
    printf("First count %d Second count %d\n", first_count, second_count);
  }
```

When you compile and execute the *prt_cnt.c* program, your screen will display the following:

```
Jamsa's C/C++ Programmer's Bible
First count 5 Second count 32
C:\>
```

USING PRINTF'S RETURN VALUE 76

In Tip 75 you learned how to use *printf*'s *%n* format specifier to determine the number of characters *printf* has written. Using the *%n* format specifier is one way to ensure that *printf* has successfully displayed its output. In addition, when *printf* completes, it returns the total number of characters that *printf* wrote. If *printf* encounters an error, it will return the constant EOF (which, as you will learn, indicates the end of a file). The following program, *printfok.c*, uses *printf*'s return value to ensure that *printf* was successful:

```c
#include <stdio.h>

void main(void)
  {
    int result;

    result = printf("Jamsa\'s C/C++ Programmer\'s Bible!\n");
    if (result == EOF)
      fprintf(stderr, "Error within printf\n");
  }
```

If the user has redirected a program's output to a file or device (such as a printer), and redirected I/O experiences an error (such as *device off-line* or *disk full*), your programs can detect the error by testing *printf*'s return value.

USING THE ANSI DEVICE DRIVER 77

Several Tips presented throughout this book have made extensive use of *printf*'s output formatting capabilities. Although *printf* provides format specifiers that you use to control the number of digits displayed, to display output in octal or hexadecimal, or to left- or right-justify text, *printf* does not provide other format specifiers. *Printf* does not provide format specifiers that let you position the cursor to a specific row and column, clear the screen, or display output in colors. However, depending on the operating system you are using, you can probably perform such operations using the ANSI device driver. The ANSI driver supports different escape sequences that direct it to use specific colors, to position the cursor, and even to clear the screen. Programmers name such formatting statements *escape sequences* because they begin with the ASCII escape character (the value 27). If you are using DOS, install the ANSI driver by placing an entry such as the following within your *config.sys* file (and then rebooting):

```
DEVICE=C:\DOS\ANSI.SYS
```

After you install the ANSI driver, your programs can write escape sequences using *printf*.

Note: *If you are running Windows 95 on the same machine on which you compile programs, adding the ANSI driver to your system's* **config.sys** *file will not interfere with Windows 95 operations.*

78 USING THE ANSI DRIVER TO CLEAR YOUR SCREEN DISPLAY

One of the most common operations each of your programs will perform when the program first begins execution is to clear the screen display. Unfortunately, the C run-time library does not provide a function that clears the screen display. To clear the screen display, use the ANSI driver discussed in Tip 77, and then invoke the following escape sequence to clear your screen display:

```
Esc[2j
```

An easy way to invoke the escape sequence is to use the octal representation of the escape character (\033). To print the escape character, as shown here:

```
printf("\033[2J");
```

79 USING THE ANSI DRIVER TO DISPLAY SCREEN COLORS

Several Tips presented throughout this book have made extensive use of the *printf* function to display output. Although *printf* provides powerful format specifiers, *printf* does not provide the means for you to display output in color. However, if you are using the ANSI driver, as discussed in Tip 77, you can use the escape sequences listed in Table 79 to display output in color.

Escape Sequence	Color
Esc[30m	Black foreground color
Esc[31m	Red foreground color
Esc[32m	Green foreground color
Esc[33m	Orange foreground color
Esc[34m	Blue foreground color
Esc[35m	Magenta foreground color
Esc[36m	Cyan foreground color
Esc[37m	White foreground color
Esc[40m	Black background color
Esc[41m	Red background color
Esc[42m	Green background color
Esc[43m	Orange background color
Esc[44m	Blue background color
Esc[45m	Magenta background color
Esc[46m	Cyan background color
Esc[47m	White background color

Table 79 ANSI escape sequences you can use to set screen colors.

The following *printf* statement selects the blue background color:

```
printf("\033[44m");
```

Similarly, the following *printf* statement selects red text on a white background:

```
printf("\033[47m\033[31m");
```

In the previous example, *printf* writes two escape sequences. The ANSI driver lets you specify the screen colors, which you separate with semicolons, as shown here:

```
printf("\033[47;31m");
```

USING THE ANSI DRIVER TO POSITION THE CURSOR C 80

As you have learned, the ANSI driver supports escape sequences that let you clear your screen and display output in color. In addition, the ANSI driver provides escape sequences that let you position the cursor to specific row and column positions, which lets you display your output at specific screen locations. Table 80 shows the ANSI driver's cursor-positioning escape sequences.

Escape Sequence	Function	Example
Esc[x;yH	Set the cursor at row *x* and column *y*	*Esc[10;25H*
Esc[xA	Move the cursor up *x* rows	*Esc[1a*
Esc[xB	Move the cursor down *x* rows	*Esc[2b*
Esc[yC	Move the cursor right *y* columns	*Esc[10c*
Esc[yD	Move the cursor left *y* columns	*Esc[10d*
Esc[S	Store the current cursor position	*Esc[S*
Esc[U	Restore the cursor position	*Esc[U*
Esc[2j	Clear the screen, moving the cursor to the home position	*Esc[2j*
Esc[K	Clear to end of the current line	*Esc[K*

Table 80 ANSI driver cursor-positioning escape sequences you can use within your programs.

PERFORMING BASIC MATH OPERATIONS IN C C 81

In all but the simplest programs, your programs will perform arithmetic operations such as addition, subtraction, multiplication, or division. To perform these basic math operations, use the operators described in Table 81.

Operator	Purpose
+	Addition
–	Subtraction
*	Multiplication
/	Division

Table 81 Basic arithmetic operators in C.

The following program, *math.c*, illustrates how you use C's basic arithmetic operators:

```
#include <stdio.h>

void main(void)
 {
   int seconds_in_an_hour;
   float average;

   seconds_in_an_hour = 60 * 60;
   average = (5 + 10 + 15 + 20) / 4;
   printf("The number of seconds in an hour %d\n", seconds_in_an_hour);
```

```
    printf("The average of 5, 10, 15, and 20 is %f\n", average);
    printf("The number of seconds in 48 minutes is %d\n",
           seconds_in_an_hour - 12 * 60);
}
```

When you compile and execute the *math.c* program, your screen will display the following output:

```
The number of seconds in an hour 3600
The average of 5, 10, 15, and 20 is 12.000000
The number of seconds in 48 minutes is 2880
C:\>
```

82 UNDERSTANDING MODULO ARITHMETIC

In Tip 81 you learned that C uses the forward slash operator (/) for division. Depending on your application, there may be times when your program needs the remainder of an integer division. In such cases, use C's modulo (remainder) operator. The following program, *modulo.c*, illustrates how you use C's modulo operator:

```
#include <stdio.h>

void main(void)
 {
    int remainder;
    int result;

    result = 10 / 3;
    remainder = 10 % 3;
    printf("10 Divided by 3 is %d Remainder %d\n", result, remainder);
 }
```

When you compile and execute the *modulo.c* program, your screen will display the following output:

```
10 Divided by 3 is 3 Remainder 1
```

83 UNDERSTANDING OPERATOR PRECEDENCE AND ASSOCIATIVITY

In Tip 81 you learned that C uses the following operators: the plus sign (+) for addition; the hyphen (-) for subtraction; the asterisk (*) for multiplication; and the forward slash (/) for division. When your programs use these operators within arithmetic expressions, you should understand C's operator precedence, which specifies the order in which C performs arithmetic operations. For example, consider the following expression:

```
result = 5 + 2 * 3;
```

If you assume that C performs the operations from left to right (the addition before the multiplication), the expression's result is 21:

```
result = 5 + 2 * 3;
       = 7 * 3;
       = 21;
```

If, however, C performs the multiplication first, the result is 11:

```
result = 5 + 2 * 3;
       = 5 + 6;
       = 11;
```

To prevent the problem of indeterminate results, C defines an *operator precedence*. An operator precedence determines which operations C executes first. Table 83 illustrates C's operator precedence.

Operator Precedence (High to Low)

()	[]	.	->							
++	--	+	-	*	&	!	~	(type)	sizeof	
*	/	%								

Table 83 C's operator precedence. (continued on following page)

Operator Precedence (High to Low)									
+	-								
>>	<<								
==	!=								
&									
^									
|									
&&									
||									
? :									
=	+=	-=	*=	/=	%=	&=	^=	|=	<<= >>=
,									

Table 83 *C's operator precedence. (continued from previous page)*

When you create an expression, C will execute the operations with the highest precedence first. If two operators have the same precedence, C performs the operations from left to right.

FORCING THE ORDER OF OPERATOR EVALUATION $\mathbb{C}$ 84

As you learned in Tip 83, C performs operations in an expression based on each operator's precedence within the expression. In many cases, the order that C will use to evaluate operators is not the order you want. For example, consider the following expression—its goal is to calculate the average of three values:

```
average = 5 + 10 + 15 / 3;
```

Mathematically, the average of the three values 5, 10, and 15 is 10. However, if you let C evaluate the previous expression, C will assign the variable *average* the value 20, as shown here:

```
average = 5 + 10 + 15 / 3;
        = 5 + 10 + 5;
        = 15 + 5;
        = 20;
```

If you examine C's operator precedence table (which Tip 83 presents), you will find that C's *division* operator (/) has a higher precedence than C's *addition* operator (+). Therefore, you need a way to change the order in which C performs the operations. When C evaluates an expression, C will always perform operations that appear within parentheses before performing other operations. When you group the values you want to sum within parentheses, C will calculate the correct average, as shown here:

```
average = (5 + 10 + 15) / 3;
        = (15 + 15) / 3;
        = (30) / 3;
        = 10;
```

C performs operations within parentheses based on its operator precedence rules. If an expression contains multiple expressions within multiple parentheses sets, C performs the operations within the innermost parentheses first, as shown here:

```
result = ((5 + 3) * 2) - 3;
       = ((8) * 2) - 3;
       = (16) - 3;
       = 13;
```

UNDERSTANDING C'S INCREMENT OPERATOR $\mathbb{C}$ 85

One very common operation programs perform is to increment a variable's current value by 1. For example, the following statement increments the value of *variable* count by 1:

```
variable = variable + 1;
```

Because increment operations are so common, C provides a shorthand notation you can use to increment variables within your programs, called the *increment operator*. The following statement uses the *increment* operator to add 1 to a value of *variable*:

```
variable++;
```

The following program, *0_to_100.c*, uses the *increment* operator to print the values 0 through 100:

```c
#include <stdio.h>

void main(void)
  {
    int value = 0;

    while (value <= 100)
      {
        printf("%d\n", value);
        value++;
      }
  }
```

C provides both a *prefix* and *postfix increment* operator. The following statements both increment the variable *count* by 1:

```
count++;
++count;
```

The first statement uses C's *postfix increment* operator. The second statement uses the *prefix increment* operator. You should distinguish between the two operators because C treats *prefix* and *postfix* operators differently. When you use the *postfix increment* operator, C first uses the variable's value and then performs the *increment* operation. On the other hand, when you use the *prefix increment* operator, C first increments the variable's value and then uses the variable. To better understand the difference between the *prefix* and *postfix increment* operators, consider the following program, *prepost.c*, which uses both operators:

```c
#include <stdio.h>

void main(void)
  {
    int value = 1;

    printf("Using postfix %d\n", value++);
    printf("Value after increment %d\n", value);
    value = 1;
    printf("Using prefix %d\n", ++value);
    printf("Value after increment %d\n", value);
  }
```

When you compile and execute the *prepost.c* program, your screen will display the following output:

```
Using postfix 1
Value after increment 2
Using prefix 2
Value after increment 2
C:\>
```

As you see, when you use the *postfix* operator, C first uses the variable's value (displaying the value 1) and then increments the variable (yielding 2). When you use the *prefix* operator, C first increments the variable (yielding 2) and then displays the already incremented value.

86 UNDERSTANDING C'S DECREMENT OPERATOR

Just as there will be many times when you want to increment a variable's value, so too will there be many times when you want to decrement a variable's current value by 1, as shown here:

```
variable = variable - 1;
```

Because decrement operations are so common, C provides a shorthand notation you can use to perform such operations—C's *decrement* operator. The following statement uses the *decrement* operator to subtract 1 from the value of *variable*:

```
variable--;
```

As was the case with C's *increment* operator, C provides both a *prefix* and a *postfix decrement* operator. The following statements both decrement the variable *count* by 1:

```
count--;
--count;
```

The first statement uses C's *postfix decrement* operator and the second statement uses the *prefix decrement* operator. You should distinguish between the two operators because C treats *prefix* and *postfix* operators differently. When you use the *postfix* operator, C first uses the variable's value and then performs the decrement operation. In the opposite manner, when you use the *prefix* operator, C first decrements the variable's value and then uses the variable. To better understand the difference between the *prefix* and *postfix increment* operators, consider the following program, *postpre.c*, which uses both operators:

```
#include <stdio.h>

void main(void)
  {
    int value = 1;

    printf("Using postfix %d\n", value--);
    printf("Value after decrement %d\n", value);
    value = 1;
    printf("Using prefix %d\n", --value);
    printf("Value after decrement %d\n", value);
  }
```

When you compile and execute the *postpre.c* program, your screen will display the following output:

```
Using postfix 1
Value after decrement 0
Using prefix 0
Value after decrement 0
C:\>
```

As you can see, when you use the *postfix decrement* operator, C first uses the variable's value (displaying the value 1) and then decrements the variable's value (yielding 0). When you use the *prefix decrement* operator, C first decrements the variable (yielding 0) and then displays the already decremented value.

UNDERSTANDING A BITWISE OR OPERATION 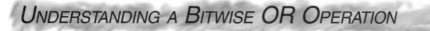 87

As the complexity of your programs increases, you may find that you can increase a program's performance or reduce a program's memory requirement by using *bitwise operations*. Bitwise operations are operations that manipulate values one or more bits at a time. When you must manipulate a value a single bit at a time, you may take advantage of C's *bitwise OR* operator (|). The *bitwise OR* operator examines each bit within two values and yields a third value as a result. For example, assume that two variables contain the values 3 and 4, whose bits are, respectively, 00000011 and 00000100. The *bitwise OR* operator returns the value 7, as shown here:

```
    3        00000011
    4        00000100
             --------
    7        00000111
```

In the value 3, bits 0 and 1 have a one value, and all the other bits have a zero value. In the value 4, bit 2 has a one value, and all the other bits have a zero value. The result of a bitwise *OR* operation will have a one value within each corresponding bit which has a one value in either of the original values. In this case, the result has a one value in bits 0, 1, and 2. The following program, *bit_or.c*, illustrates how you use C's *bitwise OR* operator:

```
#include <stdio.h>

void main(void)
  {
    printf("0 | 0 is %d\n", 0 | 0);
    printf("0 | 1 is %d\n", 0 | 1);
    printf("1 | 1 is %d\n", 1 | 1);
    printf("1 | 2 is %d\n", 1 | 2);
    printf("128 | 127 is %d\n", 128 | 127);
  }
```

When you compile and execute the *bit_or.c* program, your screen will display the following output:

```
0 | 0 is 0
0 | 1 is 1
1 | 1 is 1
1 | 2 is 3
128 | 127 is 255
C:\>
```

88 UNDERSTANDING A BITWISE AND OPERATION

As you learned in Tip 87, you may find that you can increase your program's performance or reduce your program's memory requirements by using bitwise operations. Bitwise operations are operations that manipulate values one or more bits at a time. When manipulating data one bit at a time, you may take advantage of C's *bitwise AND* operator (&). The *bitwise AND* operator examines each bit within two values and yields a third value as a result. For example, assume that two variables contain the values 5 and 7, whose bits are, respectively, 00000101 and 00000111. The *bitwise AND* operator returns the value 5, as shown here:

```
5        00000101
7        00000111
         --------
5        00000101
```

If a bit within both terms has a one value, the *bitwise AND* operator sets to one the corresponding bit within the result. If a bit within either term contains a zero value, the *bitwise AND* operator sets to zero the corresponding bit within the result. In this case, bits 0 and 2 contain one values in both terms, so the result has one values in bits 0 and 2, and zero values in the remaining bits. The following program, *bit_and.c*, illustrates the use of C's *bitwise AND* operator:

```
#include <stdio.h>
void main(void)
  {
    printf("0 & 0 is %d\n", 0 & 0);
    printf("0 & 1 is %d\n", 0 & 1);
    printf("1 & 1 is %d\n", 1 & 1);
    printf("1 & 2 is %d\n", 1 & 2);
    printf("15 & 127 is %d\n", 15 & 127);
  }
```

When you compile and execute the *bit_and.c* program, your screen will display the following output:

```
0 & 0 is 0
0 & 1 is 0
1 & 1 is 1
1 & 2 is 0
15 & 127 is 15
C:\>
```

UNDERSTANDING A BITWISE EXCLUSIVE OR OPERATION 89

As you have already learned, bitwise operations are operations that manipulate values one or more bits at a time. When you are manipulating data one bit at a time, there may be situations in which you must take advantage of C's *bitwise exclusive OR* operator (^), which examines the bits in two values and sets to 1 the bits of the result based on the truth table shown in Table 89.

X	Y	Result
0	0	0
0	1	1
1	0	1
1	1	0

*Table 89 Bit results from a **bitwise exclusive OR** operation.*

Assume that two variables contain the values 5 and 7, whose bits are, respectively, 00000101 and 00000111. The *bitwise exclusive OR* operator returns the value 2, as shown here:

```
5        00000101
7        00000111
         --------
2        00000010
```

The following program, *bit_xor.c*, illustrates the use of C's *bitwise exclusive OR* operator:

```c
#include <stdio.h>

void main(void)
 {
   printf("0 ^ 0 is %d\n", 0 ^ 0);
   printf("0 ^ 1 is %d\n", 0 ^ 1);
   printf("1 ^ 1 is %d\n", 1 ^ 1);
   printf("1 ^ 2 is %d\n", 1 ^ 2);
   printf("15 ^ 127 is %d\n", 15 ^ 127);
 }
```

When you compile and execute the *bit_xor.c* program, your screen will display the following output:

```
0 ^ 0 is 0
0 ^ 1 is 1
1 ^ 1 is 0
1 ^ 2 is 3
15 ^ 127 is 112
C:\>
```

UNDERSTANDING A BITWISE INVERSE OPERATION 90

As you have learned, bitwise operations are operations that manipulate values one or more bits at a time. When you must manipulate values one bit at a time, you may take advantage of C's *bitwise inverse* operator (~). The *bitwise inverse* operator examines each bit within a value and yields a second value as a result. The *bitwise inverse* operation makes each bit which contains a one in the original value a zero in the resulting value, and makes each bit which contains a zero in the original a one in the resulting value. As an example, assume an unsigned character variable contains the value 15. The bitwise inverse of the operation would therefore return 240, as shown here:

```
15    00001111
240   11110000
```

As you can see, each bit which was set to one in the original value is zero in the result, and each bit which was set to zero in the original value is set to one in the result. The following program, *bit_inv.c*, illustrates the use of C's *bitwise inverse* operator:

```
#include <stdio.h>

void main(void)
  {
    int value = 0xFF;

    printf("The inverse of %X is %X\n", value, ~value);
  }
```

When you compile and execute the *bit_inv.c* program, your screen will display the following output:

```
The inverse of FF is FF00
C:\>
```

91 APPLYING AN OPERATION TO A VARIABLE'S VALUE

As you perform arithmetic operations within your programs, you may find that you often assign a variable the result of an expression that includes the variable's current value. For example, consider the following statements:

```
total = total + 100;
count = count - 5;
half = half / 2;
```

For cases in which an assignment operation updates a variable with the result of an operation on the variable's current value, C provides a shorthand technique for expressing the operation. In short, you place the operator in front of the assignment operator. When you use C's shorthand assignment technique, the following statements will be equivalent to the three statements just shown:

```
total += 100;
count -= 5;
half /= 2;
```

When you use this shorthand technique, the following statements are equivalent:

```
variable += 10;        variable = variable + 10;
variable <<= 2;        variable = variable << 2;
variable &= 0xFF;      variable = variable & 0xFF;
variable *= 1.05;      variable = variable * 1.05;
```

92 UNDERSTANDING C'S CONDITIONAL OPERATOR

As you will learn, C's *if-else* statement examines a condition and performs one set of operations if the condition is true and another if the condition is false. In a similar way, C provides a *conditional* operator that examines a condition and, based on whether the condition evaluates to true or false, returns one of two values. The *conditional* operator's format is as follows:

```
(condition) ? trueResult: falseResult
```

To understand the *conditional* operator better, consider the following condition, which tests whether a test score is greater than or equal to 60. If the value is greater than or equal to 60, the statement assigns the variable *grade* a P, for pass. If the value is less than 60, the statement assigns the variable *grade* an F, for fail:

```
grade = (score >= 60) ? 'P': 'F';
```

The statement is similar to the following *if-else* statement:

```
if (score >= 60)
  grade = 'P';
else
  grade = 'F';
```

The following *printf* statement displays the string *"Pass"* or *"Fail,"* based on the test score:

```
printf("Score %d Result %s\n", score, (score >= 60) ? "Pass", "Fail");
```

When you use C's conditional operator to assign a condition's result to a variable, you can reduce the number of *if-else* statements you use within your programs.

UNDERSTANDING C'S SIZEOF OPERATOR 93

When your programs declare a variable, the C compiler allocates memory to store the variable's value. When you write programs that perform file *input/output* operations or allocate memory for dynamic lists, you will find it convenient to know the amount of memory your program has allocated for a specific variable. C's *sizeof* operator returns the number of bytes a variable or type requires. The following program, *sizeof.c*, illustrates the use of the *sizeof* operator:

```c
#include <stdio.h>

void main(void)
  {
    printf("Variables of type int use %d bytes\n", sizeof(int));
    printf("Variables of type float use %d bytes\n", sizeof(float));
    printf("Variables of type double use %d bytes\n", sizeof(double));
    printf("Variables of type unsigned use %d bytes\n", sizeof(unsigned));
    printf("Variables of type long use %d bytes\n", sizeof(long));
  }
```

Depending on your compiler and system hardware, the the *sizeof* program output may differ. When you use *Turbo C++ Lite*, your program will display the following:

```
Variables of type int use 2 bytes
Variables of type float use 4 bytes
Variables of type double use 8 bytes
Variables of type unsigned use 2 bytes
Variables of type long use 4 bytes
C:\>
```

PERFORMING A BITWISE SHIFT 94

When you work with values at the bit level, some common operations you will perform are *bitwise shifts*, either to the right (away from the most significant bit) or to the left (towards the most significant bit). To help your programs perform bitwise shifts, C provides two *bitwise shift* operators: one operator that shifts bits to the right (>>) and one that shifts bits to the left (<<). The following expression uses the *bitwise left-shift* operator to shift the values in the variable *flag* two positions to the left:

```c
flag = flag << 2;
```

Assume that the variable *flag* contains the value 2, as shown here:

```
0000 0010
```

When you shift the value two places to the left, the result will be 8, as shown here:

```
0000 1000
```

When you shift values to the left, C zero-fills the lower bit positions. When you shift values to the right, however, the value that C places in the most significant bit position depends on the variable's type. If the variable is unsigned (that is, you declared it in the program as an *unsigned* type), C zero-fills the most significant bit during a *right-shift* operation. However, if the variable is of a signed type (in other words, if you did not declare the variable as *unsigned*), C uses the value 1 if the value is currently negative or 0 if the value is positive. The following program, *shiftem.c*, illustrates the use of C's *bitwise right-shift* and *bitwise left-shift* operators:

```c
#include <stdio.h>

void main(void)
  {
    unsigned u_val = 1;
    signed int value = -1;
```

```
    printf("%u (unsigned) shifted left 2 times is %u\n", u_val, u_val << 2);
    printf("%u (unsigned) shifted right 2 times is %u\n", u_val, u_val >> 2);
    u_val = 65535;
    printf("%u (unsigned) shifted left 2 times is %u\n", u_val, u_val << 2);
    printf("%u (unsigned) shifted right 2 times is %u\n", u_val, u_val >> 2);
    printf("%d (signed) shifted left 2 times is %d\n", value, value << 2);
    printf("%d (signed) shifted right 2 times is %d\n", value, value >> 2);
}
```

95 PERFORMING A BITWISE ROTATION

In Tip 94 you learned how to use C's *left-shift* and *right-shift* operators. When you perform a *left-shift* operation, C zero-fills the least significant bit. When you perform a *right-shift* operation, on the other hand, the value C places in the most significant bit position depends on the value's type and current value. As you work at the bit level, there may be times when you may want to simply rotate bits rather than shifting bits left or right. When you rotate bits to the left, the value's most significant bit becomes the least significant, while the other bits move one position to the right. When you rotate values to the right, the value's least significant bit becomes the most significant. To help you rotate bits, many C compilers provide the _*rotl* and _*rotr* functions, which rotate the bits comprising an unsigned value to the left and the right, as shown here:

```
#include <stdlib.h>

unsigned _rotl(unsigned value, int count);
unsigned _rotr(unsigned value, int count);
```

The *count* variable specifies the number of times you want to rotate the value. The following program, *rotate.c*, illustrates the use of the _*rotl* and _*rotr* functions:

```
#include <stdio.h>
#include <stdlib.h>

void main(void)
  {
    unsigned value = 1;
    printf("%u rotated right once is %u\n", value, _rotr(value, 1));
    value = 5;
    printf("%u rotated right twice is %u\n", value, _rotr(value, 2));
    value = 65534;
    printf("%u rotated left twice is %u\n", value, _rotl(value, 2));
  }
```

When you compile and execute the *rotate.c* program, your screen will display the following:

```
1 rotated right once is 32768
5 rotated right twice is 16385
65534 rotated left twice is 65531
C:\>
```

Note: *Many C compilers also provide the _lrotl and _lrotr functions, which rotate **unsigned long** integer values left or right.*

96 UNDERSTANDING CONDITIONAL OPERATORS

All the programs previously presented in this book began their execution with the first instruction in *main* and have executed each instruction that followed in order. As your programs become more complex, there will be times when the program must perform one set of instructions if a condition is true and, possibly, other instructions if the condition is not true. For example, your program might have different instructions for different days of the week. When a program performs (or does not perform) instructions based on a specific condition, the program is performing *conditional processing*. To perform conditional processing, the program evaluates a condition that results in true or false result. For example, the condition *Today is Monday* is either true or false. To help your programs perform conditional processing, C provides the *if*, *if-else*, and *switch* statements. Several of the Tips that follow discuss these statements in detail.

UNDERSTANDING ITERATIVE PROCESSING C 97

All the programs previously presented in this book executed their instructions only one time. In some cases, a program may or may not have executed a set of instructions, based on the result of a tested condition. As your programs become more complex, there will be times when a program must repeat the same set of instructions a specific number of times or until the program meets a specific condition. For example, if you are writing a program that calculates student grades, the program must perform the same steps for each student in the class. Similarly, if a program displays a file's contents, the program will read and display each line of the file until the program finds the end-of-file marker. When programs repeat one or more statements until a given condition is met, the program is performing *iterative processing*. Each pass the program makes through the statements it is repeating is an *iteration*. To help your programs perform iterative processing, C provides the *for*, *while*, and *do while* statements. Several Tips presented in this book discuss the *for*, *while*, and *do while* statements in detail.

UNDERSTANDING HOW C REPRESENTS TRUE AND FALSE C 98

Several Tips presented in this section have discussed C's *conditional* and *iterative* constructs, which perform one set of instructions if a condition is true and, possibly, another set of instructions if the condition is false. As you work with *conditional* and *iterative* constructs, it is important that you understand how C represents a true and a false value. C interprets any value that is not 0 as true. Likewise, the value 0 represents false. The following condition, therefore, will always evaluate to true:

```
if (1)
```

Many inexperienced C programmers write their conditions as follows:

```
if (expression != 0)   // Test if expression is true
```

When you want to test if a condition is true, simply include the expression as shown here:

```
if (expression)
```

When the expression evaluates to a nonzero (true) value, then C executes the statement that immediately follows the condition. When the expression evaluates to zero (false), C does not execute the statement that immediately follows the condition. Operators which work with true and false values are *Boolean* operators. The result of a Boolean expression is always a true or false value.

TESTING A CONDITION WITH IF C 99

As your programs become more complex, they will often perform one set of statements when the condition is true and another set of statements when the condition is false. When your program must perform such *conditional processing*, you will use the C *if* statement. The *if* statement's format is as follows:

```
if (condition)
   statement;
```

The condition the *if* statement evaluates must appear within parentheses and is either true or false. When the condition is true, C performs the statement that immediately follows the condition. When the condition is false, your program does not perform the statement that follows the condition. As an example, the following *if* statement tests whether the variable *age* is greater than or equal to 21. If the condition is true, the program will execute the *printf* statement. If the condition is false, the program will not execute the *printf* statement and will continue its execution at the first statement that follows *printf* (the height assignment statement):

```
if (age >= 21)
   printf("The variable age is 21 or over\n");
height = 73;
```

100 UNDERSTANDING SIMPLE AND COMPOUND STATEMENTS

When your program performs conditional processing, there will be times when your program performs one or more statements when a condition is true and, possibly, several other statements if the condition is false. Likewise, when your program performs iterative processing, there will be times when your program repeats one statement, while at other times the program might repeat several statements. When you perform *conditional* and *iterative* processing, C classifies statements as either simple or compound. A *simple statement* is a single statement, such as a variable assignment or a call to *printf*. The following *if* statement invokes a simple statement *(printf)* when the condition is true:

```
if (condition)
   printf("The condition is true\n");
```

A *compound statement*, on the other hand, consists of one or more statements contained within right and left braces. The following *if* statement illustrates a compound statement:

```
if (condition)
   {
     age = 21;
     height = 73;
     weight = 165;
   }
```

When your program must perform multiple statements based on a condition, or when it must repeat several statements, you will use a compound statement and place the statements within the right and left braces.

101 TESTING FOR EQUALITY

As your programs become more complex, they will compare a variable's value to known conditions and determine which statements the program will execute next. To make such decisions, your programs will use the *if* or *switch* statements. As you learned in Tip 99, the format of the *if* statement is as follows:

```
if (condition)
   statement;
```

Most *if* statements will test whether a variable's value equals a second, specific value. For example, the following *if* statement tests whether the variable *age* contains the value 21:

```
if (age == 21)
   statement;
```

C uses the double equal sign (==) in tests for equality. When you write tests for equality, use the double equal sign (==) instead of the single equal sign (=) that C uses for an assignment. As you will learn in Tip 112, if you use the *assignment* operator (=), as opposed to the double equal sign, C will consider your condition correct syntax. Unfortunately, when the statement executes, C will not test to see if the variable equals the specified value. Instead, C will assign the specified value to the variable.

Note: *Depending on your compiler warning level, the compiler might display a warning message about the assignment within the expected condition.*

Just as your programs must sometimes test values for equality, they must also sometimes test values for inequality. C uses the != symbol to test for inequality. The following statement tests whether the variable *age* is not equal to 21:

```
if (age != 21)
   statement;
```

The following program, *eql_neql.c*, uses the C tests for equality (==) and inequality (!=):

```
#include <stdio.h>

void main(void)
   {
     int age = 21;
     int height = 73;
```

```
   if (age == 21)
     printf("User\'s age is 21\n");
   if (age != 21)
     printf("User\'s age is not 21\n");
   if (height == 73)
     printf("User\'s height is 73\n");
   if (height != 73)
     printf("User\'s height is not 73\n");
 }
```

When you compile and execute the *eql_neql.c* program, your screen will display the following output:

```
User's age is 21
User's height is 73
C:\>
```

To understand how to use the equality and inequality operators, experiment with the *eql_neql.c* program by changing the values of the *height* and *age* variables.

PERFORMING RELATIONAL TESTS 102

As your programs become more complex, there may be times when you must test whether a value is greater than another value, less than another value, greater than or equal to another value, or less than or equal to another value. To help you perform such tests, C provides a set of *relational operators*. Table 102 lists C's relational operators.

Operator	Function
>	*Greater-than* operator
<	*Less-than* operator
>=	*Greater-than-or-equal-to* operator
<=	*Less-than-or-equal-to* operator

Table 102 *C's relational operators.*

The following *if* statement uses C's *greater-than-or-equal-to* operator (>=) to test whether the integer variable *age* is over 20:

```
if (age >= 21)
  printf("The age is over 20\n");
```

PERFORMING A LOGICAL AND TO TEST TWO CONDITIONS 103

In Tip 99 you learned how to use C's *if* statement to test conditions within your programs. As your programs become more complex, your programs eventually will test for multiple conditions. For example, you may want an *if* statement to test whether a user has a dog and, if so, whether that dog is a Dalmatian. In cases when you want to test if two conditions are true, use C's *logical AND* operator. C represents the *logical AND* operator with two ampersands (&&), as shown in the following *if* statement:

```
if ((user_has_dog) && (dog == dalmatian))
  {
    // Statements
  }
```

When C encounters an *if* statement that uses the *logical AND* operator (&&), C evaluates the conditions from left to right. If you examine the parentheses, you will find that the previous *if* statement is in the following form:

```
if (condition)
```

In the following example, the condition is actually two conditions connected with the *logical AND* operator:

```
(user_has_dog) && (dog == dalmatian)
```

For the resulting condition to evaluate as true when your programs use the *logical AND* operator, both conditions must evaluate as true. If either condition is false, the resulting condition will evaluate as false.

Many Tips presented throughout this book will use the *logical AND* operator. In each case, to ensure that each expression evaluates with the correct operator precedence, the programs will place the conditions within parentheses.

Note: *Do not confuse C's* **logical AND** *operator (&&) with C's* **bitwise AND** *operator (&). The* **logical AND** *operator evaluates two* **Boolean** *(true or false) expressions to produce a true or false result. The* **bitwise AND** *operator, on the other hand, manipulates bits (1's and 0's).*

104 PERFORMING A LOGICAL OR TO TEST TWO CONDITIONS

In Tip 99 you learned how to use C's *if* statement to test conditions within your programs. As your programs become more complex, you eventually will test for multiple conditions. For example, you may want an *if* statement to test if a user has a dog or if the user has a computer. In cases when you want to test whether either of two conditions is true (or if both are true), you can use C's *logical OR* operator. C represents the *logical OR* with two vertical bars (||), as shown here:

```
if ((user_has_dog) || (user_has_computer))
   {
      // Statements
   }
```

When C encounters an *if* statement that uses the *logical OR* operator (||), C evaluates the conditions from left to right. If you examine the parentheses, you will find that the previous *if* statement is in the following form:

```
if (condition)
```

In this particular example, the condition is actually two conditions connected by the *logical OR* operator, as shown here:

```
(user_has_dog) || (user_has_computer)
```

For the resulting condition to evaluate as true when you use the *logical OR* operator, only one of the two conditions must evaluate as true. If either condition (or both) is true, the resulting condition evaluates as true. If both conditions evaluate as false, the result is false.

Many Tips presented throughout this book use the *logical OR* (||) operator. In each case, to ensure that each expression evaluates with the correct operator precedence, the programs will place the conditions within parentheses.

Note: *Do not confuse C's* **logical OR** *operator (||) with C's* **bitwise OR** *operator (|). The* **logical OR** *operator evaluates two* **Boolean** *(true or false) expressions to produce a true or false result. The* **bitwise OR** *operator, on the other hand, manipulates bits (1's and 0's).*

105 PERFORMING A LOGICAL NOT OPERATION

When your programs use the *if* statement to perform conditional processing, the *if* statement evaluates an expression that yields a true or false result. Depending on your program's processing, there may be times when you will only want the program to perform a set of statements when the condition evaluates as false. For example, assume that you want a program to test whether the user has a dog. If the user does not have a dog, the program should display a message telling the user to buy a Dalmatian. If the user has a dog, the program should not do anything. When you want your program to perform one or more statements when a condition is false, you should use C's *logical NOT* operator, which C represents using the exclamation mark (!). Consider the following *if* statement:

```
if (! user_has_dog)
   printf("You need to buy a dalmatian\n");
```

Conditions that use the *logical NOT* operator essentially say that when a certain condition is not true (in other words, when the condition evaluates as false), you should perform the *if* statement (or compound statements). Several Tips presented in this book use the *logical NOT* operator within conditions.

Several Tips in this section have presented different conditions that evaluate as true or false within an *if, while, for,* or other statement. In addition to letting you use conditions within C conditional and iterative control structures, C also lets you assign a condition's result to a variable. Assume, for example, that your program uses the result of the same condition more than once, as shown here:

```
if ((strlen(name) < 100) && (today == MONDAY))
  {
    // Statements
  }
else if ((strlen(name) < 100) && (today == TUESDAY))
  {
    // Statements
  }
else if (strlen(name) >= 100)
  {
    // Statements
  }
```

As you can see, the program uses the condition *(strlen(name) < 100)* three times. Each time the condition appears, the program invokes the *strlen* function. In the preceding statements, the program could (depending on *today's* value) invoke *strlen* three times. The following statements will assign the condition's result (true or false) to the variable *name_ok* and then repeatedly use the variable (as opposed to the condition). Using the variable rather than the condition, as shown here, will improve the program's performance:

```
name_ok = (strlen(name) < 100);

if (name_ok && (today == MONDAY))
  {
    // Statements
  }
else if (name_ok && (today == TUESDAY))
  {
    // Statements
  }
else if (! name_ok)
  {
    // Statements
  }
```

In Tip 100 you learned about the difference between simple and compound statements. As you have learned, a compound statement is one or more statements grouped within left and right braces. The following *while* loop, (which will read lines from a file and display the lines in uppercase letters), illustrates a compound statement:

```
while (fgets(line, sizeof(line), fp))
  {
    strupr(line);
    fputs(line, stdout);
  }
```

As your programs become more complex, sometimes the processing they perform within a compound statement will require that you use one or more variables whose values you use only within the loop (as might be the case with counter variables). When you use counter variables, for example, you usually declare those counter variables at the start of your program, immediately following the *main* statement. However, if you use a variable only within a compound statement, you can declare the variable at the start of the statement, as shown here:

```
if (condition)
  {
    int counter;
    float total;

    // Other statements
  }
```

In this case, the program declares two variables at the start of the compound statement. Within the compound statement, you can use these two variables just as though you defined the variables at the start of your program. You cannot, however, refer to these variables outside the compound statement's opening and closing braces. An advantage of declaring variables within the compound statement is that another programmer reading your program code will better understand how and when you use a variable. Several Tips presented later in this book focus on a variable's *scope*, or the locations within your program in which the program "knows" a variable. As a rule, you should limit the program's knowledge of a variable to only those locations that use the variable—in other words, you should limit the variable's scope. Declaring variables at the start of a compound statement, as this Tip describes, limits the variable's scope to the compound statement's starting and ending braces.

Note: If you declare variables within a compound statement that have the same name as variables you defined outside the statement, the C compiler will use the newly declared variables within the compound statement and the original variables outside the statement.

108 USING INDENTATION TO IMPROVE READABILITY

As you create your programs, one of the best ways you can improve program readability is to use indentation. Each time your program uses a brace (such as at the start of a compound statement), you should consider indenting your code two or more spaces. For example, consider the following program, *use_ind.c*:

```
#include <stdio.h>

void main(void)
  {
    int age = 10;
    int user_has_dog = 0;    // 0 is false

    if (age == 10)
      {
        printf("Dogs are important pets\n");
        if (! user_has_dog)
          printf("You should get a dalmatian\n");
      }
    printf("Happy is a dalmatian\n");
  }
```

You can examine only the indentation and still quickly "get a feel for" related program statements (for example, compound statements). Indentation is meaningless to the compiler. To the compiler, the following program, *no_ind.c*, is identical to the previous example:

```
#include <stdio.h>

void main(void)
{
int age = 10;
int user_has_dog = 0;    // 0 is false
if (age == 10)
{
printf("Dogs are important pets\n");
if (! user_has_dog)
printf("You should get a dalmatian\n");
}
printf("Happy is a dalmatian\n");
}
```

As you can see, the indentation makes the first program much easier for you, or another reader, to understand.

Using Extended Ctrl+Break Checking

When you create programs that use the *for*, *while*, and *do* loops for iteration and that run in the DOS environment, there may be times when you must press the Ctrl+Break keyboard combination to end a program that is stuck in an infinite loop. By default, DOS checks for a Ctrl+Break after each time it writes to the screen, the disk, or the printer, or if it reads a character from the keyboard. If your program does not perform these operations within the loop you want to break, you cannot use the Ctrl+Break command to end the program's processing. When you use the DOS BREAK command, however, you can increase the number of operations that will, upon each operation's completion, instruct DOS to check for a Ctrl+Break entry. Programmers call this additional testing *extended Ctrl+Break checking*. The following BREAK command enables extended Ctrl+Break checking:

```
C:\> BREAK ON   <ENTER>
```

If you want DOS to automatically enable extended Ctrl+Break checking as soon as the system starts, place a BREAK=ON entry in your *config.sys* file. Because DOS is performing more extended Ctrl+Break checking, your overall system performance will decrease slightly. However, while you are first getting the feel for iterative processing, you might find that your ability to end a program using Ctrl+Break is more important than the slight loss of performance.

Testing Floating-Point Values

Several Tips presented in this section have used the *if* and *while* statements to test a variable's value. For example, the following statements test several integer variables:

```
if (age == 21)
   // Statements

if (height > 73)
   // Statements
```

When you work with floating-point values, however, you must be careful when you test a variable's value. For example, the following statement tests a floating-point variable named *sales_tax*:

```
if (sales_tax == 0.065)
   // Statements
```

In Tip 51 you learned about floating-point precision and the fact that the computer must represent floating-point values using a fixed number of bits. It is impossible for the computer to represent all values exactly. In the case of the previous *if* statement, for example, the computer may represent the value 0.065 as 0.0649999. As a result, the *if* statement will never evaluate as true. To prevent such errors within your program, do not test for exact floating-point values. Instead, test for an acceptable range of values, as shown here:

```
if (fabs(sales_tax - 0.065) <= 0.0001)
   // Statements
```

In the previous example, because the difference between the value in the variable *sales_tax* and 0.065 is less than or equal to 0.0001, the program will consider the values as equal.

Looping Forever

As you have learned, C's *for*, *while*, and *do while* statements let you repeat one or more statements until they meet a given condition. Depending on your program, there may be times when you want the program to loop forever. For example, a program that detects radiation leaks at a nuclear reactor should always run. To make your program loop forever, simply place a non-zero constant within the loop, as shown here:

```
while (1)
```

Because you can use a non-zero value to force your programs to loop forever, you might want to define constants to improve your program's readability. For example, you might use the constant *FOREVER*, as shown here:

```
#define FOREVER 1
while (FOREVER)
```

To create a loop for the previous nuclear-reactor example, you might use the following:

```
#define MELT_DOWN 0
while (! MELT_DOWN)
```

112 TESTING AN ASSIGNMENT

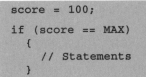

As you have learned, C uses the single equal sign as the *assignment* operator and the double equal sign to test for equality, as shown here:

```
score = 100;

if (score == MAX)
   {
      // Statements
   }
```

In the preceding code fragment, the first statement assigns the value 100 to the variable *score*. Next, the *if* statement tests the variable's value. To help you reduce the number of statements in your program, C lets you test an assignment's result. For example, the following *if* statement combines the previous assignment and condition test:

```
if ((score = 100) == MAX)
   {
      // Statements
   }
```

C will first perform the expression the parentheses contain, assigning the value 100 to the variable *score*. Next, C will compare the value you assigned to the variable *score* to the constant *MAX*. If you remove the parentheses, as shown here, C will assign a different value and perform a different test:

```
if (score = 100 == MAX)
```

Without the parentheses, C will test whether the value 100 equals the constant *MAX*, and if so, it will assign the value 1 (true) to the variable *score*. If the value 100 does not equal *MAX*, the statement will assign the value 0 (false) to the variable *score*.

You will most commonly use assignment testing when you want to test the value a function (such as *fopen* or *getchar*) returns, as shown here:

```
if ((fp = fopen("CONFIG.SYS", "r")) == NULL)
   {
      // Statements
   }

if ((letter = getchar()) == 'A')
   {
      // Statements
   }
```

113 BEWARE OF IF-IF-ELSE STATEMENTS

When you use *if-else* statements, a sneaky logic error can cause problems if you do not keep track of which *else* statement corresponds to which *if* statement. For example, consider the following code fragment:

```
test_score = 100;
current_grade = 'B';
```

```
if (test_score >= 90)
  if (current_grade == 'A')
    printf("Another A for an A student\n");
else
  printf("Should have worked harder\n");
```

The first *if* statement tests whether a student's test score was greater than or equal to 90. If so, a second *if* statement tests whether the student already has an 'A' grade and, if so, prints a message. Based on the indentation, you would expect the *else* statement to display its message if the test score was less than 90. Unfortunately, that is not how the code fragment processes the conditions. When you place an *else* statement within your program, C associates the *else* with the first *else*-less *if* statement. Although the student's test score was 100, the previous code fragment will print the message telling the student that he or she should have worked harder. In other words, the fragment executes the statements shown here:

```
if (test_score >= 90)
  if (current_grade == 'A')
    printf("Another A for an A student\n");
  else
    printf("Should have worked harder\n");
```

To prevent C from associating the *else* statement with the wrong *if* statement, place the second *if* statement within braces, forming a *compound statement*, as shown here:

```
if (test_score >= 90)
  {
    if (current_grade == 'A')
      printf("Another A for an A student\n");
  }
else
  printf("Should have worked harder\n");
```

PERFORMING STATEMENTS A SPECIFIC NUMBER OF TIMES   C114

One operation that your programs will commonly perform is to repeat a set of statements a specific number of times. For example, you might want to calculate test scores for 30 students, determine the highs and lows of 100 stock quotes, or even sound your computer's built-in speaker three times. To help your programs repeat one or more statements a specific number of times, C provides the *for* statement. You will implement the *for* statement as shown here:

```
for (starting_value; ending_condition; increment_value)
  statement;
```

When your program repeats (loops through) statements a specific number of times, you will normally use a variable, called the *control variable*, that counts the number of times you have performed the statements. The *for* statement contains four sections. The *starting_value* section assigns the control variable the variable's initial value, which is most often 0 or 1. The *ending_condition* section normally tests the control variable's value to determine if the program has performed the statements the desired number of times. The *increment_value* section normally adds the value 1 to the control variable each time the statements execute. Finally, the *for* loop's fourth section is the statement or statements you want to repeat. Because your program repeatedly performs the statement or statements you specified (loops back to the start of the statement), the *for* statement is often called a *for loop*. Consider the following *for* statement, which will display the numbers 1 through 10 on your screen:

```
for (counter = 1; counter <= 10; counter++)
  printf("%d\n", counter);
```

In the previous example, *counter* is the loop's control variable. First, the *for* statement assigns the value 1 to the variable. Second, the *for* loop immediately tests whether or not *counter's* value is less than or equal to 10 (the loop's *ending condition*). If *counter* is less than or equal to 10, the *for* loop immediately executes the next statement, which, in this example, is *printf*. After the program completes the *printf* statement, the *for* loop performs the expression you specified in the *increment_value* loop section. In this case, the *for* loop increments *counter's* value by 1. Then, the *for* loop immediately performs the *ending_value* test. If *counter's* value is less than or equal to 10, the loop continues. Therefore, the first time through the loop, the *printf* statement will display the value 1. The second time through the loop, *counter's* value is 2, then 3, and so on. After *printf* displays the value 10, the *increment_value* loop section increments *counter's* value, making it 11. When the *for* loop performs the *ending_value* test, *for* will find that *counter's* value is no longer less than or equal to 10, so the loop will end and your program will resume processing at the statement immediately following the *for* loop.

To better understand the *for* loop's processing, consider the following program, *for_test.c*:

```c
#include <stdio.h>

void main(void)
 {
   int counter;

   for (counter = 1; counter <= 5; counter++)
     printf("%d ", counter);
   printf("\nStarting second loop\n");
   for (counter = 1; counter <= 10; counter++)
     printf("%d ", counter);
   printf("\nStarting third loop\n");
   for (counter = 100; counter <= 5; counter++)
     printf("%d ", counter);
 }
```

When you compile and execute the *for_test.c* program, your screen will display the following:

```
1 2 3 4 5
Starting second loop
1 2 3 4 5 6 7 8 9 10
Starting third loop
C:\>
```

As you can see, the first *for* loop displays the numbers 1 through 5. The second *for* loop displays the values 1 through 10. The third *for* loop does not display any values. If you look closely, you will see that the program initially assigns the loop's control variable the value 100. When the *for* statement tests the value, the *for* loop immediately meets the ending condition, so the loop does not execute.

All the examples presented in this Tip have used single statements in the *for* loop. If you must repeat more than one statement, place the statements in left and right braces, forming a *compound statement*, as shown here:

```c
for (i = 1; i <= 10; i++)
  {
    // Statements
  }
```

115 PARTS OF THE FOR STATEMENT ARE OPTIONAL

In Tip 114 you learned that the *for* statement lets your program repeat one or more statements a specific number of times. As you learned, the *for* loop uses three sections within the *for* statement: an initialization, a test, and an increment (the loop's fourth section contains the statements the *for* loop repeats):

```c
for (initialization; test; increment)
```

Depending on your program, sometimes you may not need to use each of the *for* statement's sections. For example, if you have already assigned the variable *count* the initial value 0, you can skip the loop's initialization section. Then to display the numbers 0 through 999, your loop would contain the following:

```c
for (; count < 1000; count++)
  printf(" %d", count);
```

If you omit one of the *for* loop sections, however, you must include the corresponding semicolon. For example, the following *for* loop skips the initialization and increment sections:

```c
for (; count < 1000; )
  printf(" %d", count++);
```

Likewise, the following *for* statement will loop forever:

```
for (;;)
  // Statement
```

Although the *for* statement provides these optional sections, your program will become more difficult to read if you omit them. As a rule, if you do not need to use all three parts of the *for* statement, you should use a different looping construct, such as the *while* statement.

DECREMENTING VALUES IN A FOR STATEMENT 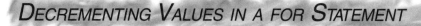 116

As you have learned, a *for* statement lets you repeat one or more statements a specific number of times. Tips 114 and 115 presented several *for* statements. In each case, the *for* loop counted up, from 1 to 5, 1 to 10, and so on. The *for* statement also lets you decrement the control variable. For example, the following *for* loop counts down the numbers 10, 9, 8 and so on to 1:

```
for (counter = 10; counter >= 1; counter--)
  printf("%d ", counter);
```

As you can see, the preceding *for* statement is nearly the opposite of the for statements you saw in previous Tips. The loop initializes the control variable *counter* to a high value and then decrements *counter* by one each time the loop repeats.

The following program, *for_down.c*, uses the *for* statement to count down, first from 5 to 1, and then from 10 to 1:

```
#include <stdio.h>

void main(void)
 {
   int counter;

   for (counter = 5; counter >= 1; counter--)
     printf("%d ", counter);
   printf("\nStarting second loop\n");
   for (counter = 10; counter >= 1; counter--)
     printf("%d ", counter);
   printf("\nStarting third loop\n");
   for (counter = 0; counter >= 1; counter--)
     printf("%d ", counter);
 }
```

When you compile and execute the *for_down.c* program, your screen will display the following output:

```
5 4 3 2 1
Starting second loop
10 9 8 7 6 5 4 3 2 1
Starting third loop
C:\>
```

As you can see, the third loop does not display any values. In this example, the *for* statement initializes *counter* to a value that is less than the ending value of 1. Therefore, the loop immediately ends.

CONTROLLING THE FOR LOOP INCREMENT 117

As you have learned, the *for* loop lets your programs repeat one or more statements a specific number of times. In previous Tips, each *for* loop has either incremented or decremented the loop's control variable by one. C, however, lets you increment the variable by any amount you want. For example, the following *for* loop increments the control variable *counter* by 10 with each iteration of the loop:

```
for (counter = 0; counter <= 100; counter += 10)
  printf("%d\n", counter);
```

In a similar way, the previous *for* loops initialized the control variable to 1 or 0. Just as you can set the increment or decrement amount to whatever size you want, C, again, lets you initialize the variable to any value you want. The following program, *for_diff.c*, uses different increment and initialization values:

```
#include <stdio.h>

void main(void)
{
  int counter;

  for (counter = -100; counter <= 100; counter += 5)
    printf("%d ", counter);
  printf("\nStarting second loop\n");
  for (counter = 100; counter >= -100; counter -= 25)
    printf("%d ", counter);
}
```

118 USING FOR LOOPS WITH CHAR AND FLOAT VALUES

As you have learned, the *for* statement lets your programs repeat a set of statements a specific number of times. Each of the *for* statements presented in the previous Tips used only values of type *int*. You can, however, use character and floating-point values in your *for* loops. For example, the following *for* loop displays the letters of the alphabet:

```
for (letter = 'A'; letter <= 'Z'; letter++)
  printf("%c", letter);
```

Likewise, the following loop increments a floating-point value by 0.5:

```
for (percent = 0.0; percent <= 100.0; percent += 0.5)
  printf("%f\n", percent);
```

The following program, *for_more.c,* illustrates the use of letters and floating-point values in a *for* loop:

```
#include <stdio.h>

void main(void)
{
  char letter;
  float percent;

  for (letter = 'A'; letter <= 'Z'; letter++)
    putchar(letter);
  for (letter = 'z'; letter >= 'a'; letter--)
    putchar(letter);
  putchar('\n');
  for (percent = 0.0; percent < 1.0; percent += 0.1)
    printf("%3.1f\n", percent);
}
```

119 UNDERSTANDING A NULL LOOP

As you have learned, the *for* loop lets you repeat one or more statements until the loop's control variable meets a specific condition. In the past when programmers wanted their programs to pause briefly, perhaps to display a message, the programmers placed a "do-nothing" or *NULL loop* in their programs. For example, the following *for* loop does nothing 100 times:

```
for (counter = 1; counter <= 100; counter++)
  ;  // Do nothing
```

When you place a *NULL* loop in your program, C will perform the loop's initialization and then repeatedly test and increment the control variable until the control variable meets the ending condition. The loop's repeated testing consumes processor time, which causes the program to delay. If the program needs a longer delay, you can increase the ending condition:

```
for (counter = 1; counter <= 10000; counter++)
  ;  // Do nothing
```

Using delay techniques such as the *NULL* loop can cause problems, however. First, if the program is running on a 286, 386, or 486 computer, the length of the delay will differ simply because of the difference in speed between the different microprocessors. Second, if the program is running in a multitasking environment, such as Windows, OS/2, or Unix, "do-nothing" loops consume time that the processor could spend doing meaningful work for another program. If your programs must use such a delay, see the functions presented in the Date and Time section of this book.

UNDERSTANDING AN INFINITE LOOP   120

As you have learned, the *for* loop lets you repeat one or more statements a specific number of times. When the *for* loop meets its ending condition, your program will continue its execution at the statement that immediately follows. When you use *for* loops, you must ensure that the loop will meet its ending condition. Otherwise, the loop will continue to execute forever. Such unending loops are called *infinite* loops. In most cases, *infinite* loops occur as the result of a programming error. For example, consider the following loop:

```
for (i = 0; i < 100; i++)
  {
     printf("%d ", i);
     result = value * --i;    // cause of error
  }
```

As you can see, the loop's second statement decrements the value of the control variable *i*. Specifically, the loop decrements the value to −1 and then later increments the value to 0. As a result, the value never reaches 100, so the loop does not end. When your program enters an infinite loop, you might be able to press CTRL+C to end the program. The following program, *infinite.c,* illustrates an infinite loop:

```
#include <stdio.h>

void main(void)
  {
     int i;
     int result = 0;
     int value = 1;

     for (i = 0; i < 100; i++)
       {
          printf("%d ", i);
          result = value * --i;
       }
     printf("Result %d\n", result);
  }
```

When you compile and execute the *infinite.c* program, it will repeatedly display the value 0. To end the program, press CTRL+C.

USING C'S COMMA OPERATOR WITHIN A FOR LOOP   121

As you have learned, when you declare variables, C lets you declare multiple variables of the same type by separating the variable names with commas:

```
int age, height, weight;
```

In addition, C lets you separate variable initializations with commas, as shown here:

```
int age = 25, height = 73, weight = 160;
```

In a similar way, C lets you initialize and increment multiple variables in a *for* loop by separating the operations with commas. Consider the following loop, which works with the variables *i* and *j*:

```
for (i = 0, j = 100; i <= 100; i++, j++)
   printf("i = %d j = %d\n", i, j);
```

You will most commonly work with multiple variables in a *for* loop (also known as *nesting for loops*) in your programs that work with arrays. You will learn more about arrays in the Arrays and Structures section of this book. The following program, *for_2var.C,* illustrates the use of C's comma operator in a *for* loop:

```
#include <stdio.h>

void main(void)
  {
    int i, j;

    for (i = 0, j = 100; i <= 100; i++, j++)
      printf("i = %d j = %d\n", i, j);
  }
```

122 AVOID CHANGING THE CONTROL VARIABLE'S VALUE IN A FOR LOOP

As you have learned, the *for* statement lets you repeat one or more statements a specific number of times. To perform such processing, the *for* loop uses a *control variable*, which works as a counter. As a rule, you should not change the control variable's value in the *for* loop's statement. The only place the control variable's value should change is in the *for* loop's initialization and increment sections. When you change the control variable's value in the program statements, you run a greater risk of creating an *infinite* loop, and you make your programs more difficult to understand.

However, there may be times when you will want the loop to end or to skip the current iteration when the *control* variable equals a certain value. For such cases, use C's *break* or *continue* statements, which later Tips in this section discuss in detail.

123 REPEATING ONE OR MORE STATEMENTS USING A WHILE LOOP

As you have learned, the *for* statement lets you repeat one or more statements a specific number of times. In many cases, however, your programs must repeat one or more statements until the loop meets a specific condition that does not necessarily involve a count. For example, if you write a program that will display a file's contents on your screen, you will want the program to display each line of the file. In most cases, you will not know in advance how many lines the file contains. Therefore, you cannot use a *for* loop to display, for example, 100 lines. The file might contain more or fewer lines. Instead, you want the program to read and display lines until it reaches the end of the file. To do so, your programs can use the *while* loop. You will format the *while* loop as follows:

```
while (condition)
  statement;
```

When C encounters a *while* loop in your program, C will test the condition specified. If the condition is true, C will perform the statements contained in the loop. If the statement is false, C will continue your program's execution at the first statement that follows. A *while* loop can repeat a single statement or a compound statement you enclose between left and right braces, as shown here:

```
while (condition)
  {
     // Statements
  }
```

The following program, *wait_yn.c*, uses the *while* loop to loop repeatedly until you press the Y or N key in response to a yes or no question:

```
#include <stdio.h>
#include <ctype.h>
#include <conio.h>

void main(void)
  {
    char letter;                              // Letter typed by the user

    printf("Do you want to continue? (Y/N): ");

    letter = getch();                         // Get the letter
    letter = toupper(letter);                 // Convert letter to uppercase

    while ((letter != 'Y') && (letter != 'N'))
      {
```

```
        putch(7);                         // Beep the speaker
        letter = getch();                 // Get the letter
        letter = toupper(letter);         // Convert letter to uppercase
    }
    printf("\nYour response was %c\n", letter);
}
```

First, the program will display the message the first *printf* statement contains. Second, the program will use *getch* to get the keystroke pressed. To simplify the loop's testing, the program will convert the letter to uppercase, so the loop will only need to test for Y or N. Third, the *while* loop will test the letter the user typed. If the letter is a Y or N, the condition will fail and the loop's statements will not execute. If the letter pressed is not Y or N, the loop's condition is true, and its statements will execute. In the loop, the program will beep the computer's built-in speaker to indicate an invalid character. Next, the program will get the new keystroke and convert the letter to uppercase. The loop will then repeat its test to determine if the user typed a Y or N. If not, the loop's statements will repeat. Otherwise, the program's execution will continue at the first statement that follows the loop.

UNDERSTANDING THE PARTS OF A WHILE LOOP   C 124

A *while* loop lets you execute one or more commands until the program meets the loop's condition. In Tip 114 you learned that a *for* loop actually contains four sections: an initialization, a test, a statement execution, and an increment. A *while* loop, on the other hand, contains only a test and the statements you want to repeat, as shown here:

```
while (condition)
   statement;
```

As you learned in Tip 120, an infinite loop is a loop whose ending condition is never met, and so the loop will continue executing forever. When you write programs that use *while* loops, you can reduce the possibility of an infinite loop by ensuring that your *while* loops perform the same four steps as those a *for* loop performs. To help you remember the four steps, you might want to use the acronym *ITEM,* as illustrated in Table 124.

Action	Description
Initialize	Initialize the loop's control variable
Test	Test the loop's control variable or condition
Execute	Execute the desired statements in the loop
Modify	Modify the control variable's value or perform an operation that will affect the condition you are testing

*Table 124 The **ITEM** acronym's components.*

Unlike the *for* loop, which lets you explicitly initialize and increment a control variable, a *while* loop requires that you include statements in the program which perform these steps for you. The following program, *item.c,* illustrates how your program performs these four steps. Unlike previous programs you have written, *item.c* uses a *while* loop to display the numbers 1 through 100:

```
#include <stdio.h>

void main(void)
 {
   int counter = 1;                  // Initialize the control variable

   while (counter <= 100)            // Test the control variable
     {
        printf("%d ", counter);      // Execute the statements
        counter++;                   // Modify the control variable
     }
 }
```

If you write a program that uses the *while* loop and the program experiences an infinite loop, one of the ITEM operations in your program is not correct.

125 Repeating One or More Statements Using do

As you have learned, C's *while* statement lets you repeat one or more statements until a specific condition is met. Likewise, C's *for* statement lets you repeat one or more statements a specific number of times. In addition, C provides the *do* statement, which lets you execute one or more statements at least one time and then, if necessary, repeat statements. The *do* statement format is as follows:

```
do
   statement;
while (condition);
```

The *do* statement is ideal for situations that require you to perform one or more statements at least one time. For example, consider the following code fragment:

```
printf("Do you want to continue? (Y/N): ");

letter = getch();            // Get the letter
letter = toupper(letter);  // Convert letter to uppercase

while ((letter != 'Y') && (letter != 'N'))
  {
    putch(7);                     // Beep the speaker
    letter = getch();           // Get the letter
    letter = toupper(letter);  // Convert letter to uppercase
  }
```

As you can see, the code prompts the user for a keystroke, gets the keystroke, and converts the keystroke to uppercase. Depending on the key the user pressed, the fragment will start a *while* loop, which performs the same commands. Note how you can simplify the statements using the *do* statement, as shown in the following code fragment:

```
printf("Do you want to continue? (Y/N): ");
do
  {
    letter = getch();            // Get the letter
    letter = toupper(letter);  // Convert letter to uppercase
    if ((letter != 'Y') && (letter != 'N'))
      putch(7);   // Sound bell for invalid letter
  }
while ((letter != 'Y') && (letter != 'N'));
```

When C encounters a *do* statement in your program, C executes the statements between the words *do* and *while*. C then tests the condition the *while* clause specifies to determine whether or not the statements should repeat. Therefore, the statements a *do* loop specifies always execute at least one time. Programs often use the *do* loop to display and process menu options. The following program, *do_menu.c*, uses the *do* statement to display and process menu options until the user selects the Quit option:

```
#include <stdio.h>
#include <conio.h>
#include <ctype.h>
#include <stdlib.h>

void main(void)
  {
    char letter;

    do
      {
        printf("A Display directory listing\n");
        printf("B Change system time\n");
        printf("C Change system date\n");
        printf("Q Quit\n");
        printf("Choice: ");
        letter = getch();
        letter = toupper(letter);
        if (letter == 'A')
```

```
          system("DIR");
        else if (letter == 'B')
          system("TIME");
        else if (letter == 'C')
          system("DATE");
     }
   while (letter != 'Q');
 }
```

UNDERSTANDING C'S CONTINUE STATEMENT

As you have learned, the *for*, *while*, and *do* statements let your programs repeat one or more statements until a specific condition evaluates to either true or false. Depending on your program's purpose, there may be times when, based on a second specific condition, you will want your program to skip the current iteration. C's *continue* statement lets you do just that. If C encounters a *continue* statement in a *for* loop, C will immediately execute the loop's increment portion and then perform the ending condition test. If C encounters a *continue* statement in a *while* or *do* loop, then C will immediately perform the ending condition test. To better understand the *continue* statement, consider the following program, *odd_even.c*, which uses *continue* in a *for* and *while* loop type to display the odd and even values between 1 and 100:

```c
#include <stdio.h>

void main(void)
 {
   int counter;

   printf("\nEven values\n");
   for (counter = 1; counter <= 100; counter++)
     {
       if (counter % 2)  // Odd
         continue;
       printf("%d ", counter);
     }
   printf("\nOdd values\n");
   counter = 0;
   while (counter <= 100)
     {
       counter++;
       if (! (counter % 2)) // Even
         continue;
       printf("%d ", counter);
     }
 }
```

The program uses the *modulo* (remainder) operator to determine if a value is even or odd. If you divide a value by 2 and get a remainder of 1, the value is odd. Likewise, if you get a remainder of 0, the value is even.

It is important to note that you can normally eliminate the need to use a *continue* statement by redesigning your program's use of *if* and *else* statements. For example, the following program *no_cont.c*, also displays even and odd values without having to use *continue*:

```c
#include <stdio.h>

void main(void)
 {
   int counter;

   printf("\nEven values\n");
   for (counter = 1; counter <= 100; counter++)
     {
       if (!(counter % 2))  // Even
         printf("%d ", counter);
     }
   printf("\nOdd values\n");
   counter = 0;
```

```
   while (counter <= 100)
    {
      counter++;
      if (counter % 2) // Odd
        printf("%d ", counter);
    }
}
```

Before you place a *continue* statement in your program, examine your code closely to determine if you can write the same statements without using *continue*. In most cases, you will find the resulting *continue*-less code easier to understand.

127 ENDING A LOOP USING C'S BREAK STATEMENT

As you have learned, the *for*, *while*, and *do* statements let your programs repeat one or more statements until a specific condition evaluates to either true or false. Depending on your program's purpose, there may be times when, based on a second specific condition, you will want the loop to end immediately, with your program continuing its processing at the statement that follows the loop. C's *break* statement lets you do just that. When C encounters a break in a loop, the loop's execution will immediately end. The next statement the program executes is the statement that immediately follows the loop. In the case of a *for* loop, C will not perform the loop's increment section—instead, the loop immediately stops. The following program, *usebreak.c*, illustrates the use of the *break* statement. The program loops through the numbers 1 through 100 and then 100 down to 1. Each time the loop reaches the value 50, the *break* statement immediately ends the loop:

```
#include <stdio.h>

void main(void)
 {
    int counter;

    for (counter = 1; counter <= 100; counter++)
     {
       if (counter == 50)
         break;
       printf("%d ", counter);
     }
    printf("\nNext loop\n");
    for (counter = 100; counter >= 1; counter--)
     {
       if (counter == 50)
         break;
       printf("%d ", counter);
     }
 }
```

As was the case with C's *continue* statement, you can usually rewrite your program's *if-else* and looping conditions to eliminate the need for the *break* statement in loops. In most cases, when you rewrite your program statements to eliminate *break*, your program will be much easier for the reader to understand. As a rule, limit your use of the *break* statement to C's *switch* statement.

128 BRANCHING WITH THE GOTO STATEMENT

If you have previously programmed in BASIC, FORTRAN, or in assembly language, you may be used to implementing *if-else* operations and loops using the GOTO statement. Like most programming languages, C provides a *goto* statement, which lets your program's execution branch go to a specific location, called a *label*. The *goto* statement's format is as follows:

```
goto label;
label:
```

The following C program, *goto_100.c*, uses the *goto* statement to display the numbers 1 through 100:

```
#include <stdio.h>
void main(void)
 {
   int count = 1;

   label:
     printf("%d ", count++);

     if (count <= 100)
       goto label;
 }
```

When you use the *goto* statement, the label must reside in the current function. In other words, you cannot use *goto* to branch from *main* to a label that appears in another function, or vice versa.

Because programmers have misused the *goto* statement in the past, you should restrict your use of *goto* whenever possible, and instead use constructs such as *if*, *if-else*, and *while*. In most cases, you can use these three constructs to rewrite a code fragment that uses *goto* and therefore produce more readable code.

TESTING MULTIPLE CONDITIONS C129

As you have learned, C's *if-else* statements let you test multiple conditions. For example, consider the following test of the variable *letter*:

```
letter = getch();
letter = toupper(letter);

if (letter == 'A')
   system("DIR");
else if (letter == 'B')
   system("TIME");
else if (letter == 'C')
   system("DATE");
```

In cases where you are testing the same variable for multiple possible values, C provides a *switch* statement, with the following format:

```
switch (expression) {
   case Constant_1: statement;
   case Constant_2: statement;
   case Constant_3: statement;
    :      :        :
 };
```

Instead of using the previous *if-else* statements, you could instead use *switch* as follows:

```
switch (letter) {
   case 'A': system("DIR");
             break;
   case 'B': system("TIME");
             break;
   case 'C': system("DATE");
             break;
 };
```

When C encounters a *switch* statement in your program, C evaluates the expression that follows to produce a result. C then compares the result to each of the constant values that you specify which follow the *case* keyword. If C finds a match, it executes the corresponding statements. The *break* statement separates corresponding statements from one case to another. You will normally place a *break* statement after the last statement that corresponds to an option. In Tip 130 you will learn the details governing the use of the *break* statement in *switch*. The following program, *swt_menu.c*, uses the *switch* statement to process a user's menu selection:

```
#include <stdio.h>
#include <conio.h>
#include <ctype.h>
#include <stdlib.h>

void main(void)
  {
    char letter;

    do {
      printf("A Display directory listing\n");
      printf("B Change system time\n");
      printf("C Change system date\n");
      printf("Q Quit\n");
      printf("Choice: ");
      letter = getch();
      letter = toupper(letter);
      switch (letter) {
        case 'A': system("DIR");
                  break;
        case 'B': system("TIME");
                  break;
        case 'C': system("DATE");
                  break;
      };
    }
    while (letter != 'Q');
  }
```

130 UNDERSTANDING BREAK WITHIN SWITCH

In Tip 129 you learned that C's *switch* statement lets you perform conditional processing. As you learned, you specify one or more possible matching cases using the *switch* statement. For each case, you specify the corresponding statements. At the end of the statements, you normally place a *break* statement to separate one *case* statement from another. If you omit the *break* statement, C will continue to execute all statements that follow, regardless of the case to which the statements belong. For example, consider the following *switch* statement:

```
switch (letter) {
  case 'A': system("DIR");
  case 'B': system("TIME");
  case 'C': system("DATE");
};
```

If the variable *letter* contains the letter A, C will match the first case, executing the DIR command. However, because no *break* statement follows, the program will also execute the TIME and DATE commands. If the variable *letter* contained the letter B, the program would execute the TIME and DATE commands. To prevent the execution of another case's statements, use the *break* statement, as shown here:

```
switch (letter) {
   case 'A': system("DIR");
             break;
   case 'B': system("TIME");
             break;
   case 'C': system("DATE");
             break;
 };
```

There may be times when you may want your programs to cascade through *case* options. For example, the following program, *vowels.c*, uses a *switch* statement to count the number of vowels in the alphabet:

```
#include <stdio.h>

void main(void)
  {
    char letter;
```

```
   int vowel_count = 0;
   for (letter = 'A'; letter <= 'Z'; letter++)
     switch (letter) {
       case 'A':
       case 'E':
       case 'I':
       case 'O':
       case 'U': vowel_count++;
     };
   printf("The number of vowels is %d\n", vowel_count);
}
```

In this case, if the variable *letter* contains the A, E, I, or O, the match occurs and the C falls through to the statement that corresponds to the letter U, which increments the variable *vowel_count*. Because the *switch* statement contains no other cases following the letter U, the program does not include the *break* statement.

USING THE SWITCH STATEMENT'S DEFAULT CASE

As you have learned, C's *switch* statement lets you perform conditional processing. When you use the *switch* statement, you specify one or more cases that you want C to match, as shown here:

```
switch (letter) {
    case 'A': system("DIR");
            break;
    case 'B': system("TIME");
            break;
    case 'C': system("DATE");
            break;
};
```

As you use the *switch* statement, you might find that sometimes you will want C to perform specific statements when the other cases do not match. To do so, you can include a *default* case with the *switch* statement, as shown here:

```
switch (expression) {
    case Constant_1: statement;
    case Constant_2: statement;
    case Constant_3: statement;
      :     :          :
    default: statement;
};
```

If C does not match any of the case options that precede the default, C will execute the default statements. The following program, *con_vowl.c*, uses the *default* case to track the number of consonant letters in the alphabet:

```
#include <stdio.h>

void main(void)
{
   char letter;
   int vowel_count = 0;
   int consonant_count = 0;

   for (letter = 'A'; letter <= 'Z'; letter++)
     switch (letter) {
       case 'A':
       case 'E':
       case 'I':
       case 'O':
       case 'U': vowel_count++;
                 break;
       default: consonant_count++;
     };
   printf("The number of vowels is %d\n", vowel_count);
   printf("The number of vowels is %d\n", consonant_count);
}
```

132 DEFINING CONSTANTS IN YOUR PROGRAMS

As a rule, you can improve your program's readability and portability by replacing references to numbers, such as 512, with a more meaningful constant name. A *constant* is a name the C compiler associates with a value that does not change. To create a constant, you use the *#define* directive. For example, the following directive creates a constant named *LINE_SIZE*, and assigns to the constant the value 128:

```
#define LINE_SIZE 128
```

When the C preprocessor later encounters the *LINE_SIZE* constant name in your program, the preprocessor will replace the constant name with the constant's value. For example, consider the following character string declarations:

```
char line[128];
char text[128];

char current_line[LINE_SIZE];
char user_input[LINE_SIZE];
```

The first two declarations create character strings that contain 128-byte character strings. The second two declarations create character strings that are based on a constant named *LINE_SIZE*. When other programmers read your program code, one of the first questions they might ask is why you used 128 in your string declarations. In the case of the second declaration, however, the programmer knows that you declared all your strings in terms of a predefined *LINE_SIZE*. Within your programs, you might include loops similar to the following:

```
for (i = 0; i < 128; i++)
  // statements
for (i = 0; i < LINE_SIZE; i++)
  // statements
```

The second *for* loop makes your program more readable and easier to change. Assume, for example, that your program uses the value 128 throughout to refer to the string size. Should you later want to change the size to 256 characters, you must change every occurrence of the value 128 in your program—a time-consuming process. On the other hand, if you are using a constant such as *LINE_SIZE*, you only need to change the *#define* directive—a one-step process—as shown here:

```
#define LINE_SIZE 256
```

133 UNDERSTANDING MACRO AND CONSTANT EXPANSION

In Tip 132 you learned that your programs can use the *#define* directive to define a constant within your program. The following program, *sho_mac.c*, for example, uses three constants:

```
#define LINE 128
#define TITLE "Jamsa\'s C/C++ Programmer\'s Bible"
#define SECTION "Macros"

void main(void)
 {
    char book[LINE];
    char library_name[LINE];

    printf("This book's title is %s\n", TITLE);
    printf(SECTION);
 }
```

When you compile a C program, a *preprocessor* program runs first. The preprocessor's purpose is to include any specified header files and to expand macros and constants. Before the C compiler actually begins compiling your program, the preprocessor will substitute each constant name with the constant's value, as shown here:

```
void main(void)
 {
    char book[128];
    char library_name[128];
```

```
      printf("This book\'s title is %s\n", "Jamsa\'s C/C++ Programmer\'s Bible");
      printf("Macros");
   }
```

Because the preprocessor works with *#define*, *#include*, and other *#* statements, these statements are often called *preprocessor directives*.

NAMING CONSTANTS AND MACROS  134

As you have learned, a constant is a name the C compiler associates with a value that does not change. In Tip 144, you will learn about C macros. When you use constants and macros within your programs, you should use meaningful names that accurately describe their use. To help programmers who read your code differentiate between constants and variables, you should usually use uppercase letters for your constant and macro names. The following *#define* directives illustrate several macro definitions:

```
#define TRUE 1
#define FALSE 0
#define PI 3.1415
#define PROGRAMMER "Kris Jamsa"
```

As you can see, constants can contain *int*, *float*, or even *char* values.

USING THE __FILE__ PREPROCESSOR CONSTANT 135

When you work on a large project, sometimes you may want the preprocessor to know the name of the current source file. For example, you might use the filename within a processor directive that includes a message to the user stating that the program is still under development, as shown here:

```
The program PAYROLL.C is still under development and testing.
This is a BETA release only.
```

To help your programs perform such processing, the C preprocessor defines the *__FILE__* constant as equal to the name of the current source file. The following program, *filecnst.c*, illustrates the use of the *__FILE__* constant:

```
#include <stdio.h>

void main(void)
  {
    printf("The file %s is under Beta testing\n", __FILE__);
  }
```

When you compile and execute the *filecnst.c* program, your screen will display the following:

```
The file filecnst.c is under Beta testing
C:\>
```

Note: *While many preprocessor constants will change from compiler to compiler, the __FILE__ constant is consistent within **Turbo C++ Lite**, **Visual C++**, Borland's **C++ 5.02** and Borland's **C++ Builder**.*

USING THE __LINE__ PREPROCESSOR CONSTANT 136

When you work on a large project, sometimes you may want the preprocessor to know, and potentially use, the current line number of the current source file. For example, if you are debugging a program, you might want the compiler to display messages from various points within your program, as shown here:

```
Successfully reached line 10
Successfully reached line 301
Successfully reached line 213
```

The following program, *linecnst.c*, illustrates the use of the *__LINE__* preprocessor constant:

```
#include <stdio.h>

void main(void)
  {
    printf("Successfully reached line %d\n", __LINE__);
    // Other statements here
    printf("Successfully reached line %d\n", __LINE__);
  }
```

When you compile and execute this program, your screen will display the following output:

```
Successfully reached line 5
Successfully reached line 7
C:\>
```

Note: *While many preprocessor constants will change from compiler to compiler, the __LINE__ constant is consistent with* **Turbo C++ Lite,** **Visual C++,** **Borland's C++ 5.02** *and* **Borland's C++ Builder.**

137 CHANGING THE PREPROCESSOR'S LINE COUNT

In Tip 136 you learned how to use the preprocessor's *__LINE__* constant within your programs. When you use the *__LINE__* constant, sometimes you may want to change the preprocessor's current line number. For example, assume you are using *__LINE__* to help debug your program, as discussed in Tip 136. If you have narrowed down the error to a specific set of instructions, you might want the preprocessor to display line numbers relative to a specific location. To help you perform this processing, the C preprocessor provides the *#line* directive that lets you change the current line number. The following directive, for example, directs the preprocessor to set its line number to 100:

```
#line 100
```

You can also use the *#line* directive to change the name of the source code filename which the *__FILE__* constant will display:

```
#line 1 "FILENAME.C"
```

The following program, *chg_line.c*, illustrates how you use the *#line* directive:

```
#include <stdio.h>

void main(void)
  {
    printf("File %s: Successfully reached line %d\n", __FILE__, __LINE__);

    // Other statements here
#line 100 "FILENAME.C"

    printf("File %s: Successfully reached line %d\n", __FILE__, __LINE__);
  }
```

When you compile and execute the *chg_line.c* program, your screen will display the following output:

```
File chg_line.c: Successfully reached line 6
File FILENAME.C: Successfully reached line 102
C:\>
```

138 GENERATING AN UNCONDITIONAL PREPROCESSOR ERROR

As your programs become complex and use a large number of header files, sometimes you may not want the program to successfully compile if the program has not defined one or more constants. Likewise, if you are working with a group of programmers and you want them to be aware of a change you have made to the program, you can use the *#error* preprocessor directive to display an error message and end the compilation. The following directive, for example, ends the compilation, displaying a message to the user about the update:

```
#error The routine string_sort now uses far strings
```

Before the other programmers can successfully compile the program, they must remove the *#error* directive, therefore becoming aware of change.

OTHER PREPROCESSOR CONSTANTS 139

Several Tips in this section presented preprocessor constants most compilers support. Some compilers define many other preprocessor constants. The Microsoft *Visual C++* compiler, for example, uses over 15 other preprocessor constants this book does not discuss. Refer to the documentation that accompanied your compiler to determine if your programs can take advantage of other preprocessor constants. Additionally, consult the on-line help documentation, under the *Predefined Macros* heading.

RECORDING THE PREPROCESSOR DATE AND TIME 140

As you work on large programs, you may want your preprocessor to work with the current date and time. For example, you might want the program to display a message that states the date and time that you last compiled the program, as shown here:

```
Beta Testing: PAYROLL.C Last compiled Nov 4 1997 12:00:00
```

To help you perform such processing, the C preprocessor assigns the constants *__DATE__* and *__TIME__* to the current date and time. The following program, *datetime.c*, illustrates how you might use the *__DATE__* and *__TIME__* constants:

```c
#include <stdio.h>
void main(void)
  {
    printf("Beta Testing: Last compiled %s %s\n", __DATE__, __TIME__);
  }
```

TESTING FOR ANSI C COMPLIANCE 141

Although most C compilers are very similar, every compiler provides unique capabilities. To help you write programs that you can easily move from one system to another, the American National Standards Institute (ANSI) defines standards for operators, constructs, statements, and functions a compiler should support. Compilers that comply with these standards are called *ANSI C compilers*. As you build programs, sometimes you may want to determine whether or not you are using an ANSI compiler. To help you do so, ANSI C compilers define the constant *__STDC__* (for STandarD C). If the compiler is compiling for ANSI C compliance, the compiler will define the constant. Otherwise, the compiler does not define the constant. The following program, *chk_ansi.c*, uses the *__STDC__* constant to determine if the current compiler complies to the ANSI standards:

```c
#include <stdio.h>
void main(void)
  {
    #ifdef __STDC__
      printf("ANSI C compliance\n");
    #else
      printf("Not in ANSI C mode\n");
    #endif
  }
```

Note: *Most compilers provide command-line switches or inline pragmas that direct it to use ANSI compliance. You will learn about both command-line switches and inline pragmas later in this book.*

TESTING FOR C++ VERSUS C 142

You can use several of the Tips this book presents for both C programming and C++ programming, while other Tips only apply to C++. As you create your own programs, there may be times when you want the preprocessor to determine if you are using C or C++ and process your statements accordingly. To help you perform such testing, many C++ compilers define the *__cplusplus* constant. If you use a standard C compiler, the constant will be undefined. The following program, *chk_cpp.c*, uses the *__cplusplus* constant to determine the compiler's current mode:

```
#include <stdio.h>

void main(void)
 {
   #ifdef __cplusplus
     printf("Using C++\n");
   #else
     printf("Using C\n");
   #endif
 }
```

If you examine the header files the compiler provides, you will find many uses of the *__cplusplus* constant.

Note: Many C++ compilers provide command-line switches that direct them to compile using C++, as opposed to standard C.

143 UNDEFINING A MACRO OR CONSTANT

Several Tips this section presented discussed constants and macros the preprocessor defines or a header file contains. Depending on your program, you may want the preprocessor to remove the definition of one or more of these constants from your programs. Alternately, you may want the preprocessor to redefine one or more of these constants. For example, the following macro redefines the macro *_toupper*, which is defined in the header file *ctype.h*:

```
#define _toupper(c) ((((c) >= 'a')&&((c)<='z')) ? (c)-'a' + 'A': c)
```

When you compile this program, many preprocessors will display a warning message stating that you have redefined the macro. To avoid display of this warning message, use the *#undef* directive to remove the macro's current definition before you redefine the macro, as shown here:

```
#undef _toupper
#define _toupper(c) ((((c)>='a')&&((c)<='z')) ? (c) - 'a' + 'A': c)
```

144 COMPARING MACROS AND FUNCTIONS

New C programmers often become confused as to when they should use macros or functions because of the similarities between the two. As you have learned, each time the preprocessor encounters a macro reference within your program, the preprocessor replaces the reference with the macro statements. Therefore, if your program uses a macro 15 times, the program will have 15 different copies of the macro placed in its statements. As a result, the executable program's size will grow. When your program uses a function, on the other hand, the program only contains one copy of code, which reduces the program's size. When the program uses the function, the program calls (branches to) the function's code. The disadvantage of using functions, however, is that each function call incurs additional processing that makes the function call take slightly longer to execute than a comparable macro. Therefore, if you want fast performance, use a macro. However, if program size concerns you more, use a function.

145 UNDERSTANDING COMPILER PRAGMAS

Several Tips in this section presented different preprocessor directives such as *#define*, *#include*, and *#undef*. Depending on your compiler, your preprocessor may support various compiler directives, called *pragmas*. The format of a pragma is as follows:

```
#pragma compiler_directive
```

For example, the *Turbo C++ Lite* compiler provides the *startup* and *exit* pragmas, which let you specify the functions that you want your program to automatically execute when the program starts or ends:

```
#pragma startup load_data
#pragma exit close_all_files
```

Note that the function you name within the *startup* pragma will actually execute *before main*, so you should not use the *startup* pragma too often. Depending on your compiler, the available pragmas will differ. Refer to the documentation that accompanies your compiler for a complete description of the pragmas available for your program use.

Note: *When you use the* **startup** *and* **exit** *pragmas, the function you name within the pragma must take no parameters and return no value; in other words, you must write the function in the following manner:*

```
void function(void)
```

LEARNING ABOUT PREDEFINED VALUES AND MACROS   146

Several Tips in this section discussed macros, constants, and various preprocessor directives. One of the most effective ways of learning how to better use macros, constants, and other preprocessor directives is to thoroughly examine how the C compiler uses these options. The C compiler places macros and constants within header files that reside in the compiler's *include* subdirectory. Many of the header files present ways to use various preprocessor directives. You should examine the contents of various header files to help you learn many ways to improve your programs by taking advantage of these preprocessor capabilities.

CREATING YOUR OWN HEADER FILES   147

As you know, the C compiler provides different header files that contain related macros, constants, and function prototypes. As the number of programs you create increases, you may find that many of your programs use the same constants and macros. Rather than repeatedly typing these macros and constants into your programs, you might consider creating your own header file and placing into the file the corresponding macros and constants. Assuming that you create a header file named *my_defs.h,* you can include the file at the start of your programs using the *#include* preprocessor directive, as shown here:

```
#include "my_defs.h"
```

When you include your macros and constants in a header file in this way, you can quickly change several programs by editing the header file and then recompiling the programs that include the file.

USING #INCLUDE <FILENAME.H> OR #INCLUDE "FILENAME.H"   148

All the programs presented throughout this book have included the header file *stdio.h,* as shown here:

```
#include <stdio.h>
```

In Tip 147 you learned how to create and include your own header file, *my_defs.h*. You can include *stdio.h* and *my_defs.h* within you programs with the following statements:

```
#include <stdio.h>
#include "my_defs.h"
```

As you examine the two *include* statements, note that left and right brackets <> enclose the header file *stdio.h,* while double quotes enclose *my_defs.h*. When you enclose a header filename within the left and right brackets, the C compiler will first search its header file directory for the specified file. If the compiler locates the file, the preprocessor will use the file. If the compiler does not find the file, the compiler will search the current directory or a directory you specify. When you enclose a header filename in double quotes, on the other hand, the compiler will only search the current directory for the file.

149 TESTING WHETHER A SYMBOL IS DEFINED

Several Tips in this section presented predefined C compiler symbols. In addition, some Tips have discussed how you can define your own constants and macros. Depending on your program, there may be times when you want the preprocessor to test whether the program has previously defined a symbol and, if so, process a specific set of statements. To help your program test whether or not the program has previously defined a symbol, the C preprocessor supports the *#ifdef* directive. The format of the *#ifdef* directive is as follows:

```
#ifdef symbol
   // statements
#endif
```

When the preprocessor encounters the *#ifdef* directive, the preprocessor tests whether or not the program has previously defined the specified symbol. If so, the preprocessor processes the statements that follow the directive up to the *#endif* statement. There may be times when you want the preprocessor to process statements if the program has not defined a symbol. In such cases, you can use the *#ifndef* directive. The following statements use *#ifndef* to direct the preprocessor to define the *_toupper* macro if a similar macro is not defined:

```
#ifndef _toupper
   #define _toupper(c) ((((c)>='a')&&((c)<='z')) ? (c) - 'a' + 'A': c)
#endif
```

150 PERFORMING IF-ELSE PREPROCESSING

In Tip 149, you learned how to use the *#ifdef*, *#ifndef*, and *#endif* statements to specify a set of statements you want the preprocessor to perform if a program has previously defined (*#ifdef*) or not defined (*#ifndef*) a symbol. There may be times when you want to take this processing one step further and include a set of statements you want the preprocessor to perform when the condition tested within the *#ifdef* statement is true, and a different set if the condition is false. To perform such processing, you can use the *#else* directive, shown here:

```
#ifdef symbol
   // Statements
#else
   // Other statements
#endif
```

For example, both the Microsoft *Visual C++* and the Borland *C++ 5.02* compilers include unique preprocessor constants that indicate which compiler and version you are using to compile the program. You can use each compiler's unique constants to respond to different compilers. For example, the following code fragment will print *Microsoft* if the compiler is *Visual C++* and *Borland* if the compiler is Borland *C++ 5.02*:

```
#ifdef _MSC_VER
   printf ("Microsoft");
#endif
#ifdef __BORLANDC__
   printf ("Borland");
#endif
```

151 PERFORMING MORE POWERFUL PREPROCESSOR CONDITION TESTING

In Tip 149 you learned how to use the *#ifdef* and *#ifndef* statements to direct the preprocessor to test whether a program has previously defined or not defined a symbol and then to process the statements that follow based on the test's result. In some cases, you may need the processor to test if several symbols are defined, not defined, or some combination of both. The following directives first test to see if the symbol *MY_LIBRARY* is defined. If your program has previously defined *MY_LIBRARY*, the preprocessor directives test whether your program has also previously defined the symbol *MY_FUNCTIONS*. If your program has not already defined *MY_FUNCTIONS*, the code directs the preprocessor to include the header file *my_code.h*:

```
#ifdef MY_LIBRARY
#ifndef MY_ROUTINES
#include "my_code.h"
#endif
#endif
```

Although the directives perform the desired processing, the nested conditionals make it potentially difficult for another programmer to follow your intent. As an alternative, your programs can use the *#if* directive with the *defined* operator to test if the program has previously defined the symbol, as shown here:

```
#if defined(symbol)
   // Statements
#endif
```

Your advantage in using the *#if* directive is that you can combine testing, unlike with the *#ifdef* or *#ifndef* directives. The following directive performs the same testing as the first example in this Tip:

```
#if defined(MY_LIBRARY) && !defined(MY_ROUTINES)
#include "my_code.h"
#endif
```

You can use *#if defined* to build conditions that use C's logical operators (including &&, ||, and !).

PERFORMING IF-ELSE AND ELSE-IF PREPROCESSING `C`152

In Tip 151 you learned how to use the *#if* preprocessor directive to test whether or not your program has previously defined a symbol. When you use the *#if* directive, there may be times when you want the preprocessor to process one set of statements when a symbol is defined and another set if the symbol is undefined (*conditional preprocessing*). You can perform conditional preprocessing using the *#else* directive:

```
#if defined(symbol)
   // Statements
#else
   // Statements
#endif
```

Taking the previous preprocessing example one step further, there may be times when you will want the preprocessor to test the status of other symbols when a specified condition fails. The following directives, for example, instruct the preprocessor to process one set of statements if the symbol *MY_LIBRARY* is defined; another set if *MY_LIBRARY* is not defined but *MY_ROUTINES* is defined; and a third set if neither symbol is defined:

```
#if defined(MY_LIBRARY)
   // Statements
#else if defined (MY_ROUTINES)
   // Statements
#else
   // Statements
#endif
```

As you can see, when you use *#if* and *#else* directives you significantly increase your control over the preprocessor.

Note: *Some compilers, including* **Turbo C++ Lite***, support the* **#elif** *preprocessor directive, which performs the same processing as the* **#else if** *construction.*

DEFINING MACROS AND CONSTANTS THAT REQUIRE MULTIPLE LINES `C`153

Several Tips presented throughout this section have defined constants and macros. As your constants and macros become more complex, sometimes a definition will not fit on one line. When you must wrap a constant or macro definition to the next line, place a backslash character at the end of the line, as shown here:

```
#define very_long_character_string "This extremely long string constant\
requires two lines"

#define _toupper(c) ((((c) >= 'a') && ((c) <= 'z'))\
 ? (c) - 'a' + 'A': c)
```

154 CREATING YOUR OWN MACROS

As you have learned, macros provide a way for you to define constants that the preprocessor substitutes throughout your program before compilation begins. In addition, macros let you create function-like operations that work with *parameters*. Parameters are values that you pass to the macro. For example, the following macro, *SUM*, returns the sum of the two values that you pass to the macro:

```
#define SUM(x, y) ((x) + (y))
```

The following program, *show_sum.c*, uses the *SUM* macro to add several values:

```
#include <stdio.h>
#define SUM(x, y) ((x) + (y))

void main(void)
 {
    printf("Adding 3 + 5 = %d\n", SUM(3, 5));
    printf("Adding 3.4 + 3.1 = %f\n", SUM(3.4, 3.1));
    printf("Adding -100 + 1000 = %d\n", SUM(-100, 1000));
 }
```

Within the *SUM* macro's definition, the *x* and *y* represent macro parameters. When you pass two values to the macro, such as *SUM(3, 5)* the preprocessor substitutes the parameters into the macro, as shown in Figure 154.

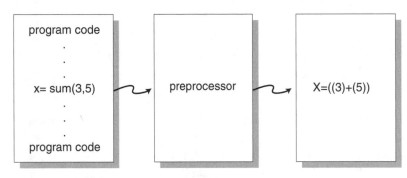

Figure 154 The parameter substitution for SUM.

In the program *show_sum.c*, the preprocessor's substitutions will result in the following code:

```
    printf("Adding 3 + 5 = %d\n", ((3) + (5)));
    printf("Adding 3.4 + 3.1 = %f\n", ((3.4) +  (3.1)));
    printf("Adding -100 + 1000 = %d\n", ((-100) + (1000)));
```

155 DO NOT PLACE SEMICOLONS IN MACRO DEFINITIONS

When you examine the macro definition of the following *SUM* macro, note that the macro does not include a semicolon:

```
#define SUM(x, y) ((x) + (y))
```

If you include a semicolon within your macro, the preprocessor will place the semicolon at each macro occurrence throughout your program. Assume, for example, you placed a semicolon at the end of the *SUM* macro definition, as shown here:

```
#define SUM(x, y) ((x) + (y));
```

When the preprocessor expands the macro, the preprocessor will include the semicolon, as shown here:

```
      printf("Adding 3 + 5 = %d\n", ((3) + (5)););
      printf("Adding 3.4 + 3.1 = %f\n", ((3.4) + (3.1)););
      printf("Adding -100 + 1000 = %d\n", ((-100) + (1000)););
```

Because the semicolon now occurs in the middle of the *printf* statement (indicating the statement's end), the compiler will generate errors.

Note: *Unless you want the preprocessor to include a semicolon in the macro expansion, do not include a semicolon in the macro definition.*

CREATING MIN AND MAX MACROS   C156

In Tip 154 you created the *SUM* macro, which added two values together. The following macros, *MIN* and *MAX*, return the minimum and maximum of two values:

```
#define MIN(x, y) (((x) < (y)) ? (x): (y))
#define MAX(x, y) (((x) > (y)) ? (x): (y))
```

The following program, *min_max.c*, illustrates how to use *MIN* and *MAX* macros:

```
#include <stdio.h>

#define MIN(x, y) (((x) < (y)) ? (x): (y))
#define MAX(x, y) (((x) > (y)) ? (x): (y))

void main(void)
  {
    printf("Maximum of 10.0 and 25.0 is %f\n", MAX(10.0, 25.0));
    printf("Minimum of 3.4 and 3.1 is %f\n", MIN(3.4, 3.1));
  }
```

When you execute the *min_max.c* program, the preprocessor's substitutions result in the following code:

```
printf("Maximum of 10.0 and 25.0 is %d\n", (((10.0) < (25.0)) ? (10.0): (25.0)));
printf("Minimum of 3.4 and 3.1 is %f\n", (((3.4) > (3.1)) ? (3.4): (3.1)));
```

CREATING SQUARE AND CUBE MACROS   C157

As you have learned, C lets you define and pass values to macros. The last two macros you will examine in this section are the *SQUARE* and *CUBE* macros, which return, respectively, a value squared (x * x) and a value cubed (x * x * x) results:

```
#define SQUARE(x) ((x) * (x))
#define CUBE(x) ((x) * (x) * (x))
```

The following program, *sqr_cube.c*, illustrates how to use the *SQUARE* and *CUBE* macros:

```
#include <stdio.h>
#define SQUARE(x) ((x) * (x))
#define CUBE(x) ((x) * (x) * (x))

void main(void)
  {
    printf("The square of 2 is %d\n", SQUARE(2));
    printf("The cube of 100 is %f\n", CUBE(100.0));
  }
```

In the *sqr_cube.c* program, the preprocessor's substitutions result in the following code:

```
      printf("The square of 2 is %d\n", ((2) * (2)));
      printf("The cube of 100 is %f\n", ((100.0) * (100.0) * (100.0)));
```

Note: *To avoid overflow, the **sqr_cube.c** program uses the floating-point value 100.0 within the **CUBE** macro.*

158 BE AWARE OF SPACES IN MACRO DEFINITIONS

Several previous Tips have presented macros that support parameters. When you define macros that support parameters, you must be careful of white space in the macro definition. Do not place a space between the macro name and its parameters. For example, consider the following macro definition, *SQUARE*:

```
#define SQUARE (x) ((x) * (x))
```

When the preprocessor examines your program, the spaces between the macro name cause the preprocessor to assume that is should replace each occurrence of the name *SQUARE* with *(x) ((x) * (x))*, rather than with *((x) * x))*. As a result the macro will not evaluate correctly, and in most cases, the compiler will generate syntax error messages or warnings because of the substitution. To understand the preprocessor's macro substitution process better, experiment with the program *sqr_cube.c* (presented in Tip 157), by placing a space after each macro name.

159 UNDERSTANDING HOW TO USE PARENTHESES

Several of the previous Tips have presented macros to which your programs will pass values (parameters). If you take a close look at each macro's definitions, you will find that parentheses enclose the values:

```
#define SUM(x, y) ((x) + (y))
#define SQUARE(x) ((x) * (x))
#define CUBE(x) ((x) * (x) * (x))
#define MIN(x, y) (((x) < (y)) ? (x): (y))
#define MAX(x, y) (((x) > (y)) ? (x): (y))
```

Macro definitions enclose parameters within parentheses in order to support expressions. As an example, consider the following statement:

```
result = SQUARE(3 + 5);
```

The statement should assign the variable *result* the value 64 (8 * 8). Assume, for example, that you define the *SQUARE* macro as follows:

```
#define SQUARE(x) (x * x)
```

When the preprocessor substitutes the expression 3 + 5 for *x*, the substitution becomes the following:

```
result = (3 + 5 *  3 + 5);
```

Recall C's operator precedence and note that multiplication has higher precedence than does addition. Therefore, the program would calculate the expression as follows:

```
result = (3 + 5 * 3 + 5);
       = (3 + 15 + 5);
       = 23;
```

When you enclose each parameter within parentheses, however, you ensure that the preprocessor evaluates the expression correctly:

```
result = SQUARE(3 + 5);
       = ((3 + 5) * (3 + 5));
       = ((8) * (8));
       = (64);
       = 64;
```

Note: As a rule, you should always enclose your macro parameters within parentheses.

160 MACROS ARE TYPELESS

In the Functions section of this book, you will learn how to create functions that perform specific operations. You will learn that C lets you pass parameters to your functions, just as you have passed values to macros. If your function performs an operation and returns a result, you must specify the result's type (such as *int, float,* and so on). For example, the following function, *add_values*, adds two integer values and returns a result of type *int*:

```
int add_values(int x, int y)
  {
    return(x + y);
  }
```

Within your program you can only use the *add_values* function to add two values of type *int*. If you try to add two floating-point values, an error will occur. As you have seen, macros let you work with values of any type. The *SUM* macro that you previously created, for example, supported values of both type *int* and type *float*:

```
printf("Adding 3 + 5 = %d\n", SUM(3, 5));
printf("Adding 3.4 + 3.1 = %f\n", SUM(3.4, 3.1));
```

When you use macros for simple arithmetic operations, you eliminate the need to duplicate functions simply because you want to work with values of different types. However, as you will learn in this book's Functions section, there are other tradeoffs to consider when deciding whether you are going to use macros or functions.

VISUALIZING A C STRING   161

Your computer requires a byte of memory to store a single ASCII character. As you have learned, a *string* is a sequence of ASCII characters. When you declare a string constant, C automatically assigns the *NULL* character. When your programs create their own strings by reading characters from the keyboard, your programs must assign the *NULL* character to the end of the string to indicate the string's end. Therefore, the best way for you to visualize a string is as a collection of bytes terminated by a *NULL* character, as shown in Figure 161.

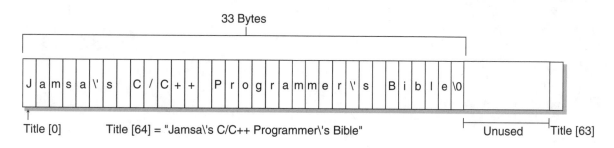

Figure 161 C stores strings in consecutive byte locations in memory.

When functions work with strings, the function usually only receives the location at which the string starts. After the function knows the string's start location, the function can traverse successive memory locations until the function encounters *NULL* character (which indicates the string's end).

HOW THE COMPILER REPRESENTS A CHARACTER STRING   162

Several Tips presented throughout this book use character string constants enclosed by double quotes, as in the following example:

```
"Jamsa\'s C/C++ Programmer\'s Bible"
```

When you use a character string constant within your program, the C compiler automatically assigns the *NULL* character (\0) at the end of the string. Given the previous string constant, the C compiler will actually store the constant in memory, as shown in Figure 162.

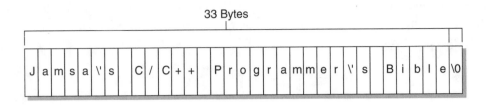

Figure 162 *C automatically appends the NULL character to string constants.*

163 HOW C STORES CHARACTER STRINGS

Many of the Tips this book presents make extensive use of character strings. For example, some programs use strings to read files and keyboard input and to perform other operations. In C, a character string is a *NULL-* or zero-terminated array of characters. To create a character string, you simply declare a character array, as shown here:

```
char string[256];
```

C will create a string capable of storing 256 characters, which C indexes from *string*[0] through *string*[255]. Because the string may contain less than 256 characters, C uses the *NULL* (ASCII 0) character to represent the string's last character. C does not typically place the *NULL* character after the last character in the string. Instead, functions such as *fgets* or *gets* place the *NULL* character at the string's end. As your programs manipulate strings, it is your responsibility to ensure that the *NULL* character is present. The following program, *buildabc.c*, defines a 256-character string and then assigns the uppercase letters of the alphabet to the first twenty-six digits of the string:

```
#include <stdio.h>

void main(void)
  {
    char string[256];
    int i;

    for (i = 0; i < 26; i++)
      string[i] = 'A' + i;
    string[i] = NULL;
    printf ("The string contains %s\n", string);
  }
```

The *buildabc.c* program uses the *for* loop to assign the letters A through Z to the string. The program then places the *NULL* character after the letter Z to indicate the string's end. The *printf* function will then display each character in the string up to the *NULL* character. The C functions that work with strings use the *NULL* character to determine the string's end. The following program, *a_thru_j.c*, also assigns the letters A through Z to a character string. However, the program then assigns the *NULL* character to *string*[10], which is the location that immediately follows the letter J. When *printf* displays the string's contents, it will stop at the letter J:

```
#include <stdio.h>

void main(void)
  {
    char string[256];
    int i;

    for (i = 0; i < 26; i++)
      string[i] = 'A' + i;
    string[10] = NULL;
    printf ("The string contains %s\n", string);
  }
```

Note: *As you work with strings, you must make sure you correctly include the NULL character to represent the end of the string.*

LEARNING HOW 'A' DIFFERS FROM "A"

164

As you learned in Tip 161, a character string is a sequence of zero or more ASCII characters that C typically terminates with *NULL* (an ASCII 0). When you work with characters within C, you can use a character's numeric ASCII value or you can place the character within single quotes, such as 'A'. On the other hand, when you use double quotes, such as "A," C creates a character string that contains the specified letter (or letters) and terminates the string with the *NULL* character. Figure 164 illustrates how C stores the constants 'A' and "A".

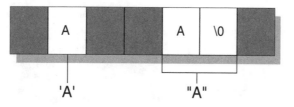

Figure 164 *How C stores the constants 'A' and "A".*

Because C stores them differently, character and string constants are not the same and you should be sure to treat the two sets of constants differently within your programs.

REPRESENTING A QUOTE WITHIN A STRING CONSTANT

165

As you have learned, to create a string constant your program must place the desired characters within double quotes:

```
"This is a string constant"
```

Depending on your programs, there may be times when a string constant will contain a double quote character. For example, assume you must represent the following string:

```
"Stop!", he said.
```

Because C uses the double quotes to define the string constants, you must have a way to tell the compiler that you want to include a quote within the string. To do so, use the escape sequence \", as shown here:

```
"\"Stop!\", he said."
```

The following program, *quotes.c,*, uses the \" escape sequence to place quotes within a string constant:

```c
#include <stdio.h>

void main(void)
  {
    char string[] = "\"Stop!\", he said.";
    printf(string);
  }
```

DETERMINING THE LENGTH OF A STRING

166

In Tip 163 you learned that C functions usually use the *NULL* character to represent the end of a string. Functions such as *fgets* and *cgets* automatically assign the *NULL* character to indicate the end of a string. The following program, *show_str.c*, uses the *gets* function to read a character string from the keyboard. The program then uses a *for* loop to display the string's characters one at a time until the conditional *string[i] != NULL* evaluates to false:

```c
#include <stdio.h>

void main(void)
  {
    char string[256];   // String input by user
    int i;               // Index into the string
```

```
    printf("Type a string of characters and press Enter:\n");
    gets(string);
    // Display each string character until NULL is found
    for (i = 0; string[i] != NULL; i++)
      putchar(string[i]);
    printf("\nThe number of characters in the string is %d\n", i);
  }
```

167 USING THE STRLEN FUNCTION

As you work with strings within your programs, you will perform many operations based on the number of characters in the string. To help you determine the number of characters in a string, most C compilers provide a *strlen* function, which returns the number of characters in a string. The format of the *strlen* function is as follows:

```
#include <string.h>

size_t strlen(const char string);
```

The following program, *strlen.c*, illustrates how to use the *strlen* function:

```
#include <stdio.h>
#include <string.h>

void main(void)
  {
    char book_title[] = "Jamsa\'s C/C++ Programmer\'s Bible";

    printf("%s contains %d characters\n", book_title, strlen(book_title));
  }
```

When you compile and execute the *strlen.c* program, your screen will display the following:

```
Jamsa's C/C++ Programmer's Bible contains 32 characters
C:\>
```

To better understand how the *strlen* function works, consider the following implementation. The function simply counts the characters in a string up to, but not including, the *NULL* character:

```
size_t strlen(const char string)
  {
    int i = 0;
    while (string[i])
        i++;
    return(i);
  }
```

168 COPYING ONE STRING'S CHARACTERS TO ANOTHER STRING

As your programs work with strings, there may be times when you must copy the contents of one character string to another string. To help you perform character string operations, most C compilers provide a *strcpy* function, which copies the characters in one string (the *source* parameter) to another string (the *destination* parameter):

```
#include <string.h>

char *strcpy(char *destination, const char *source);
```

The *strcpy* function returns a pointer to the beginning of the destination string. The following program, *strcpy.c*, illustrates how you will use the *strcpy* function within your programs:

```
#include <stdio.h>
#include <string.h>

void main(void)
  {
    char title[] = "Jamsa\'s C/C++ Programmer\'s Bible";
    char book[128];
```

```
    strcpy(book, title);
    printf("Book name %s\n", book);
}
```

To better understand how the *strcpy* function works, consider the following implementation:

```
char *strcpy(char *destination, const char *source)
  {
     while (*destination++ = *source++)
         ;
     return(destination-1);
  }
```

The *strcpy* function simply copies letters from the source string to the destination, up to and including the *NULL* character.

APPENDING ONE STRING'S CONTENTS TO ANOTHER STRING   C169

As your programs work with strings, there may be times when you must append one string's contents to another string. For example, if one string contains a subdirectory name and another contains a filename, you might append the filename to the subdirectory to create a complete pathname. C programmers often refer to the process of appending one string to another as *concatenating* strings. To help you append one string to another, most C compilers provide a function named *strcat*, which concatenates (appends) a source string to a target string, as shown here:

```
#include <string.h>
char *strcat (char target, const char *source);
```

The following program, *strcat.c*, illustrates how to use the *strcat* function:

```
#include <stdio.h>
#include <string.h>

void main(void)
  {
    char name[64] = "Triggerhill\'s I\'m so";
    strcat(name, " Happy");
    printf("Happy\'s full name is %s\n", name);
  }
```

When you compile and execute the *strcat.c* program, your screen will display the following:

```
Happy's full name is Triggerhill's I'm so Happy
C:\>
```

To better understand the *strcat* function, consider the following implementation:

```
char *strcat(char *target, const char *source)
  {
    char *original = target;

    while (*target)
      target++;        // Find the end of the string
    while (*target++ = *source++)
      ;
    return (original);
  }
```

As you can see, the *strcat* function loops through the destination string's characters until the function finds the *NULL* character. The *strcat* function then appends each character in the source string, up to and including the *NULL* character, to the destination string.

APPENDING N CHARACTERS TO A STRING   C170

In Tip 169 you learned that the *strcat* function lets you append (concatenate) the characters in one string to another. In some cases, you will not want to append all the characters in a string, but rather only the first two, three, or *n* characters in the string. To help you append *n* characters to a string, most C compilers provide a function named *strncat*, which appends the first *n* characters of a source string to a destination string, as shown here:

```
#include <stding.h>

char *strncat(char *destination, const *source, size_t n);
```

If *n* specifies a number of characters greater than the number of characters in the source string, *strncat* will copy characters up to the end of the string and no more. The following program, *strncat.c*, illustrates how to use the *strncat* function:

```
#include <stdio.h>
#include <string.h>

void main(void)
  {
    char name[64] = "Bill";

    strncat(name, " and Hillary", 4);
    printf("Did you vote for %s?\n", name);
  }
```

When you compile and execute the *strncat.c* program, your screen will display the following:

```
Did you vote for Bill and?
C:\>
```

To help you better understand the *strncat* function, consider the following implementation:

```
char *strncat(char *destination, const char *source, int n)
  {
    char *original = destination;
    int i = 0;

    while (*destination)
      destination++;
    while ((i++ < n) && (*destination++ = *source++))
      ;
    if (i > n)
      *destination = NULL;
    return(original);
  }
```

171 TRANSFORMING ONE STRING TO ANOTHER STRING

Several of the Tips in this book have shown you ways to copy the contents of one string to another. The *strxfrm* function copies the contents of one string to another (up to the number of characters you specify within the *n* parameter) and then returns the length of the resultant string:

```
#include <string.h>

size_t strxfrm(char *target, char *source, size_t n);
```

The *target* parameter is a pointer to which the *strxfrm* function copies the source string. The *n* parameter specifies the maximum number of characters to copy. The following program, *strxfrm.c*, illustrates how to use the *strxfrm* function:

```
#include <stdio.h>
#include <string.h>

void main(void)
  {
    char buffer[64] = "Jamsa\'s C/C++ Programmer\'s Bible";
    char target[64];
    int length;

    length = strxfrm(target, buffer, sizeof(buffer));
    printf("Length %d Target %s Buffer %s\n", length, target, buffer);
  }
```

DO NOT OVERWRITE A STRING'S BOUNDS 172

Several of the Tips in this section have presented functions that copy or append characters from one string to another. When you perform character string operations, you must ensure that you do not overwrite a string's memory locations. As an example of problems with overwriting a string's bounds, consider the following declaration, which creates a character string capable of storing 10 characters:

```
char string[10];
```

If you assign more than 10 characters to the string, your operating system may not detect the error. Rather, the characters you intended to assign to the string may overwrite the memory locations that correspond to other variables. Not only is correcting an overwrite error very difficult, but an overwrite error might also cause both your program and the operating system to cease execution. As a rule, declare your strings slightly larger than you think you will need. Doing so lets you reduce the likelihood of overwriting a string. If your programs experience intermittent errors, examine your program code to determine if your program may be overwriting a character string.

DETERMINING WHETHER TWO STRINGS ARE THE SAME 173

As your programs work with strings, you will often compare two strings to determine if the strings are the same. To help you determine if two strings contain the same characters, you can use the *streql* function, shown here:

```
int streql(char *str1, char *str2)
  {
    while ((*str1 == *str2) && (*str1))
      {
        str1++;
        str2++;
      }
    return((*str1 == NULL) && (*str2 == NULL));
  }
```

The *streql* function will return the value 1 if the two strings are equal, and 0 if the strings are not equal. The following C program, *streql.c*, illustrates how to use the *streql* function:

```
#include <stdio.h>

void main(void)
  {
    printf("Testing Abc and Abc %d\n", streql("Abc", "Abc"));
    printf("Testing abc and Abc %d\n", streql("abc", "Abc"));
    printf("Testing abcd and abc %d\n", streql("abcd", "abc"));
  }
```

When you compile and execute the *streql.c* program, your screen will display the following output:

```
Testing Abc and Abc 1
Testing abc and Abc 0
Testing abcd and abc 0
C:\>
```

IGNORING CASE WHEN DETERMINING WHETHER STRINGS ARE EQUAL 174

In Tip 173 you created the function *streql*, which lets your programs quickly determine whether two strings are equal. When the *streql* function compares two strings, *streql* considers upper- and lowercase characters as distinct. There may be times when you will want to compare two strings without considering case. To compare strings without considering case, you can create the function *strieql*, as shown here:

```
#include <ctype.h>

int strieql(char *str1, char *str2)
  {
    while ((toupper(*str1) == toupper(*str2)) && (*str1))
      {
        str1++;
        str2++;
      }
    return((*str1 == NULL) && (*str2 == NULL));
  }
```

As you can see, the *strieql* function converts each character in each string to uppercase before comparing the two strings. The following program, *strieql.c*, illustrates how to use *strieql*:

```
#include <stdio.h>
#include <ctype.h>

void main(void)
  {
    printf("Testing Abc and Abc %d\n", strieql("Abc", "Abc"));
    printf("Testing abc and Abc %d\n", strieql("abc", "Abc"));
    printf("Testing abcd and abc %d\n", strieql("abcd", "abc"));
  }
```

When you compile and execute the *strieql.c* program, your screen will display the following:

```
Testing Abc and Abc 1
Testing abc and Abc 1
Testing abcd and abc 0
C:\>
```

175 CONVERTING A CHARACTER STRING TO UPPER- OR LOWERCASE

When your programs work with strings, there may be times when you may want to convert the string to uppercase. For example, when a user types in a filename or customer name, you may want the program to convert the entered string to uppercase to simplify string compare operations or to ensure that the program stores data in a consistent format. To help you perform these conversions, most C compilers provide the functions *strlwr* and *strupr*, as shown here:

```
#include <string.h>

char *strlwr(char *string);
char *strupr(char *string);
```

The following program, *strcase.c*, illustrates how to use the *strlwr* and *strupr* functions:

```
#include <stdio.h>
#include <string.h>

void main(void)
  {
    printf(strlwr("Jamsa\'s C/C++ Programmer\'s Bible!\n"));
    printf(strupr("Jamsa\'s C/C++ Programmer\'s Bible!\n"));
  }
```

To help you better understand these two functions, consider the following implementation of *strlwr*:

```
#include <ctype.h>

char *strlwr(char *string)
  {
    char *original = string;

    while (*string)
      {
        *string = tolower(*string);
        string++;
      }
    return(original);
  }
```

As you can see, both *strlwr* and *strupr* loop through the characters in a string, converting each character to either upper- or lowercase, depending upon the invoked function.

OBTAINING THE FIRST OCCURRENCE OF A CHARACTER IN A STRING 176

As your programs work with strings, there may be times when you will want to find the first (leftmost) occurrence of a specific character within a string. For example, if you are working with a string that contains a pathname, you might search the string for the first backslash (\) character. To help you search for the first occurrence of a string, most compilers provide a function named *strchr*, which returns a pointer to the first occurrence of a specific character within a string, as shown here:

```
#include <string.h>

char *strchr(const char *string, int character);
```

If *strchr* does not find the specified character within the string, *strchr* returns a pointer to the *NULL* character that marks the end of the string. The following program, *strchr.c*, illustrates how to use the *strchr* function:

```
#include <stdio.h>
#include <string.h>

void main(void)
 {
   char title[64] = "Jamsa\'s C/C++ Programmer\'s Bible!";
   char *ptr;

   ptr = strchr(title, 'C');
   if (*ptr)
     printf("First occurrence of C is at offset %d\n", ptr - title);
   else
     printf("Character not found\n");
 }
```

When you compile and execute the *strchr.c* program, your screen will display the following:

```
The first occurrence of C is at offset 5
C:\>
```

You should note that *strchr* does not contain an index to the first occurrence of a character; rather, *strchr* contains a pointer to the character. To help you better understand the *strchr* function, consider the following implementation:

```
char *strchr(const char *string, int letter)
 {
   while ((*string != letter) && (*string))
     string++;
   return((string);
 }
```

RETURNING AN INDEX TO THE FIRST OCCURRENCE OF A STRING 177

In Tip 176 you learned how to use the function *strchr* to obtain a pointer to the first occurrence of a character within a string. If you treat strings as arrays, as opposed to pointers, however, you probably prefer to work with an index to the character, rather than with a pointer. You can use the *strchr* function to obtain an index to the desired character by subtracting the string's starting address from the pointer *strchr* returns, as shown here:

```
char_ptr = strchr(string, character);
index = char_ptr - string;
```

If *strchr* does not find the character in the string, then the value *strchr* assigns to the index will be equal to the string's length. In addition to using *strchr* in the manner this Tip details, you can also use the function *str_index*, as shown here:

```
int str_index(const char *string, int letter)
 {
   char *original = string;

   while ((*string != letter) && (*string))
     string++;
   return(string - original);
 }
```

178 FINDING THE LAST OCCURRENCE OF A CHARACTER IN A STRING

As your programs work with strings, there may be times when you will want to find the last (rightmost) occurrence of a specific character within a string. For example, if you are working with a string that contains a pathname, you might search the string for the last backslash (\) character in order to find the location where the filename begins. To help you search for the last occurrence of a character within a string, most compilers provide a function named *strrchr*, which returns a pointer to the last occurrence of a specific character within a string, as shown here:

```
#include <string.h>

char *strrchr(const char *string, int character);
```

If *strrchr* does not find the character you specify within the string, *strrchr* returns a pointer to the *NULL* character that marks the end of the string. The following program, *strrchr.c*, illustrates how to use the *strrchr* function:

```
#include <stdio.h>
#include <string.h>

void main(void)
 {
   char title[64] = "Jamsa\'s C/C++ Programmer\'s Bible!";
   char *ptr;

   if (ptr = strrchr(title, 'C'))
     printf("Rightmost occurrence of C is at offset %d\n", ptr - title);
   else
     printf("Character not found\n");
 }
```

You should note that *strrchr* does not contain an index to the last occurrence of a character, but rather contains a pointer to the character. To help you better understand the *strrchr* function, consider the following implementation:

```
char *strrchr(const char *string, int letter)
 {
   char *ptr = NULL;

   while (*string)
    {
       if (*string == letter)
         ptr = string;
       string++;
    }
   return(ptr);
 }
```

179 RETURNING AN INDEX TO THE LAST OCCURRENCE OF A STRING

In Tip 178 you learned how to use the function *strrchr* to obtain a pointer to the last occurrence of a character within a string. If you treat a string as an array, as opposed to a pointer, however, you probably prefer to work with an index to the character rather than a pointer. If you use the *strrchr* function, you can obtain an index to the desired character by subtracting the string's starting address from the pointer *strrchr* returns:

```
char_ptr = strrchr(string, character);

index = char_ptr - string;
```

If *strrchr* does not find the character in the string, the value *strrchr* assigns to the index will be equal to the string's length. In addition to using *strrchr*, you can use the function *strr_index*, as shown here:

```
int strr_index(const char *string, int letter)
  {
    char *original = string;
    char *ptr = NULL;

    while (*string)
     {
      if (*string == letter)
        ptr = string;
      string++;
     }
    return((*ptr) ? ptr-original: string-original);
  }
```

WORKING WITH FAR STRINGS C180

As discussed in the Memory section of this book, *far* pointers let DOS programs access data that reside outside of the current 64Kb data segment. When you are working with *far* pointers, you must also use functions that expect their parameters to be *far* pointers. Unfortunately, none of the string manipulation routines this section presents anticipate *far* pointers to strings. Passing a *far* pointer to one of the string manipulation functions this section details will make an error occur. To support *far* pointers, however, many compilers provide *far*-pointer implementations of these functions. For example, to determine the length of a string a *far* pointer references, you might use the function *_fstrlen*, as shown here:

```
#include <string.h>
size_t _fstrlen(const char *string)
```

To determine which *far* functions your compiler supports, refer to your compiler documentation.

Note: As you have learned previously, **Visual C++** does not support **far** declarations (either functions or pointers), so you can use the **strlen** function with **char** pointers of any size in **Visual C++**.

WRITING STRING FUNCTIONS FOR FAR STRINGS C181

In Tip 180 you learned that several compilers provide functions that support strings which *far* pointers reference. If your compiler does not provide such functions, you can create the *far* string functions yourself by modifying the functions in this section. As an example, the following function, *fstreql*, illustrates a *far* pointer-based implementation of *streql* (rather than the standard, local pointer-based implementation):

```
int fstreql(char far *str1, char far *str2)
  {
    while ((*str1 == *str2) && (*str1))
      {
        str1++;
        str2++;
      }
    return((*str1 == NULL) && (*str2 == NULL));
  }
```

Note: As you have learned previously, **Visual C++** does not support **far** declarations, so you can use the **streql** function with **char** pointers of any size in **Visual C++**.

COUNTING THE NUMBER OF CHARACTER OCCURRENCES IN A STRING C182

As your programs work with strings, there may be times when you will want to know the number of times a character occurs within a string. To help you count the number of times a character occurs within a string, your programs can use the *charcnt* function, as shown here:

```
int charcnt(const char *string, int letter)
  {
    int count = 0;

    while (*string)
      if (*string == letter)
        count++;
    return(count);
  }
```

183 REVERSING A STRING'S CONTENTS

As your programs perform different string operations, there may be times when you must reverse the order of characters within a string. To simplify such operations, most compilers provide a *strrev* function, as shown here:

```
#include <string.h>

char *strrev(char *string);
```

To better understand the *strrev* function, consider the following implementation:

```
char *strrev(char *string)
  {
    char *original = string;
    char *forward = string;
    char temp;

    while (*string)
      string++;
    while (forward < string)
      {
        temp = *(--string);
        *string = *forward;
        *forward++ = temp;
      }
    return(original);
  }
```

184 ASSIGNING A SPECIFIC CHARACTER TO AN ENTIRE STRING

As your programs work with strings, there may be times when you will want to set all the characters in a string to a specific character. For example, there may be times when you want to overwrite a string's current value before passing the string to a function. To simplify the overwriting of every character within a string, most C compilers provide a *strset* function, which assigns every character in the string a specified character, as shown here:

```
#include <string.h>

char *strset(char *string, int character);
```

The *strset* function assigns the specified character to each string location until the *strset* function encounters the *NULL* character. To better understand the *strset* function, consider the following implementation:

```
char *strset(char *string, int letter)
  {
    char *original = string;

    while (*string)
      *string++ = letter;
    return(original);
  }
```

As you can see, the function loops through the string assigning the specified character until the function finds the *NULL* character.

COMPARING TWO CHARACTER STRINGS 185

In Tip 173 you created the *streql* function, which let your programs test whether or not two character strings are equal. Depending on the processing your program must perform, there will be times (such as when your program performs a *sort* operation) when you must know if one string is greater than another. To help your programs perform operations that determine the value of various strings, most C compilers provide a function named *strcmp*, which compares two character strings, as shown here:

```
#include <string.h>

int strcmp(const char *str1, const *char str2);
```

If the strings are equal, *strcmp* returns the value 0. If the first string is greater than the second, *strcmp* returns a value less than 0. Likewise, if the second string is greater than the first, *strcmp* returns a value greater than 0. The following program, *strcmp.c*, illustrates how to use the *strcmp* function:

```
#include <stdio.h>
#include <string.h>

void main(void)
{
   printf("Comparing Abc with Abc %d\n", strcmp("Abc", "Abc"));
   printf("Comparing abc with Abc %d\n", strcmp("abc", "Abc"));
   printf("Comparing abcd with abc %d\n", strcmp("abcd", "abc"));
   printf("Comparing Abc with Abcd %d\n", strcmp("Abc", "Abcd"));

   printf("Comparing abcd with abce %d\n", strcmp("abcd", "abce"));
   printf("Comparing Abce with Abcd %d\n", strcmp("Abce", "Abcd"));
}
```

To better understand the *strcmp* function, consider the following implementation:

```
int strcmp(const char *s1, const char *s2)
{
   while ((*s1 == *s2) && (*s1))
     {
       s1++;
       s2++;
     }
   if ((*s1 == *s2) && (! *s1))     // Same strings
     return(0);
   else if ((*s1) && (! *s2))       // Same but s1 longer
     return(-1);
   else if ((*s2) && (! *s1))       // Same but s2 longer
     return(1);
   else
     return((*s1 > *s2) ? -1: 1); // Different
}
```

COMPARING THE FIRST N CHARACTERS OF TWO STRINGS 186

In Tip 185 you learned how to use the *strcmp* function to compare two strings. Depending on your program's function, there may be times when you may only want to compare the first *n* characters of two strings. To make comparing only *n* characters with two strings easier to perform, most C compilers provide a function named *strncmp*, as shown here:

```
#include <string.h>

int strncmp(const char *s1, const char *s2, size_t n);
```

Like *strcmp*, the *strncmp* function returns the value 0 if the strings are equal and a value less than or greater than 0, depending on whether the first or second string is greater. The following program, *strncmp.c*, illustrates how to use the *strncmp* function:

```
#include <stdio.h>
#include <string.h>

void main(void)
  {
    printf("Comparing 3 letters Abc with Abc %d\n", strncmp("Abc", "Abc", 3));
    printf("Comparing 3 letters abc with Abc %d\n", strncmp("abc", "Abc", 3));
    printf("Comparing 3 letters abcd with abc %d\n", strncmp("abcd", "abc", 3));
    printf("Comparing 5 letters Abc with Abcd %d\n", strncmp("Abc", "Abcd", 5));
    printf("Comparing 4 letters abcd with abce %d\n", strncmp("abcd", "abce", 4));
  }
```

To understand the *strncmp* function better, consider the following implementation:

```
int strncmp(const char *s1, const char *s2, int n)
  {
    int i = 0;

    while ((*s1 == *s2) && (*s1) && i < n)
      {
        s1++;
        s2++;
        i++;
      }
    if (i == n)                              // Same strings
      return(0);
    else if ((*s1 == *s2) && (! *s1))        // Same strings
      return(0);
    else if ((*s1) && (! *s2))               // Same but s1 longer
      return(-1);
    else if ((*s2) && (! *s1))               // Same but s2 longer
      return(1);
    else
      return((*s1 > *s2) ? -1: 1);
  }
```

187 COMPARING STRINGS WITHOUT CONSIDERING CASE

In Tip 185 you learned how to use the *strcmp* function to compare two strings. Likewise, in Tip 186 you learned how to use the function *strncmp* to compare the first *n* characters of two strings. Both *strcmp* and *strncmp* consider upper- and lowercase letters as distinct. Depending on the function your program performs, there may be times when you may want the string comparison to ignore case. For such operations, most C compilers provide the functions *stricmp* and *strncmpi*, as shown here:

```
#include <string.h>

int stricmp(const char s1, const char s2);
int strncmpi(const char *s1, const char *s2, size_t n);
```

The following program, *cmpcase.c*, illustrates how to use the *stricmp* and *strncmpi* functions:

```
#include <stdio.h>
#include <string.h>

void main(void)
  {
    printf("Comparing Abc with Abc %d\n", stricmp("Abc", "Abc"));
    printf("Comparing abc with Abc %d\n", stricmp("abc", "Abc"));
    printf("Comparing 3 letters abcd with ABC %d\n", strncmpi("abcd", "ABC", 3));
    printf("Comparing 5 letters abc with Abcd %d\n", strncmpi("abc", "Abcd", 5));
  }
```

When you compile and execute the *cmpcase.c* program, your screen will display the following output:

```
Comparing ABC with ABC 0
Comparing abc with Abc 0
Comparing 3 letters abcd with ABC 0
Comparing 5 letters abc with Abcd -1
C:\>
```

CONVERTING A CHARACTER-STRING REPRESENTATION OF A NUMBER 188

When your programs work with strings, one of the most common operations you must perform is to convert an ASCII representation of a value to a numeric value. For example, if you prompt the user to input his or her salary, you might need to convert the character string input into a floating-point value. To help you convert ASCII values, most C compilers provide a set of run-time library functions that perform ASCII to numeric conversion. Table 188 briefly describes the standard ASCII conversion functions.

Function	Purpose
atof	Converts a character string representation of a floating-point value
atoi	Converts a character string representation of an integer value
atol	Converts a character string representation of a long integer value
strtod	Converts a character string representation of a double precision value
strtol	Converts a character string representation of a long value

Table 188 *Run-time library functions your programs can use to convert ASCII representations of a numeric value.*

The following program, *asciinum.c*, illustrates how to use the ASCII-to-numeric functions:

```
#include <stdio.h>
#include <stdlib.h>

void main(void)
  {
    int int_result;
    float float_result;
    long long_result;

    int_result = atoi("1234");
    float_result = atof("12345.678");
    long_result = atol("1234567L");
    printf("%d %f %ld\n", int_result, float_result, long_result);
  }
```

DUPLICATING A STRING'S CONTENTS 189

When your programs work with strings, sometimes you want to duplicate a string's contents quickly. If there are times when your program will need to copy the string and other times when your program might not, you might want the program to allocate the memory *dynamically* (during the program's execution) to hold the string copy as needed. To let your programs allocate memory during execution (dynamically) in order to create a character string copy, most C compilers provide the *strdup* function, as shown here:

```
#include <string.h>

char *strdup(const char *some_string);
```

When you invoke *strdup*, the function uses *malloc* to allocate memory and then copies the string's location to the memory location. When your program has finished using the string copy, it can release the memory using the *free* statement. The following program, *strdup.c*, illustrates how to use the *strdup* function:

```
#include <stdio.h>
#include <string.h>

void main(void)
  {
    char *title;

    if ((title = strdup("Jamsa\'s C/C++ Programmer\'s Bible")))
      printf("Title: %s\n", title);
    else
      printf("Error duplicating string");
  }
```

To better understand the *strdup* function, consider the following implementation:

```
#include <string.h>
#include <malloc.h>

char *strdup(const char *s1)
  {
    char *ptr;

    if ((ptr = malloc(strlen(s1)+1)))   // Allocate buffer
      strcpy(ptr, s1);
    return(ptr);
  }
```

190 FINDING A CHARACTER FROM A GIVEN SET'S FIRST OCCURRENCE

In Tip 176 you learned how to use the function *strchr* to find the first occurrence of a specific character. Depending on the function your program performs, there may be times when you may want to search a string for the first occurrence of any one character from a given character set. To help you search a string for any character in a set, most C compilers provide the *strspn* function, as shown here:

```
#include <string.h>

size_t strspn(const char *s1, const char *s2);
```

Within the *s1* string, the function returns the offset of the first character not contained within the *s2* string. The following program, *strspn.c*, illustrates how to use the *strspn* function:

```
#include <stdio.h>
#include <string.h>

void main(void)
  {
    printf("Searching for Abc in AbcDef %d\n", strspn("AbcDef", "Abc"));
    printf("Searching for cbA in AbcDef %d\n", strspn("AbcDef", "cbA"));
    printf("Searching for Def in AbcAbc %d\n", strspn("AbcAbc", "Def"));
  }
```

When you compile and execute the *strspn.c* program, your screen will display the following:

```
Searching for Abc in AbcDef 3
Searching for cbA in AbcDef 3
Searching for Def in AbcAbc 0
C:\>
```

To better understand *strspn*, consider the following implementation:

```
size_t strspn(const char *s1, const char *s2)
  {
    int i, j;

    for (i = 0; *s1; i++, s1++)
      {
        for (j = 0; s2[j]; j++)
          if (*s1 == s2[j])
            break;
        if (s2[j] == NULL)
          break;
      }
    return(i);
  }
```

191 LOCATING A SUBSTRING WITHIN A STRING

As your programs work with strings, there will be times when you must search a string for a specific substring. To help you search a string for a substring, most C compilers provide a function named *strstr*, as shown here:

```
#include <string.h>
strstr(string, substring);
```

If the substring exists within the string, *strstr* returns a pointer to the first occurrence of the string. If *strstr* does not find the substring, the function returns *NULL*. The following program, *strstr.c*, illustrates how to use *strstr*:

```
#include <stdio.h>
#include <string.h>

void main(void)
  {
    printf("Looking for Abc in AbcDef %s\n",
      (strstr("AbcDef", "Abc")) ? "Found" : "Not found");
    printf("Looking for Abc in abcDef %s\n",
      (strstr("abcDef", "Abc")) ? "Found" : "Not found");
    printf("Looking for Abc in AbcAbc %s\n",
      (strstr("AbcAbc", "Abc")) ? "Found" : "Not found");
  }
```

To help you better understand *strstr*, consider the following implementation:

```
char *strstr(const char *s1, const char *s2)
  {
    int i, j, k;

    for (i = 0; s1[i]; i++)
      for (j = i, k = 0; s1[j] == s2[k]; j++, k++)
        if (! s2[k+1])
          return(s1 + i);
    return(NULL);
  }
```

COUNTING THE NUMBER OF SUBSTRING OCCURRENCES $\mathbb{C}$192

In Tip 191 you learned how to use the function *strstr* to locate a substring within a string. You may sometimes want to know the number of times a substring appears within a string. The following function, *strstr_cnt*, lets you determine how many times a given substring occurs within a string:

```
int strstr_cnt(const char *string, const char *substring)
  {
    int i, j, k, count = 0;

    for (i = 0; string[i]; i++)
      for (j = i, k -= 0; string[j] == substring[k]; j++, k++)
        if (! substring[k + 1])
          count++;
    return(count);
  }
```

OBTAINING AN INDEX TO A SUBSTRING $\mathbb{C}$193

In Tip 191 you learned how to use the function *strstr* to obtain a pointer to a substring within a string. If you treat character strings as arrays, instead of using pointers, there may be times when you will want to know the character index at which a substring begins within a string. Using the value *strstr* returns, you can subtract the string's address to produce an index:

```
index = strstr(string, substr) - string;
```

If *strstr* does not find the substring, the index value will be equal to the length of the string. In addition, your programs can use the function *substring_index* to obtain an index to a substring, as shown here:

```
int substring_index(const char *s1, const char *s2)
  {
    int i, j, k;
```

```
for (i = 0; s1[i]; i++)
    for (j = i, k = 0; s1[j] == s2[k]; j++, k++)
        if (! s2[k+1])
            return(i);
    return(i);
}
```

194 OBTAINING THE RIGHTMOST OCCURRENCE OF A SUBSTRING

In Tip 191 you used the function *strstr* to determine the first occurrence of a substring within a string. Depending on your program's function, there may be times when you will want to know the last (rightmost) occurrence of a substring within a string. The following function, *r_strstr*, returns a pointer to the rightmost occurrence of a substring within a string or the value *NULL* if the substring does not exist:

```
char *r_strstr(const char *s1, const char *s2)
{
    int i, j, k, left = 0;
    for (i = 0; s1[i]; i++)
        for (j = i, k = 0; s1[j] == s2[k]; j++, k++)
            if (! s2[k+1])
                left = i;
    return((left) ? s1+left: NULL);
}
```

195 DISPLAYING A STRING WITHOUT THE %S FORMAT SPECIFIER

Several of the Tips in this section have used the *%s* format specifier to display character strings. The following statement, for example, uses *printf* to display the contents of the character string variable named *title*:

```
printf("%s", title);
```

The first argument passed to the *printf* statement is a character string, which may contain one or more format specifiers. When your programs use *printf* to display only one character string, as the previous example shows, you can omit the character string that contains the format specifier and pass to *printf* the character string you want to display, as shown here:

```
printf(title);
```

As you can see, *printf's* first argument is nothing more than a character string that contains one or more special symbols.

196 REMOVING A SUBSTRING FROM WITHIN A STRING

In Tip 191 you used the *strstr* function to determine the starting location of a substring within a string. In many cases, your program must remove a substring from within a string. To do so, you can use the function *strstr_rem*, which removes the first occurrence of a substring, as shown here:

```
char *strstr_rem(char *string, char *substring)
{
    int i, j, k, loc = -1;
    for (i = 0; string[i] && (loc == -1); i++)
        for (j = i; k = 0; str[j] == substring[k]; j++, k++)
            if (! substring[k + 1])
                loc = i;
    if (loc != -1)   // Substring was found
    {
        for (k = 0; substr[k]; k++)
            ;
        for (j = loc, i = loc + k, string[i]; j++, i++)
            string[j] = string[i];
        string[i] == NULL;
    }
    return(string);
}
```

REPLACING ONE SUBSTRING WITH ANOTHER

197

In Tip 196 you used the function *strstr_rem* to remove a substring from within a string. In many cases, your programs must replace the first occurrence of one substring with another substring. You can do so with the following function, *strstr_rep*, as shown here:

```c
#include <string.h>
char *strstr_rep(char *source, char *old, char *new)
  {
    char *original = source;
    char temp[256];
    int old_length = strlen(old);
    int i, j, k, location = -1;

    for (i = 0; source[i] && (location == -1); ++i)
      for (j = i; k = 0; source[j] == old[k]; j++, k++
        if (! old[k+1])
          location = i;
    if (location != -1)
      {
        for (j=0; j < location; j++)
          temp[j] = source[j];
        for (i=0; new[i]; i++, j++)
          temp[j] = new[i];
        for (k = location + old_length; source[k]; k++, j++)
          temp[j] = source[k];
        temp[j] = NULL;
        for (i = 0; source[i] = temp[i]; i++;        // NULL Loop
      }
    return(original);
}
```

CONVERTING AN ASCII NUMERIC REPRESENTATION

198

When your programs work with character strings, your programs must often convert an ASCII representation of a value, such as 1.2345, to the corresponding *int, float, double, long,* or *unsigned* value. To help you perform such operations, C provides the functions defined in Table 198.

Function	Purpose
atof	Converts an ASCII representation of a value of type *float*
atoi	Converts an ASCII representation of a value of type *int*
atol	Converts an ASCII representation of a value of type *long int*

Table 198 C functions which you can use to convert ASCII numeric representations.

The formats of the functions Table 198 details are as follows:

```c
#include <stdlib.h>

double atof(char *string);
int atoi(char *string);
int atol(char *string);
```

If a function is unable to convert the character string to a numeric value, the function returns 0. The following program, *ascii_to.c*, illustrates how to use the *ato* functions:

```c
#include <stdio.h>
#include <stdlib.h>

void main(void)
  {
    int int_value;
```

```
    float flt_value;
    long long_value;

    int_value = atoi("12345");
    flt_value = atof("33.45");
    long_value =atol("12BAD");
    printf("int %d float %5.2f long %ld\n", int_value, flt_value, long_value);
}
```

When you compile and execute the *ascii_to.c* program, your screen will display the following output:

```
int 12345 float 33.45 long 12
C:\>
```

Note the program's function call to *atol*. As you can see, when the function encounters the non-numeric value (the letter B), the function ends the conversion, returning the value that the function had already converted up to that point.

199 DETERMINING WHETHER A CHARACTER IS ALPHANUMERIC

An *alphanumeric* character is either a letter or a digit. In other words, an alphanumeric character is an uppercase letter from A through Z, a lowercase letter from a through z, or a digit from 0 through 9. To help your programs determine whether a character is alphanumeric, the header file *ctype.h* contains a macro named *isalnum*. The macro examines a letter and returns the value 0 if the character is not alphanumeric and a non-zero value for alphanumeric characters, as shown here:

```
    if (isalnum(letter))
```

To better understand the macro *isalnum*, consider the following implementation:

```
#define isalnum(c) ((toupper((c)) >= 'A' && (toupper((c)) <= 'Z') || ((c) >= '0'
&& ((c) <= '9'))
```

200 DETERMINING WHETHER A CHARACTER IS A LETTER

As your programs work with characters within strings, there may be times your programs must test whether a character contains a letter of the alphabet (either upper- or lowercase). To help your programs determine whether a character is a letter of the alphabet, the header file *ctype.h* provides the macro *isalpha*. The macro examines a letter and returns the value 0 if the character does not contain a letter from uppercase A through Z or lowercase a through z. If the character contains a letter of the alphabet, then the macro returns a non-zero value:

```
    if (isalpha(character))
```

To better understand the *isalpha* macro, consider the following implementation:

```
#define isalpha(c) (toupper((c)) >= 'A' && (toupper((c)) <= 'Z')
```

201 DETERMINING WHETHER A CHARACTER CONTAINS AN ASCII VALUE

An ASCII value is a value in the range 0 through 127. When your programs work with a string's characters, there may be times when you must determine whether a character contains an ASCII value. To help your programs determine an ASCII value, the header file *ctype.h* contains the macro *isascii*, which examines a letter and returns the value 0 if the character does not contain an ASCII character, and a non-zero value if the character does contain an ASCII value, as shown here:

```
    if (isascii(character))
```

To better understand the *isascii* macro, consider the following implementation:

```
#define isascii(ltr) ((unsigned) (ltr) < 128)
```

As you can see, the *isascii* macro considers a value in the range 0 through 127 as ASCII.

DETERMINING WHETHER A CHARACTER IS A CONTROL CHARACTER 202

A *control character* is a value from ^A through ^Z or ^a through ^z. Different applications use control characters differently. For example, DOS uses the CTRL+Z character to represent the end of a file. Other word processors use control characters to represent boldface or italics. When you work with characters in a string, there may be times when you must determine whether a character is a control character. To help your programs perform such testing, the header file *ctype.h* contains the macro *iscntrl*, which returns a non-zero value for a control character and 0 if the letter is not a control character, as shown here:

```
if (iscntrl(character))
```

DETERMINING WHETHER A CHARACTER IS A DIGIT 203

A *digit* is an ASCII value from 0 through 9. When you work with strings, there may be times when you must determine if a character is a digit. To help you test whether a character is a digit, the header file *ctype.h* provides the macro *isdigit*. The *isdigit* macro examines a letter and returns the value 0 if the character is not a digit and a non-zero value for characters in the range 0 through 9, as shown here:

```
if (isdigit(letter))
```

To better understand the macro *isdigit*, consider the following implementation:

```
#define isdigit(c) ((c) >= '0' && (c) <= '9')
```

DETERMINING WHETHER A CHARACTER IS A GRAPHICS CHARACTER 204

A *graphics character* is a printable character (see *isprint*), excluding the space character (ASCII 32). When your programs perform character output operations, there may be times when you may want to know whether a character is a graphics character. To help your programs perform such testing, the header file *ctype.h* provides the macro *isgraph*. The *isgraph* macro examines a letter and returns the value 0 if the character is not a graphic and a non-zero value for graphics characters:

```
if (isgraph(letter))
```

To better understand the *isgraph* macro, consider the following implementation:

```
#define isgraph(ltr) ((ltr) >= 33) && ((ltr) <= 127)
```

As you can see, a graphics character is any ASCII character in the range 33 to 127.

DETERMINING WHETHER A CHARACTER IS UPPER- OR LOWERCASE 205

As your programs work with characters within a string, there may be times when you must know whether a character is an upper- or lowercase letter. To help your programs test for case, the header file *ctype.h* provides the macros *islower* and *isupper*. These macros examine a character and return a 0 value for characters that are not lowercase *(islower)* or uppercase *(isupper)*, and a non-zero value otherwise:

```
if (islower(character))
if (isupper(character))
```

To better understand the *islower* and *isupper* macros, consider the following implementations:

```
#define islower(c) ((c) >= 'a' && (c) <= 'z')
#define isupper(c) ((c) >= 'A' && (c) <= 'Z')
```

206 DETERMINING WHETHER A CHARACTER IS PRINTABLE

When your programs perform character output, you might want to examine each character to ensure that you only output *printable characters*. A printable character is any character in the range 32 (the space character) through 127 (the DEL character). To help your programs test for a printable character, the header file *ctype.h* provides the macro *isprint*. The *isprint* macro returns a non-zero value for printable characters and a 0 value for characters that are not printable:

```
if (isprint(character))
```

To better understand the *isprint* macro, consider the following implementation:

```
#define isprint(ltr) ((ltr) >= 32) && ((ltr) <= 127)
```

As you can see, the *isprint* macro considers any ASCII character in the range 32 through 127 as a printable character.

207 DETERMINING WHETHER A CHARACTER IS A PUNCTUATION SYMBOL

Within a book, punctuation symbols include commas, semicolons, periods, question marks, and so on. Within C, however, a punctuation symbol is any graphics ASCII character that is not alphanumeric. As your programs work with characters in a string, there may be times when you must test whether a character contains a punctuation symbol. To help your programs test for punctuation symbols, the header file *ctype.h* defines the macro *ispunct*. This macro examines a character and returns a non-zero value for a character that contains a punctuation symbol and a 0 value for a character that does not contain a punctuation symbol:

```
if (ispunct(character))
```

To better understand the *ispunct* macro, consider the following implementation:

```
#define ispunct(c) (isgraph(c)) && ! isalphanum((c)))
```

208 DETERMINING WHETHER A CHARACTER CONTAINS WHITESPACE

The term *whitespace characters* includes the following characters: space, tab, carriage-return, newline, vertical tab, and formfeed. When your programs perform character output, sometimes you must test whether or not a character contains a whitespace character. To help your programs test for whitespace, the header file *ctype.h* provides the macro *isspace*. This macro examines a character and returns a non-zero value for whitespace characters and a 0 value for non-whitespace characters:

```
if (isspace(character))
```

To better understand the *isspace* macro, consider the following implementation:

```
#define isspace(c)   (((c) == 32) || ((c) == 9) || ((c) == 13))
```

209 DETERMINING WHETHER A CHARACTER IS A HEXADECIMAL VALUE

A *hexadecimal value* is a digit in the range 0 through 9 or a letter from uppercase A through F or lowercase a through f. When your programs work with characters in a string, sometimes you must determine whether a character contains a hexadecimal digit. To help your programs test for hexadecimal digits, the header file *ctype.h* defines the macro *isxdigit*. This macro examines a character and returns a non-zero value if the character is a hexadecimal value and a 0 value if the character is not:

```
if (isxdigit(character))
```

To better understand the *isxdigit* macro, consider the following implementation:

```
#define isxdigit(c) (isnum((c)) || (toupper((c)) >= 'A' && toupper((c)) <= 'F'))
```

CONVERTING A CHARACTER TO UPPERCASE 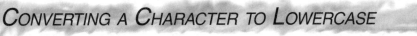 210

As you work with character strings, a common operation your programs must perform is to convert a character from lowercase to uppercase. When you want to convert cases, your programs have two choices. Your programs can use the macro *_toupper*, which is defined in the header file *ctype.h*, or they can use the run-time library function *toupper*. The macro and function formats are as follows:

```
#include <ctype.h>

int _toupper(int character);
int toupper(int character);
```

Although the macro and function both convert a character to uppercase, the macro and function work differently. The macro *_toupper* does not test to make sure the character it is converting is lowercase. If you invoke the macro with a character that is not lowercase, the macro will cause an error. The function *toupper*, on the other hand, only converts lowercase letters and leaves all other characters unchanged. If you are sure that the character contains a lowercase letter, use the *_toupper* macro; this macro will execute faster than the function. If you are not sure if the character is lowercase, however, use the *toupper* function. The following program, *toupper.c*, illustrates the use of *_toupper* and *toupper*, as well as the errors that can occur when you use the macro with characters that are not lowercase:

```
#include <stdio.h>
#include <ctype.h>

void main(void)
  {
    char string[] = "Jamsa\'s C/C++ Programmer\'s Bible";
    int i;

    for (i = 0; string[i]; i++)
      putchar(toupper(string[i]));
    putchar('\n');
    for (i = 0; string[i]; i++)
      putchar(_toupper(string[i]));
    putchar('\n');
  }
```

When you compile and execute this program, your screen will display the first string (using *toupper*) in correct uppercase letters. The second string, however, will contain non-standard characters (symbols, graphics, and so on) because *_toupper* tries to convert uppercase characters as it does lowercase characters.

CONVERTING A CHARACTER TO LOWERCASE 211

As you work with character strings, a common operation your programs must perform is to convert a character from uppercase to lowercase. When you want to convert cases, your programs have two choices. Your programs can use the macro *_tolower*, which is defined in the header file *ctype.h*, or your programs can use the run-time library function *tolower*. The macro and function formats are as follows:

```
#include <ctype.h>

int _tolower(int character);
int tolower(int character);
```

Although the macro and function both convert a character to lowercase, the macro and the function work differently. The macro *_tolower* does not test to make sure the character it converts is uppercase. If you invoke the macro with a character that is not uppercase, you will cause an error. The function *tolower*, on the other hand, only converts uppercase letters and leaves all other characters unchanged. If you are sure that the character contains an uppercase letter, then use the *_tolower* macro, which will execute faster than the function. If you are not sure if the character is uppercase, however, use the *tolower* function. The following program, *tolower.c*, illustrates the use of *_tolower* and *tolower*, as well as the errors that can occur if you use the macro with characters that are not uppercase:

```
#include <stdio.h>
#include <ctype.h>

void main(void)
 {
    char string[] = "Jamsa\'s C/C++ Programmer\'s Bible";
    int i;

    for (i = 0; string[i]; i++)
      putchar(tolower(string[i]));
    putchar('\n');
    for (i = 0; string[i]; i++)
      putchar(_tolower(string[i]));
    putchar('\n');
 }
```

When you compile and execute this program, your screen will display the first string (using *tolower*) in correct lowercase letters. The second string, however, will contain non-standard characters (symbols, graphics, and so on) because *_toupper* tries to convert uppercase characters as it does lowercase characters.

212 WORKING WITH ASCII CHARACTERS

When you work with character strings and different character functions, sometimes you must ensure that a character is a valid ASCII character; that is, that the value is in the range 0 through 127. To ensure a character is a valid ASCII character, you can use the *toascii* macro, which is defined in the header file *ctype.h*, as shown here:

```
#include <ctype.h>

int toascii(int character);
```

To better understand the *toascii* macro, consider the following implementation:

```
#define toascii(character) ((character) & 0x7F)
```

To improve its performance, the *toascii* macro performs a *bitwise AND* operation that clears the most significant bit of the character's byte value. The *bitwise AND* operation helps the macro ensure that the value falls in the range 0–127.

213 WRITING FORMATTED OUTPUT TO A STRING VARIABLE

As you know, the *printf* function lets you write formatted output to the screen display. Depending on your program's requirements, there may be times when you must work with a character string that contains formatted output. For example, say that your employees have a five-digit employee number and a three-character region identifier (such as Sea for Seattle). Assume that you store information about each employee in a file you name with a combination of these two values (such as SEA12345). The *sprintf* function lets you write formatted output to a character string. The format of the *sprintf* function is as follows:

```
#include <stdio.h>

int sprintf(char *string, const char *format [,arguments...]);
```

The following program, *sprintf.c*, uses the *sprintf* function to create an eight-character employee filename:

```
#include <stdio.h>

void main(void)
 {
    int employee_number = 12345;
    char region[] = "SEA";
    char filename[64];

    sprintf(filename, "%s%d", region, employee_number);
    printf("Employee filename: %s\n", filename);
 }
```

READING INPUT FROM A CHARACTER STRING

As you have learned, the *scanf* function lets you read formatted input from *stdin*. Depending on your program's processing, there may be times when a character string will contain fields you want to assign to specific variables. The *sscanf* function lets your programs read values from a string and assign the values to the specified variables. The format of the *sscanf* function is as follows:

```
#include <stdio.h>

int sscanf(const char *string, const char *format [,arguments]);
```

The arguments your program passes to the *sscanf* function must be pointers to variable addresses. If *sscanf* successfully assigns fields, it returns the number of fields it assigned. If *sscanf* does not assign fields, then it returns 0 or *EOF* if *sscanf* encountered the string's end. The following program, *scanf.c*, illustrates the *sscanf* function:

```
#include <stdio.h>

void main(void)
  {
    int age;
    float salary;
    char string[] = "33 25000.00";

    sscanf(string, "%d %f\n", &age, &salary);
    printf("Age: %d Salary %f\n", age, salary);
  }
```

TOKENIZING STRINGS TO SAVE SPACE

Tokenizing strings is the process of using a unique value to represent a string. For example, assume that you have a program that works with a large number of character strings. Say the program contains a database of your customer accounts by city and state. Depending on how the program performs its processing, you might end up with many different tests, as the following example illustrates:

```
if (streql(city, "Seattle"))
  // Statement
else if (streql(city, "New York"))
  // Statement
else if (streql(city, "Chicago"))
  // Statement
```

Within each of your program's functions that perform repetitive *else if* testing, the program consumes a considerable amount of space for the string constants, as well as a considerable amount of time performing the string comparisons. Rather than using repetitive string calls, you can create a function called *tokenize_string*, which returns a unique token for each string. Within the example function, your program testing will become the following:

```
int city_token;

city_token = tokenize_string(city);
if (city_token == Seattle_token)
  // Statement
else if (city_token == NewYork_token)
  // Statement
else if (city_token == Chicago_token)
  // Statement
```

Using tokens in this way will help you eliminate the amount of data space the string consonants consume. Eliminating the string comparisons will also improve your program's performance.

216 INITIALIZING A STRING

In the Arrays and Pointers section of this book you will learn how to assign values to arrays while your program is declaring the array. C represents character strings as an array of bytes. When you declare a string, you will generally specify an initial value, as shown here:

```
char title[] = "Jamsa\'s C/C++ Programmer\'s Bible";
char section[64] = "Strings";
```

In the *title* string, the C compiler will allocate an array large enough to hold the specified characters (plus the *NULL* character). Because the string "Jamsa's C/C++ Programmer's Bible" is 32 characters long, the *title* string can hold 32 printable characters plus the *NULL* character. If you later assign more than 33 characters to the string, you will overwrite the memory that stores another variable's value. In the *section* string, the compiler will allocate a string capable of storing 64 characters. The compiler will assign to the first seven bytes of the string the letters in the word "Strings" and to the eighth byte the *NULL* character. The compiler usually initializes the remaining 56 characters to *NULL*.

217 UNDERSTANDING FUNCTIONS

Most programs presented throughout this book thus far use only the *main* function. As your programs become larger and more complex, you can simplify your work and improve your program's clarity by breaking the program into smaller pieces, called *functions*. For example, assume that you are creating an accounting program. You might have a function that performs the general ledger operations, a different function for accounts payable, a third for accounts receivable, and a fourth to generate a balance sheet. If were to you place all your program's statements within *main*, your program would become very large and difficult to understand. As a program's size and complexity increases, so too does the chance of program errors. If you divide the program into smaller, more manageable blocks, you can avoid errors. A *function* is a named collection of statements that perform a specific task. For example, the following function, *hello_world*, uses *printf* to display a message:

```
void hello_world(void)
  {
    printf("Hello, world!\n");
  }
```

The keyword *void* tells C that the function does not return a value. In many cases, your functions will use *return* to return a calculation's result to the calling function. If the function does not use *return* to return a result, you should precede the function's name with *void*. The *void* that appears in parentheses tells C that the function does not use any parameters. A *parameter* is information the program passes to the function. When your programs invoke *printf*, for example, the information you specify within the parentheses are *parameters*. When a function does not use parameters, you should place the word *void* within the parentheses. To use a function, you simply specify the function's name followed by parentheses, much as you use *printf*. Programmers refer to using a function as a *function call*. The following program, *use_func.c*, uses the *hello_world* function:

```
#include <stdio.h>
void hello_world(void)
  {
    printf("Hello, world!\n");
  }
void main(void)
  {
    hello_world();
  }
```

When you execute this program, the *main* function executes first. As you can see, the only statement in *main* is the function call to the *hello_world* function. When C encounters the function call, C immediately transfers the program's execution to the function, beginning the program's execution with the first statement in the function. After the last statement in the function completes, C transfers the execution to the statement that immediately follows the function call. To better understand this process, change the *main* function within the *usefunc.c* program, as shown here:

```
void main(void)
 {
   printf("About to call function\n");
   hello_world();
   printf("Back from the function call\n");
 }
```

When you compile and execute the *use_func.c* program, your screen will display the following:

```
About to call function
Hello, world!
Back from the function call
C:\>
```

USING VARIABLES WITHIN FUNCTIONS 218

As you create useful functions, you will find that many functions require variables to generate valuable results. To use a variable within a function, you must first declare the variable, just as you do in *main*. For example, the following program, *three_hi.c*, calls the function *three_hellos*, which uses the variable *counter* in a *for* loop to display a message three times:

```
#include <stdio.h>

void three_hellos(void)
 {
   int counter; // Variable

   for (counter = 1; counter <= 3; counter++)
     printf("Hello, world!\n");
 }

void main(void)
 {
   three_hellos();
 }
```

When you declare variables within a function, the names you use for these variables are unique to the function. Therefore, if your program uses 10 different functions and each function uses a variable named *counter*, C considers each function's variable as distinct. If your function requires many variables, you should declare the variables at the function's start, just as you would within *main*.

UNDERSTANDING MAIN AS A FUNCTION 219

When you create a C program, C uses the function name *main* to determine the first statement the program will execute. Actually, *main* is a function, so if you have questions about the types of operations you can perform within your functions, the rule is fairly simple: *Anything you can do in main, you can do in a function.* Just as you can declare variables in *main*, you can also declare variables in your functions. You can also use constructs such as *if*, *while*, and *for* in your functions. Finally, one function can call (use) another. For example, the following program, *call_2.c*, uses two functions. When the program begins, *main* calls the function *three_hellos*, which in turn calls the function *hello_world* three times to display messages on your screen, as shown here:

```
#include <stdio.h>

void hello_world(void)
 {
   printf("Hello, world!\n");
 }

void three_hellos(void)
 {
   int counter;
```

```
   for (counter = 1; counter <= 3; counter++)
     hello_world();
 }

void main(void)
 {
   three_hellos();
 }
```

220 GETTING STARTED WITH PARAMETERS

A *parameter* is a value passed to a function. Most of the programs presented throughout this book have passed parameters to the *printf* function, as shown here:

```
printf("The value is %d\n", result);
```

As you use functions on a regular basis, you can pass parameters to a function to improve the function's usefulness. For example, consider the following construction of the *three_hellos* function, which calls the *hello_world* function three times:

```
void three_hellos(void)
 {
   int counter;

   for (counter = 1; counter <= 3; counter++)
     hello_world();
 }
```

A more useful function might let you specify, as a parameter, the number of times you want the program to display the message. To use a parameter, your function must specify the parameter's name and type, as shown here:

```
void hello_count(int message_count)
```

In this case, the function *hello_count* supports one parameter of type *int* named *message_count*. When another function, such as *main*, wants to use *hello_count*, the function must specify the value C assigns to the parameter *message_count*:

```
hello_count(2);     // Displays the message twice
hello_count(100);   // Displays the message 100 times
hello_count(1);     // Displays the message 1 time
```

The following program, *useparam.c*, illustrates how you might use a function with a parameter:

```
#include <stdio.h>

void hello_world(void)
 {
   printf("Hello, world!\n");
 }

void hello_count(int message_count)
 {
   int counter;

   for (counter = 1; counter <= message_count; counter++)
     hello_world();
 }

void main(void)
 {
   printf("Display the message twice\n");
   hello_count(2);
   printf("Display the message five times\n");
   hello_count(5);
 }
```

As you can see, in *main*, the function call to *hello_count* includes the value that C is to assign to the *message_count* parameter.

Note: *When you pass a parameter to a function, the type of value you pass to the parameter (such as **int, float, char**, and so on), must match the parameter type. Depending on your C compiler, the compiler might detect parameter type mismatches. If your compiler does not detect parameter type mismatches, errors may emerge that are often difficult to detect and correct.*

USING MULTIPLE PARAMETERS

As you have learned, a *parameter* is a value you pass to a function. In general, you can pass an unrestricted number of parameters to a function. However, research has shown that when the number of parameters exceeds seven, the function becomes more difficult to understand and use correctly, therefore making the function more susceptible to error. When your function uses more than one parameter, you must specify each parameter's type and name and separate the parameters with commas, as shown here:

```
void some_function(int age, float salary, int job_number)
   {
      // Function statements
   }
```

When your program wants to call the function, you must specify values for each parameter, as shown here:

```
some_function(33, 40000.00, 534);
```

C, in turn, will assign the values to the parameters, as shown in Figure 221.

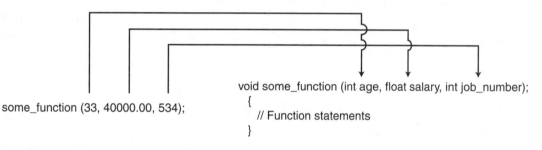

Figure 221 *Mapping parameter values.*

UNDERSTANDING PARAMETER DECLARATIONS IN OLDER C PROGRAMS

When you create a function that uses parameters, you will usually specify each parameter's type and name, separated by commas, within the function header, as shown here:

```
void some_function(int age, float salary, int job_number)
   {
      // Function statements
   }
```

If you work with older C programs, you might find that the programmer declared the parameters as follows:

```
void some_function(age, salary, job_number)
   int age;
   float salary;
   int job_number;
   {
      // Function statements
   }
```

If you encounter such parameter declarations, you should understand that although the declaration format differs slightly, the purpose remains the same—to specify the parameter's type and name. If you feel tempted to update the function's format, make sure that your compiler fully supports the new format. Also, remember that the more changes you make to your program, the greater your chances are of introducing an error. As a general rule, "*If it ain't broke, don't fix it!*"

RETURNING A VALUE FROM A FUNCTION

As your functions become more complex, they will usually perform a calculation and return a result. To provide a result to the caller, a function must use the *return* statement, which you will implement as shown here:

```
   return(result);
```

The type of value the function returns (*int, float, char*, and so on) determines the function's type. If a function returns a value of type *int*, for example, you must precede the function name with the type name, as shown here:

```
int some_function(int value)
{
   // Function statements
}
```

The following function, *i_cube*, returns the cube of the integer value the program specifies as its parameter. For example, if the calling function passes the value 5 to the function, *i_cube* will return the value 5 * 5 * 5 or 125:

```
int i_cube(int value)
{
   return(value * value * value);
}
```

As you can see, the function uses the *return* statement to pass back the calculation's result to the caller. The code within the calling function can assign the called function's result (also known as a *return value*) to a variable, or the code can use the return value within a third function, such as *printf*, as shown here:

```
result = i_cube(5);
printf("The cube of 5 is %d\n", i_cube(5));
```

The following program, *i_cube.c*, uses the *i_cube* function to determine several different cube values:

```
#include <stdio.h>

int i_cube(int value)
{
   return(value * value * value);
}

void main(void)
{
   printf("The cube of 3 is %d\n", i_cube(3));
   printf("The cube of 5 is %d\n", i_cube(5));
   printf("The cube of 7 is %d\n", i_cube(7));
}
```

The values you pass to a function must match the parameter types contained within that function's declaration. If you want to determine the cube of a floating-point value, for example, you would create a second function called *f_cube*, as shown here (note that the return value is also of type *float*):

```
float f_cube(float value)
{
   return (value * value * value);
}
```

224 UNDERSTANDING THE RETURN STATEMENT

As you have learned, for a function to provide its caller with a result, the function must use the *return* statement. When C encounters a *return* statement in a function, C immediately ends the function's execution, and returns the specified value to the calling function. The program does not execute any statements within the function that follow the *return* statement. Instead, the program resumes execution in the calling function.

As you examine other C programs, you might encounter functions that contain multiple *return* statements, each of which returns a value for a specific condition. For example, consider the function *compare_values*, shown here:

```
int compare_values(int first, int second)
{
   if (first == second)
      return(0);
```

```
     else if (first > second)
       return(1);
     else if (first < second)
       return(2);
   }
```

The function *compare_values* examines two integer values and returns one of the values listed in Table 224.

Result	Meaning
0	The values are the same.
1	The first value is greater than the second value.
2	The second value is greater than the first value.

*Table 224 Values the **compare_values** function returns.*

As a rule, you should try to limit your functions to one *return* statement. As your functions become larger and more complex, having multiple *return* statements often will make the functions more difficult to understand. In most cases, you can rewrite your function so that it only uses one *return* statement, as shown here:

```
int compare_values(int first, int second)
  {
    int result;

    if (first == second)
      result = 0;
    else if (first > second)
      result = 1;
    else if (first < second)
      result = 2;

    return(result);
  }
```

In this case, because the function is so simple, you may have difficulty understanding the advantage you gain by using only one *return* statement. As your functions become more complex, however, the advantage might become more clear. You should note, however, that sometimes using more than one *return* statement produces more readable code than the single *return* alternative. You should write the most readable and modifiable code possible; if using multiple *return* statements achieves that goal, then use as many *return* statements as necessary.

UNDERSTANDING FUNCTION PROTOTYPES 225

If you take a close look at each preceding program, you will find that the calling functions always appear in the program source code following the functions they call. Most new C compilers require knowledge of a function's return and parameter types before the program calls the function. By placing the functions in front of their callers within your program code, you let the C compiler know the information it must have before it encounters the function call. As your programs become more complex, however, it might become impossible for you to always place the functions in the correct order. Therefore, C lets you place *function prototypes* in your program that describe a function's return and parameter types. For example, consider a program that uses the functions *i_cube* and *f_cube*, presented in Tip 223. Before the functions' first use, the program can include a prototype similar to the following:

```
int i_cube(int);      // Returns an int--one int parameter
float f_cube(float);  // Returns a float--one float parameter
```

As you can see, the function prototype specifies the function's return and parameter types. The following program, *useproto.c*, uses two function prototypes to eliminate the need for function ordering:

```
#include <stdio.h>

int i_cube(int);
float f_cube(float);
```

```
void main(void)
  {
    printf("The cube of 3 is %d\n", i_cube(3));
    printf("The cube of 3.7 is %f\n", f_cube(3.7));
  }

int i_cube(int value)
  {
    return(value * value * value);
  }

float f_cube(float value)
  {
    return(value * value * value);
  }
```

If you examine the *.h* header files, such as *stdio.h*, you will find that these files contain many function prototypes.

226 UNDERSTANDING THE RUN-TIME LIBRARY

As you write your own functions, you will often find that a function you created for one program meets the needs of a second program. The ability to reuse functions in more than one program can save you considerable programming and testing time. In the Tools section of this book, you will learn how to place your commonly-used functions within a library to make them easier to use in multiple programs. For now, however, you may need to cut and paste the function's statements from one source code file to another.

Before you spend a great deal of time writing a wide variety of all-purpose functions, make sure you examine the functions your compiler provides. Many compilers refer to these built-in functions as the *run-time library*. Most C compilers provide hundreds of run-time library functions with purposes ranging from opening and working with files to accessing disk or directory information to determining a character string's length. The hour or two you spend reading your compiler's run-time library documentation will save you many programming hours that you might have otherwise spent "reinventing the wheel."

227 UNDERSTANDING FORMAL AND ACTUAL PARAMETERS

As you read different books on C, you might encounter the terms *formal* and *actual* parameters. In short, formal parameters are the parameter names that appear in the function definition. For example, the names *age*, *salary*, and *job_number* are the formal parameters for the *job_information* function, as shown here:

```
void job_information(int age, float salary, int job_number)
  {
    // Function statements
  }
```

When a function calls another function, the values the calling function passes are the actual parameters. In the case of the following function invocation, the values 30, 42000.00, and 321 are the actual parameters:

```
job_information(30, 42000.00, 321);
```

The actual parameters you pass to a function can be constant values or variables. The value or variable's type must match that of the formal parameter. For example, the following code fragment illustrates how to use variables as actual parameters:

```
int workers_age = 30;
float workers_salary = 42000.00;
int job_number = 321;

job_information(workers_age, workers_salary, job_number);
```

When you invoke a function with variables as the actual parameters, the variable names used for the actual parameters have no relationship to the names of the formal parameters. Instead, C concerns itself only with the values the variables contain.

RESOLVING NAME CONFLICTS 228

As you have learned, most C compilers provide an extensive library of functions you can call to perform specific tasks. For example, to obtain the absolute value of an integer expression, you can use the *abs* function. Likewise, to copy one string's contents to another, you can use the *strcpy* function. As you create your own functions, sometimes a function you define will have the same name as a run-time library function. For example, the following program, *mystrcpy.c*, creates and uses a function named *strcpy*:

```c
#include <stdio.h>
char *strcpy(char *destination, const char *source)
{
   char *start = destination;
   while (*destination++ = *source++)
     ;
   return(start);
}
void main(void)
{
   char title[64];
   strcpy(title, "Jamsa\'s C/C++ Programmer\'s Bible");
   printf(title);
}
```

When a function name that you declare within your program conflicts with a run-time library function, C uses your program's function, not the run-time library function.

FUNCTIONS THAT DO NOT RETURN int 229

Several of the functions you saw earlier returned values of type *int*. When your function does not return a value type *int* (rather, it might return *float*, *double*, *char*, and so on), you must tell the compiler the function's return type. The following program, *show_avg.c*, uses the function *average_value* to determine the average of three values of type *int*. The function returns the average using a value of type *float*:

```c
#include <stdio.h>
float average_value(int a, int b, int c)
 {
   return ((a + b + c) / 3.0);
 }
void main(void)
 {
   printf("The average of 100, 133, and 155 is %f\n", average_value(100, 133, 155));
 }
```

As you can see, the function header specifies the function's return type:

```c
float average_value(int a, int b, int c)
```

Note: If you do not specify a function's return type, the C compiler will assume that the function returns the type **int**.

UNDERSTANDING LOCAL VARIABLES 230

C lets you declare variables within your functions. Such variables are called *local variables* because their names and values only have meaning within the function that contains the variable declaration. The following program, *localerr.c*, illustrates the concept of a local variable. The function *local_values* declares three variables, *a*, *b*, and *c*, and assigns to the variables the values 1, 2, and 3, respectively. The function *main* tries to print each variable's value. However, because the variable names are local to the function *local_values*, the compiler generates errors that state that the symbols *a*, *b*, and *c* are undefined, as shown here:

```
#include <stdio.h>

void local_values(void)
  {
    int a = 1, b = 2, c = 3;

    printf("a contains %d b contains %d c contains %d\n", a, b, c);
  }

void main(void)
  {
    printf("a contains %d b contains %d c contains %d\n", a, b, c);
  }
```

231 HOW FUNCTIONS USE THE STACK

The Memory section of this book describes the *stack*, which programs use to temporarily hold detailed information. The stack's primary purpose is to support function invocations. When your program invokes a function, C places the address of the instruction that follows the function invocation (called the *return address*) onto the stack. Next, C places the function's parameters, from right to left, onto the stack. Finally, if the function declares local variables, C allocates stack space that the function then uses to hold the variable's value. Figure 231 shows how C uses the stack for a simple function call.

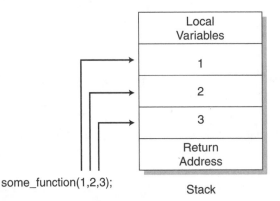

Figure 231 C uses the stack for a function call.

When the function ends, C discards the stack space that contained the local variables and parameters. Next, C uses the return value to determine the instruction that the program executes next. C removes the return value from the stack and places the address into the IP (instruction pointer) register.

232 UNDERSTANDING FUNCTION OVERHEAD

As you learned in Tip 231, when your program uses a function, C pushes the return address, parameters, and local variables onto the stack. When the function completes, C discards (pops) the stack space that contained the local variables and parameters and then uses the return value to resume executing the program at the correct location.

Although C's use of the stack is powerful because it lets the program invoke and pass information to functions, C's use also consumes processing time. Programmers call the amount of time the computer requires to push and pop stack information *function overhead*. To better understand function overhead's impact on your program's performance, consider the following program, *functovr.c*. The program first uses a loop to sum the values 1 through 100,000. Next, the program loops again, but instead uses a function to add the values, as shown here:

```
#include <stdio.h>
#include <time.h>
```

```
float add_em(long int a, float b)
  {
    float result;

    result = a + b;
    return(result);
  }

void main(void)
  {
    long int i;
    float result = 0;
    time_t start_time, stop_time;

    printf("Working...\n");
    time(&start_time);
    for (i = 1; i <= 100000L; i++)
      result += i;
    time(&stop_time);
    printf("Using loop %d seconds\n", stop_time - start_time);
    printf("Working...\n");
    time(&start_time);
    for (i = 1; i <= 100000L; i++)
      result = add_em(i, result);
    time(&stop_time);
    printf("Using function %d seconds\n", stop_time - start_time);
  }
```

On most systems, the function-based calculations might require almost twice as much processing time. When you use functions within your programs, therefore, you must consider the benefits the functions provide (such as ease of use, reuse of an existing function, reduction of testing, ease of understanding, and so on) versus the performance overhead they introduce.

UNDERSTANDING WHERE C PLACES LOCAL VARIABLES 233

As you have learned, C lets you declare variables within your functions. These variables are *local* to the function, which means only the function in which you declared the variables knows their values and existence. The following function, *use_abc*, declares three local variables named *a*, *b*, and *c*:

```
void use_abc(void)
  {
    int a, b, c;

    a = 3;
    b = a + 1;
    c = a + b;
    printf("a contains %d b contains %d c contains %d\n", a, b, c);
  }
```

Each time your program invokes the function, C allocates stack space to hold the local variables *a*, *b*, and *c*. When the function ends, C discards both the previously allocated stack space and the values that the local variables contained. Even if your function declares many local variables, C stores each variable's value on the stack.

DECLARING GLOBAL VARIABLES 234

In Tip 218 you learned that local variables are variables defined within a function whose names and existence are known only to the function. In addition to local variables, C also lets your programs use *global variables*, whose names, values, and existence are known throughout your program. In other words, all your C programs can use global variables. The following program, *global.c*, illustrates the use of three global variables, *a*, *b*, and *c*:

```
#include <stdio.h>
int a = 1, b = 2, c = 3;  // Global variables
```

```
void global_values(void)
  {
    printf("a contains %d b contains %d c contains %d\n", a, b, c);
  }

void main(void)
  {
    global_values();
    printf("a contains %d b contains %d c contains %d\n", a, b, c);
  }
```

When you compile and execute this program, the functions *global_values* and *main* both display the global variable values. Note that you declare the variables outside all the functions. When you declare global variables in this way, all your program's functions can use and change the global variable values simply by referring to the global variable name. Although global variables might at first appear convenient, misusing them can lead to errors that are very difficult to debug, as you will learn in Tip 235.

235 Avoid Using Global Variables

In Tip 234 you learned how to declare global variables, which your program knows throughout all its functions. At first glance, using global variables seems to simplify your programming because it eliminates the need for function parameters and, more importantly, the need to understand *call by value* and *call by reference*. Unfortunately, however, global variables often create more errors than they fix. Because your code can change a global variable's value at virtually any location within your program, it is very difficult for another programmer who is reading your program to find each location in the program where the global variable changes. Therefore, other programmers might make changes to your program without fully understanding the effect the change has on a global variable. As a rule, functions should only change those variables passed to the functions as parameters. This lets programmers study the function prototypes to quickly determine which variables a function changes.

If you find that your program uses global variables, you may want to reconsider your program design. Your goal should be to eliminate (and definitely minimize) your use of global variables.

236 Resolving Global and Local Variable Name Conflicts

As you have learned, local variables are variables you declare within a function whose names are known only to that function. On the other hand, when you declare global variables outside all functions, every function throughout your program will know their names. If your program uses global variables, there may be times when a global variable's name is the same as a that of a local variable your program declares within a function. For example, the following program, *conflict.c*, uses the global variables *a*, *b*, and *c*. The *conflict_a* function uses a local variable named *a* and the global variables *b* and *c*:

```
#include <stdio.h>
int a = 1, b = 2, c = 3;   // Global variables

void conflict_a(void)
  {
    int a = 100;
    printf("a contains %d b contains %d c contains %d\n", a, b, c);
  }

void main(void)
  {
    conflict_a();
    printf("a contains %d b contains %d c contains %d\n", a, b, c);
  }
```

When you compile and execute the *conflict.c* program, your screen will display the following:

```
a contains 100 b contains 2 c contains 3
a contains 1 b contains 2 c contains 3
C:\>
```

When global variable names and local variable names conflict, C will always use the local variable. As you can see, the changes the function *conflict_a* made to the variable *a* only appear within the function.

*Note: Although this program's purpose is to illustrate how C resolves name conflicts, it also illustrates the confusion that can occur when you use global variables. In this case, a programmer who is reading your code must pay close attention to determine that the function does not change the global variable **a**, but rather a local variable. Because the function combines the use of global and local variables, the code can become difficult to understand.*

BETTER DEFINING A GLOBAL VARIABLE'S SCOPE 237

In Tip 234 you learned that a global variable is a variable that all the functions throughout your program know. Depending on where you define a global variable, you can control which functions are actually able to reference the variable. In other words, you can control the global variable's *scope*. When your program declares a global variable, any functions that follow the variable declaration can reference that variable, up to the end of the source file. Functions that have definitions that appear prior to the global variable's definition cannot access the global variable. As an example, consider the following program, *gloscope.c*, which defines the global variable *title*:

```
#include <stdio.h>

void unknown_title(void)
  {
    printf("The book's title is %s\n", title);
  }

char title[] = "Jamsa\'s C/C++ Programmer\'s Bible";

void main(void)
  {
    printf("Title: %s\n", title);
  }
```

As you can see, the *unknown_title* function will try to display the variable *title*. However, because the global variable declaration occurs after the function definition, the global variable is unknown within the function. When you try to compile this program, your compiler will generate an error. To correct the error, move the global variable declaration to before the function.

UNDERSTANDING CALL BY VALUE 238

As you have learned, your programs pass information to functions using parameters. When you pass a parameter to a function, C uses a technique known as *call by value* to provide the function with a copy of the parameter's value. Using call by value, any changes the function makes to the parameter exist only within the function itself. When the function completes, the value of variables the calling function passed to the function are not changed within the calling function. For example, the following program, *nochange.c*, passes three parameters (the variables *a*, *b*, and *c*) to the function *display_and_change*. The function, in turn, will display the values, add 100 to the values, and then display the result. When the function ends, the program will display the values of the variables. Because C uses call by value, the function does not change the values of the variables within the calling function, as shown here:

```
#include <stdio.h>

void display_and_change(int first, int second, int third)
  {
    printf("Original function values %d %d %d\n", first, second, third);
    first += 100;
    second += 100;
    third += 100;
    printf("Ending function values %d %d %d\n", first, second, third);
  }

void main(void)
  {
    int a = 1, b = 2, c = 3;
```

```
    display_and_change(a, b, c);
    printf("Ending values in main %d %d %d\n", a, b ,c);
}
```

When you compile and execute the *nochange.c* program, your screen will display the following:

```
Original function values 1 2 3
Ending function values 101 102 103
Ending values in main 1 2 3
C:\>
```

As you can see, the changes the function makes to the variables are only visible within the function itself. When the function ends, your variables within *main* are unchanged.

Note: When you use call by reference (which Tip 240 presents in detail), a function can change a parameter's value so that the change is visible outside of the function.

239 PREVENTING PARAMETER VALUE CHANGE WITH CALL BY VALUE

In Tip 238 you learned that by default C uses call by value to pass parameters to functions. As a result, any changes to the parameter's value only occur within the function itself. When the function ends, the values of variables the program passed to the function are unchanged. As the "Getting Started with C" section of this book details, a variable is essentially a name assigned to a memory location. Every variable has two attributes of interest—its current value and its memory address. In the case of the program *nochange.c,* presented in Tip 238, the variables *a, b,* and *c* might use the memory addresses shown in Figure 239.1.

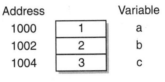

Figure 239.1 Variables store a value and reside in a specific memory location.

When you pass parameters to a function, C places the corresponding values onto the stack. In the case of the variables *a, b,* and *c,* the stack contains the values 1, 2, and 3. When the function accesses the variable's values, the function references the stack locations, as shown in Figure 239.2.

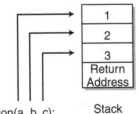

Figure 239.2 Functions reference parameter values stored on the stack.

Any changes the function makes to the parameter values actually change the stack values, as shown in Figure 239.3.

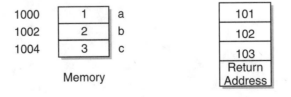

Figure 239.3 Changes functions make to parameter values affect only those values on the stack.

When the function ends, C discards the values on the stack as well as the changes the function has made to the stack locations. The function never references the memory locations that contain each variable's value, so your functions cannot make changes that exist after the function ends to any parameter the function receives using call by value.

UNDERSTANDING CALL BY REFERENCE   240

As you have learned, C passes parameters to functions using call by value by default. Using call by value, functions cannot change the value of a variable passed to a function. In most programs, however, your functions will change variables in one way or another. For example, a function that reads information from a file must place the information in a character string array. Likewise, a function such as *strupr* (presented in the Strings section of this book) must convert the letters in a character string to uppercase. When your functions change a parameter's value, your programs must pass the parameter to the function using *call by reference*. The difference between call by value and call by reference is that using call by value, functions receive a copy of a parameter's value. With call by reference, on the other hand, functions receive the variable's memory address. Therefore, the functions can make changes to the value stored at a specific memory location (in other words, the variable's value), which changes remain after the function ends. To use call by reference, your program must use *pointers*. The Pointers section of this book discusses pointers in detail. For now, however, think of a pointer simply as a memory address. To assign a variable's address to a pointer, use C's address operator (&). To later access the value in the memory location to which the pointer points, use C's redirection operator (*). Tips 241 and 242 discuss these operators in detail.

GETTING AN ADDRESS   241

A variable is essentially a name assigned to one or more memory locations. When your program runs, each variable resides in its own memory location. Your program locates variables in memory using the variable's *memory address*. To determine a variable's address, you use C's address operator (&). The following program, *showaddr.c,* for example, uses the address operator to display the addresses (in hexadecimal format) of the variables *a*, *b*, and *c*:

```
#include <stdio.h>

void main(void)
 {
    int a = 1, b = 2, c = 3;

    printf("The address of a is %x the value of a is %d\n", &a, a);
    printf("The address of b is %x the value of b is %d\n", &b, b);
    printf("The address of c is %x the value of c id %d\n", &c, c);
 }
```

When you compile and run this program, your program will display output similar to the following (the actual address values shown may differ):

```
The address of a is fff4 the value of a is 1
The address of b is fff2 the value of b is 2
The address of c is fff0 the value of c is 3
C:\>
```

When your programs later pass parameters to functions for variables whose value the function must change, your programs will pass the variables by reference (memory address), using the address operator, as shown here:

```
some_function(&a, &b, &c);
```

USING A VARIABLE'S ADDRESS   242

In Tip 241 you learned how to use C's address operator to obtain a variable's memory address. When you pass an address to a function, you must tell the C compiler that the function will be using a pointer (the memory address) of a variable, as opposed to the variable's value. To do so, you must declare a *pointer variable*. Declaring a pointer variable is very similar to a standard variable declaration, in that you specify a type and variable name. The difference, however, is that an asterisk (*) precedes pointer variable names. The following declarations create pointer variables to values of type *int*, *float*, and *char*:

```
int *i_pointer;
float *f_pointer;
char *c_pointer;
```

After you declare a pointer variable, you must assign to the variable a memory address. The following statement, for example, assigns the address of the integer variable *a* to the pointer variable *i_pointer*:

```
i_pointer = &a;
```

Next, to use the value pointed to by the pointer variable, your programs must use C's redirection operator—the asterisk (*). For example, the following statement assigns the value 5 to the variable *a* (whose address is contained in the variable *i_pointer*):

```
*i_pointer = 5;
```

In a similar way, the following statement assigns to the variable *b* the value to which the variable *i_pointer* currently points:

```
b = *i_pointer;
```

When you want to use the value pointed to by a pointer variable, use the redirection operator (*). When you want to assign a variable's address to a pointer variable, you use the address operator (&). The following program, *use_addr.c*, illustrates the use of a pointer variable. The program assigns the pointer variable *i_pointer* the address of the variable *a*. The program then uses the pointer variable to change, display, and assign the variable's value:

```
#include <stdio.h>

void main(void)
  {
    int a = 1, b = 2;
    int *i_pointer;

    i_pointer = &a;                // Assign an address
    *i_pointer = 5;                // Change the value pointed to by i_pointer to 5

    // Display the value
    printf("Value pointed to by i_pointer %d the variable a %d\n", *i_pointer, a);
    b = *i_pointer;                // Assign the value
    printf("Value of b is %d\n", b);
    printf("Value of i_pointer %x\n", i_pointer);
  }
```

Remember that a pointer is nothing more than a memory address. Your program must assign the value the pointer (the address) contains. In the program *use_addr.c*, the program assigned the pointer the address of the variable *a*. The program could have just as easily assigned the address of the variable *b*.

*Note: When you use pointers, you must still keep in mind value types, such as **int**, **float**, and **char**. Your programs should only assign the address of integer values to integer pointers, and so on.*

243 CHANGING A PARAMETER'S VALUE

As you have learned, to change a parameter's value within a function, your programs must use call by reference, passing the variable's address. Within the function, you must use pointers. The following program, *chgparam.c*, uses pointers and addresses (call by reference) to display and then change the parameters the program passes to the *display_and_change* function:

```
#include <stdio.h>

void display_and_change(int *first, int *second, int *third)
  {
    printf("Original function values %d %d %d\n", *first, *second, *third);
    *first += 100;
    *second += 100;
```

```
    *third += 100;
    printf("Ending function values %d %d %d\n", *first, *second, *third);
}

void main(void)
{
    int a = 1, b = 2, c = 3;

    display_and_change(&a, &b, &c);
    printf("Ending values in main %d %d %d\n", a, b ,c);
}
```

As you can see, when the program invokes the function, it passes as parameters the addresses of the variables *a*, *b*, and *c*. Within *display_and_change*, the function uses pointer variables and C's redirection operator to change and display the parameter's values. When you compile and execute the *display_and_change* program, your screen will display the following output:

```
Original function values 1 2 3
Ending function values 101 102 103
Ending values in main 101 102 103
C:\>
```

CHANGING ONLY SPECIFIC PARAMETERS   244

As you have learned, your functions can change a parameter's value using call by reference. Tip 243, for example, presented the *display_and_change* function, which used call by reference to change the value of each of its parameters. In many cases, however, your functions may change one parameter's value while leaving a second parameter's value unchanged. For example, the following program, *chgfirst.c*, uses the *change_first* function to assign to the *first* parameter the value of the *second* parameter:

```
#include <stdio.h>
void change_first(int *first, int second)
{
    *first = second;   // Assign value of second to first
}

void main(void)
{
    int a = 0, b = 5;

    change_first(&a, b);
    printf("Value of a %d value of b %d\n", a, b);
}
```

As you can see, the *change_first* function uses call by reference to change the first parameter's value, and call by value for the second parameter. When your functions use both techniques—and they will—you must keep in mind when to use pointers and when to directly reference the variable. As a rule, the parameters whose values you want to change will require call by reference. To better understand the impact of call by reference versus call by value, change the *change_first* function, as shown here:

```
void change_first(int *first, int second)
{
    *first = second;   // Assign the value of second to first
    second = 100;
}
```

When you compile and execute this program, you will see that the value of *first* has changed but the value of *second* has not. Because the parameter *second* is passed using call by value, the change to the parameter is not visible outside the function.

CALL BY REFERENCE STILL USES THE STACK   245

As you have learned, when C passes parameters to functions, C places the parameter's values on the stack. C uses the stack to hold parameters whether you are using call by value or call by reference. When you pass a parameter by value, C places the parameter's *value* on the stack. When you pass a parameter by reference, C places the parameter's *address* on the stack. Tip 244 presented the *chgfirst.c* program, which used the *change_first* function to assign the value of the function's second parameter to the function's first parameter. When the program invokes the function, C places the address of variable *a* and the value of variable *b* on the stack, as shown in Figure 245.

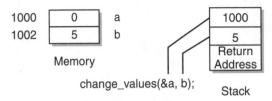

Figure 245 *C places an address and a value on the stack.*

Because the *change_values* function actually references the memory location that contains the value of variable *a*, the changes *change_values* makes to the variable exist after the function ends.

246 INTRODUCING FUNCTION VARIABLES THAT REMEMBER

In C, the variables you declare within functions are often called *automatic* because the C compiler automatically creates them when the function begins and then destroys them when the function ends. The variable's automatic life occurs because the compiler stores function variables temporarily on the stack. As a result, should a function assign a value to a variable during one invocation, the variable loses its value when the function completes. The next time you invoke the function, the variable's value is again undefined. Depending on the processing your function performs, sometimes you may want the function's variables to remember the last value they were assigned within the function.

For example, assume that you have written a function called *print_reportcard*, which prints a report card for every student in a school. Your function might use the variable *student_id* to hold the student identification number of the last student whose report card the function printed. In this way, without being told to, the function can begin with the next student. To make your function's local variables remember their values in this way, you must declare the variables using the keyword *static*, as shown here:

```
void print_reportcard(int printer_number)
  {
    static int student_id;

    // Other statements
  }
```

The following program, *static.c*, illustrates the use of a *static* variable within a function. The program, which uses the *print_reportcard* function, begins by assigning the variable *student_id* the value 100. Each time the program invokes the function, the function will display the variable's value and then will increment the value by 1, as shown here:

```
#include <stdio.h>
void print_reportcard(int printer_number)
  {
    static int student_id = 100;

    printf("Printing report card for student %d\n", student_id); student_id++;
    // Other statements here
  }
void main(void)
  {
    print_reportcard(1);
    print_reportcard(1);
    print_reportcard(1);
  }
```

When you compile and execute the *static.c* program, your screen will display the following output:

```
Printing report card for student 100
Printing report card for student 101
Printing report card for student 102
C:\>
```

As you can see, the *student_id* variable retains its value from one invocation to the next.

Note: *When you declare static variables, the C compiler does not store the variables on the stack. Instead, the compiler places the variables within the data segment so their values can remain.*

UNDERSTANDING HOW C INITIALIZES STATIC VARIABLES 247

In Tip 246 you learned that the *static* keyword directs the compiler to retain a variable's value from one function invocation to the next. When your function declares a static variable, C lets you initialize the variable, as shown here:

```
void print_reportcard(int printer_number)
  {
    static int student_id = 100;  // Initialized once
    // Other statements
  }
```

When you declare a variable as *static*, the C compiler will initialize the variable to the value you specify. When you invoke the function later, C *will not perform* the initialization assignment again. This function variable initialization is different from the processing that C usually performs within a function. In the case of the following function, C will initialize the variable *count* every time the program calls the function:

```
void some_function(int age, char *name)
  {
    int count = 1;  // Initialized on every call
    // Other statements
  }
```

USING THE PASCAL CALLING SEQUENCE 248

As you create C programs, you might find that you would like to use a function that you have previously created in Pascal. Depending on your compiler, linker, and library type, you might still be able to call the Pascal function from your C program. The steps you must perform to do so, however, will depend on your compiler. Additionally, within your program code, you must include a function prototype at the start of your program that includes the *pascal* keyword, as shown here:

```
int pascal some_function(int score, int grade);
```

If you program in the Windows environment, you will find that many run-time library functions use the Pascal calling sequence. Functions that use the *pascal* keyword cannot support a variable number of arguments (as can *printf* and *scanf*).

UNDERSTANDING THE PASCAL KEYWORD'S EFFECT 249

You learned in Tip 248 that when your programs invoke a function, C passes parameters to the function using the stack. C places parameters on the stack from right to left. Figure 249.1 illustrates the stack contents for a C function call.

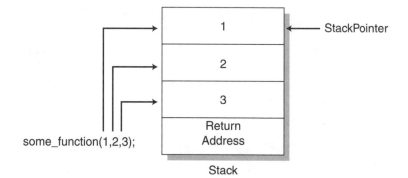

Figure 249.1 The stack contents for a C function call.

Pascal, on the other hand, pushes arguments onto the stack from left to right. Figure 249.2 illustrates the stack contents for a Pascal function call.

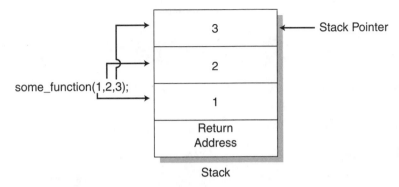

Figure 249.2 The stack contents for a Pascal function call.

If you are using a Pascal function from within your C program, use the *pascal* keyword to direct the C compiler to place the parameters on the stack from left to right, in the order that Pascal expects.

250 WRITING A MIXED LANGUAGE EXAMPLE

As you have learned, many C compilers let you invoke functions that were written in a different programming language. If you are calling a Pascal function from within your C program, for example, you can precede the function prototype using the *pascal* keyword. As you have learned, the *pascal* keyword directs the compiler to push parameters onto the stack from left to right. To illustrate the processing the *pascal* keyword performs, create the following function, *show_values*, and precede the function with the *pascal* keyword:

```
#include <stdio.h>
void pascal show_values(int a, int b, int c)
  {
     printf("a %d b %d c %d\n", a, b, c);
  }
```

Next, call the function using the following program code:

```
void main(void)
  {
     show_values(1, 2, 3);
     show_values(100, 200, 300);
  }
```

To experiment with the *show_values* function, remove the *pascal* keyword and note the change in the order of the parameter values C displays. Should your programs later call a Pascal routine, you must use the *pascal* keyword in the function prototype.

251 UNDERSTANDING THE CDECL KEYWORD

In Tip 250 you learned that if you use functions written in Pascal, you will use the *pascal* keyword to inform the compiler so that the compiler will place parameters onto the stack in the correct order. When you use functions written with multiple programming languages, you will probably want to include the keyword *cdecl* within your function prototypes to indicate C functions and to provide clarity to the reader. For example, the following function prototype informs the compiler that the function *change_values* uses the C calling structure:

```
int cdecl change_values(int *, int *, int *);
```

When the compiler encounters the *cdecl* keyword within a function header, the compiler will ensure that parameters passed to the function are placed on the stack from right to left. In addition, the compiler will ensure that the linker uses the C format for the function's name.

UNDERSTANDING RECURSION 252

As you have learned, C lets you divide your program into smaller pieces called functions. Using functions, your program becomes easier to understand, program, and test. In addition, you can often use the functions you create for one program within another program. As your programs execute, one function may call another, which calls another, which may, in turn, call several other functions. Within the series, each function performs a specific operation. As it turns out, C even lets a function call itself! A *recursive function* is a function that calls itself to perform a specific operation. The process of a function calling itself is named *recursion*. As the complexity of your programs and functions increases, you might find that you can easily define many operations in terms of themselves.

When you use complex programs and functions, you might want to create a recursive function. Many programming books, for example, use the factorial problem to illustrate how recursion works. The factorial of the value 1 is 1. The factorial of the value 2 is 2*1. The factorial of the value 3 is 3*2*1. Likewise, the factorial of the value 4 is 4*3*2*1. The factorial process can essentially go on indefinitely. If you take a close look at the processing that the factorial performs, you will find that the factorial of 4, for example, is actually 4 times the factorial of 3 (3*2*1). Likewise, the factorial of 3 is actually 3 times the factorial of 2 (2*1). The factorial of 2 is 2 times the factorial of 1 (1). Table 252 illustrates the factorial processing.

Value	Calculation	Result	Factorial
1	1	1	1
2	2*1	2	2 * Factorial(1)
3	3*2*1	6	3 * Factorial(2)
4	4*3*2*1	24	4 * Factorial(3)
5	5*4*3*2*1	120	5 * Factorial(4)

Table 252 Factorial processing.

The following program, *fact.c*, creates the recursive function *factorial* and then uses the function to return the factorial values for the values 1 through 5:

```
#include <stdio.h>

int factorial(int value)
 {
   if (value == 1)
     return(1);
   else
     return(value * factorial(value-1));
 }

void main(void)
 {
   int i;

   for (i = 1; i <= 5; i++)
     printf("The factorial of %d is %d\n", i, factorial(i));
 }
```

As you can see, the *factorial* function returns a result that is based on the result of the function itself. Tip 253 examines the *factorial* function in detail.

UNDERSTANDING THE RECURSIVE FACTORIAL FUNCTION 253

In Tip 252 you learned that a recursive function is a function that calls itself to perform a specific task. Tip 252 presented the *factorial* function to illustrate recursion. The *factorial* function receives a specific parameter value. When the function begins, it first checks whether the value is 1, which by factorial definition is 1. If the value is 1, the function returns the value 1. If the value is not 1, the function returns the result of the value times the factorial of the value minus 1.

Assume, for example, that the program invokes the function with the value 3. The function will return the result of 3 * *factorial(3–1)*. When C encounters the function call within the *return* statement, C will invoke the function a second time—this time with the value of 3–1 or 2. Again, because the value is not 1, the function returns the result of the 2 * *factorial(2–1)*. On the third invocation of the function, the value is 1. As a result, the function returns the value 1 to the calling function, which, in turn, returns the result of 2*1 to its calling function. That calling function then returns the result of 3*2*1 to *its* calling function. Figure 253 illustrates the chain of recursive function invocations and return values for the factorial(3) function call.

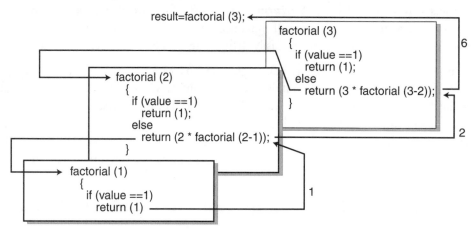

Figure 253 *The chain of function calls and value returns for the recursive **factorial** function.*

A recursive function is somewhat like a looping construct, in that you must specify an ending condition. If you do not specify an ending condition, the function will never end. In the factorial problem, the ending condition is the factorial of 1, which is, by definition, 1.

254 PROGRAMMING ANOTHER RECURSIVE EXAMPLE

In Tip 252 you learned that a recursive function is a function that calls itself in order to perform specific processing. Tip 253, in turn, presented and explained the recursive *factorial* function. Because recursion can be a difficult concept, this Tip presents one more recursive function, *display_backward*, which will display a string's letters in reverse order. Given the letters ABCDE, the function will display the letters on your screen as EDCBA. The following program, *backward.c*, uses the *display_backward* function:

```c
#include <stdio.h>

void display_backward(char *string)
 {
   if (*string)
    {
       display_backward(string+1);
       putchar(*string);
    }
 }

void main(void)
 {
    display_backward("ABCDE");
 }
```

255 DISPLAYING VALUES TO BETTER UNDERSTAND RECURSION

As you have learned, a *recursive* function is a function that calls itself to perform a specific operation. Tip 252 presented the recursive *factorial* function. To help you to better understand the recursion process, the program *showfact.c* includes *printf* statements within the *factorial* function that illustrate the function's recursive processing within the program:

```
#include <stdio.h>

int factorial(int value)
  {
    printf("In factorial with the value %d\n", value);
    if (value == 1)
      {
        printf("Returning the value 1\n");
        return(1);
      }
    else
      {
        printf("Returning %d * factorial(%d)\n", value, value-1);
        return(value * factorial(value-1));
      }
  }
void main(void)
  {
    printf("The factorial of 4 is %d\n", factorial(4));
  }
```

When you compile and execute the *showfact.c* program, your screen will display the following output:

```
In factorial with the value 4
Returning 4 * factorial(3)
In factorial with the value 3
Returning 3 * factorial(2)
In factorial with the value 2
Returning 2 * factorial(1)
In factorial with the value 1
Returning the value 1
The factorial of 4 is 24
C:\>
```

Inserting *printf* statements throughout your recursive functions will help you to better understand the processing the functions perform.

UNDERSTANDING DIRECT AND INDIRECT RECURSION   256

A recursive function is a function that calls itself to perform a specific operation. Several previous Tips in this section have presented recursive functions. When a function invokes itself to perform a task, the function performs a *direct recursion*. After you have examined a few recursive functions, you should be able to understand most functions that use direct recursion. A more difficult form of recursion, *indirect recursion*, occurs when a function (function A) calls another function (function B), which, in turn, calls the original function (function A). Because indirect recursion can result in code that is very difficult to understand, as a rule you should avoid using indirect recursion whenever possible.

DECIDING WHETHER TO USE RECURSION   257

A recursive function is a function that calls itself to perform a specific task. When you create functions, you can use recursion to create elegant solutions to many problems. However, you should avoid recursion whenever possible for two reasons. First, recursive functions can be difficult for novice programmers to understand. Second, as a rule, recursive functions are often considerably slower than their non-recursive counterparts. The following program, *no_recur.c*, invokes the non-recursive function *string_length* with the string "Jamsa's C/C++ Programmer's Bible" 100,000 times and then displays the amount of time required to perform the processing:

```
#include <stdio.h>
#include <time.h>
```

```
int string_length(const char *str)
{
   int length = 0;

   while (*str++)
     length++;
   return(length);
}

void main(void)
{
   long int counter;

   time_t start_time, end_time;
   time(&start_time);
   for (counter = 0; counter < 100000L; counter++)
     string_length("Jamsa\'s C/C++ Programmer\'s Bible");
   time(&end_time);
   printf("Processing time %d\n", end_time - start_time);
}
```

Next, the program *ok_recur.c* uses a recursive implementation of the *string_length* function to perform the same processing:

```
#include <stdio.h>
#include <time.h>
int string_length(const char *str)
{
   if (*str)
     return(1 + string_length(str+1));
   else
     return(0);
}

void main(void)
{
   long int counter;

   time_t start_time, end_time;
   time(&start_time);
   for (counter = 0; counter < 100000L; counter++)
     string_length("Jamsa\'s C/C++ Programmer\'s Bible");
   time(&end_time);
   printf("Processing time %d\n", end_time - start_time);
}
```

Experiment with these programs by, for example, changing the number of function calls to one or two million. As you will find, the non-recursive function executes considerably faster than its recursive counterpart. Therefore, when you design a recursive function, keep in mind that you may be adding significant overhead to your program's execution time.

258 UNDERSTANDING WHY RECURSIVE FUNCTIONS ARE SLOW

A recursive function is a function that calls itself to perform a specific task. As you learned in Tip 257, one reason to avoid using recursion is that recursive functions are usually considerably slower than their non-recursive counterparts. Recursive functions are slow because the function *call overhead* occurs with every invocation. As Tip 231 details, each time your program calls a function, the C compiler pushes onto the stack the address of the statement that immediately follows the function call (named the *return address*). Next, the compiler pushes the parameter values onto the stack. When the function completes, the computer's operating system pops the return address off the stack into the CPU's program counter. Although computers can perform these push and pop operations very quickly, the operations still require time.

As an example, assume that you invoke the recursive *factorial* function with the value 50. The function will then invoke itself 49 times. If each function call adds 10 milliseconds to your program, the function will be a half-second slower than a non-recursive counterpart, which only has the overhead of one function invocation. A half-second of overhead does not seem like much, yet assume that the program calls the function ten times. The half-second delay quickly turns into five seconds. If the program uses the function 100 times, the delay becomes 50 seconds, and so on. If you are writing a program that requires maximum performance, you should try to eliminate recursive functions whenever possible.

Note: With newer, faster microprocessors (such as the 200 MHz processors), the operating-system slowdown from recursive functions is not as important as it once was. However, the impact of recursive functions is still significant, and you should try to write effective, readable code without recursion whenever possible.

UNDERSTANDING HOW TO REMOVE RECURSION 259

A recursive function is a function that calls itself to perform a specific task. As you have learned, you can improve your program's performance using non-recursive functions. As a rule, any function you are able to write recursively you can also write in terms of looping constructs, such as a *for* or *while* statement. The following program, *loopfact.c,* uses a *for* loop to implement the *factorial* function:

```c
#include <stdio.h>

int factorial(int value)
  {
    int result = 1;
    int counter;

    for (counter = 2; counter <= value; counter++)
      result *= counter;
    return(result);
  }

void main(void)
  {
    int i;

    for (i = 1; i <= 5; i++)
      printf("Factorial of %d is %d\n", i, factorial(i));
  }
```

Whenever you eliminate recursion within your programs using a looping construct, you will generally improve your program's performance. However, keep in mind that users may more easily understand some operations your programs will perform when you implement the operations with recursion. Just as there are times when you must make tradeoffs between your program's speed and memory consumption, there may also be times when you must choose between readability and performance.

PASSING STRINGS TO FUNCTIONS 260

As you have learned, when you pass parameters to functions, C, by default, passes the parameters *by value*. Therefore, any changes that your function makes to the parameter do not exist outside of the function. To change a parameter's value, you must pass the parameter *by reference*. The exception to this rule is character strings. When you invoke a function with a character string, you are simply passing a byte array to the function. When C passes an array (any type of array—not just a string), C passes the array's starting address to the function. In other words, *C always uses call by reference for arrays*, so you do not need to use the *address* operator.

PASSING SPECIFIC ARRAY ELEMENTS 261

As you learned in Tip 260, C always passes arrays to functions using call by reference. As you work with character strings, there may be times when you want a function to work with specific array elements. For example, the following program, *halfcaps.c,* uses the *strupr* function to convert a section of a character string to uppercase:

```
#include <stdio.h>
#include <string.h>

void main(void)
  {
    char alphabet[] = "abcdefghijklmnopqrstuvwxyz";

    strupr(&alphabet[13]);
    printf(alphabet);
  }
```

The *strupr* expects the starting address of a *NULL*-terminated string to be a parameter. In this case, the program passes to *strupr* the address of the letter n, which the function call then follows with several *NULL*-terminated characters. By passing the address of a specific array element, your programs can use functions to manipulate specific array elements.

262 UNDERSTANDING CONST IN FORMAL PARAMETERS

If you examine the function prototypes for the string manipulation functions presented in the Strings section of this book, you will find that many of the parameter declarations place the keyword *const* before character string arguments, as shown here:

```
char *strcpy(char *destination, const char *source);
```

In the *strcpy* function's definition example, the *const* keyword specifies that the function code should not change the variable *source* within the function. Should your function code try to change the string's value, the compiler will generate an error. The following program, *chkconst.c*, uses the *const* keyword for the parameter *string*:

```
#include <stdio.h>

void no_change(const char *string)
  {
    while (*string)
      *string++ = toupper(*string);
  }

void main(void)
  {
    char title[] = "Jamsa\'s C/C++ Programmer\'s Bible";

    no_change(title);
    printf(title);
  }
```

As you can see, the function *no_change* tries to convert the string's letters to uppercase. However, because the program uses the *const* keyword, the compiler will display an error message and the code will not successfully compile. You should use the *const* keyword before parameters that a function receives by reference when you do not want the parameter's value changed. Because C normally passes non-pointer parameters by value, parameters by value do not require the *const* keyword.

263 USING CONST WILL NOT PREVENT PARAMETER MODIFICATION

As you learned in Tip 262, the *const* keyword informs the compiler that the function should not change a specific parameter's value. Should a function try to modify such a parameter's value, the compiler will generate an error, and the program will not compile. However, you should note that just because the function's header specifies a parameter as a constant, it does not mean that function cannot change the parameter's value. The following program, *chgconst.c*, uses a pointer to the constant parameter *string* to convert the string's contents to uppercase:

```
#include <stdio.h>
#include <ctype.h>

void no_change(const char *string)
  {
    char *alias = string;
```

```
   while (*alias)
     *alias++ = toupper(*alias);
 }
void main(void)
 {
   char title[] = "Jamsa\'s C/C++ Programmer\'s Bible";

   no_change(title);
   printf(title);
 }
```

When you compile and execute the *chgconst.c* program, the function *no_change* will convert the string's characters to uppercase. Because you used *pointer aliasing* (referring to a variable's memory locations using a different name), the compiler does not detect the parameter value change. Depending on your compiler type, the compiler may generate a warning message. If you are creating your own functions, do not use aliasing to change a parameter's value as does the *chgconst.c* program. If a parameter is truly a constant, its value should not change. The program within this Tip should teach you that the *const* keyword cannot actually prevent a parameter's value from changing.

UNDERSTANDING UNBOUNDED STRING DECLARATIONS 264

In C, a character string is an array of character values. You learned in the Strings section of this book that you specify the maximum number of characters the string will ever hold to create a string, as shown here:

```
char name[64];
char title[32];
char buffer[512];
```

When you pass a character string to a function, you actually pass the string's starting address. Because the *NULL* character terminates the string, C functions do not care how many characters the string contains. As a result, many functions declare character string parameters as unbounded arrays (arrays that do not specify a size), as shown here:

```
int strlen(char string[])
```

The declaration *char string[]* tells the compiler that the function will receive a pointer to a *NULL*-terminated string. The string might contain 64 characters, 1,024 characters, or maybe just the *NULL* character. The following program, *strarray.c*, uses an unbounded array to implement the *strlen* function:

```
#include <stdio.h>
int strlen(char str[])
 {
   int i = 0;

   while (str[i] != NULL)
     i++;
   return(i);
 }
void main(void)
 {
   printf("Length of ABC is %d\n", strlen("ABC"));
   printf("Length of C/C++ Programmer\'s Bible is %d\n",
     strlen("C/C++ Programmer\'s Bible"));
   printf("Length of a NULL string is %d\n", strlen(""));
 }
```

When you compile and execute the *strarray.c* program, you will see that the function works for any size string. However, like most C functions that work with strings, the function will fail if the string is not terminated by the *NULL* character.

USING POINTERS VERSUS STRING DECLARATIONS 265

As you examine different C functions that manipulate strings, you may find the character strings declared as either unbounded arrays or as pointers, as shown here:

```
char *strcpy(char destination[], char source[]);
char *strcpy(char *destination, char *source);
```

Both declarations in the previous example inform the compiler that it is working with strings. Both are functionally identical, and both are correct. If you are creating your own functions, the format you choose should depend on how you reference the parameter within the function. If you treat the parameter as a pointer, use the *pointer-style* declaration. If you instead treat the parameter as an array, use the array. By treating the parameter in a consistent way, you will make your programs easier to understand.

266 HOW C USES THE STACK FOR STRING PARAMETERS

As you have learned, when your programs pass a parameter to functions, C places the parameter's value or address on the stack. When you pass a character string to a function, C places the string's starting address on the stack. For example, Tip 264 presented the program *strarray.c*, which passed several strings to the *strlen* function. Figure 266 illustrates the parameter value C places on the stack for the first function invocation.

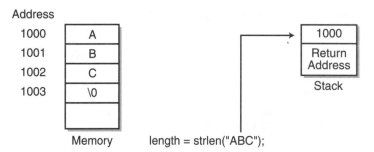

Figure 266 *How C passes string parameters to functions.*

As you can see, C does not place the string's characters onto the stack. Instead, C simply places the address of the *NULL*-terminated string on the stack. Because the function receives only an address (as opposed to an array of bytes), the function does not care how many characters the string contains.

267 UNDERSTANDING EXTERNAL VARIABLES

You can often use the functions you create for one program within another. To simplify function reuse, programmers often place functions in *object code libraries*. The Tools section of this book discusses the use of such libraries. In some cases, a library might define a global variable, such as the *_fmode*, *_psp*, or *errno* variables discussed throughout this book. When code outside of the current program defines a global variable and you want to use the global variable within your program, you must declare the variable using the *extern* keyword. The *extern* keyword tells the compiler that another program has declared the variable *externally* (outside of the current source file). If you examine the header file *dos.h*, for example, you will find several external variable declarations, including those shown here:

```
extern int const _Cdecl _8087;
extern int _Cdecl _argc;
extern char **_Cdecl _argv;
extern char **_Cdecl environ;
```

If you do not use the *extern* keyword, the compiler will assume that you are creating a variable with the name specified. When you include the *extern* keyword, on the other hand, the compiler will search for the global variable you specified.

268 PUTTING EXTERN TO USE

Tip 267 introduced the *extern* keyword, which you will use within your programs to tell the compiler to use a global variable that another program has declared outside of the current program. To better understand how the *extern* keyword works, compile the file *external.c*, which contains the declaration of the variable *tip_count* and the function *show_title*:

```
#include <stdio.h>

int tip_count = 1500;   // Global variable

void show_title(void)
  {
     printf("Jamsa\'s C/C++ Programmer\'s Bible");
  }
```

When you compile the *external.c* program, C will create the object file *external.obj*. The program *showext.c*, shown here, uses the external variable *tip_count* within the *external.obj* file:

```
#include <stdio.h>

void main(void)
  {
     extern int tip_count;
     printf("The number of tips is %d\n", tip_count);
  }
```

When you compile the *showext.c* program, perform the following steps within the *Turbo C++ Lite* compiler (if you are not using *Turbo C++ Lite,* check your compiler documentation):

1. Select the Project menu Open Project option.
2. Change to the directory which contains the *showext.c* program and enter the project's name as *showext*. Click your mouse on OK to create the project.
3. Select the Project menu Add Item option.
4. Add the *external.obj* file to the project.
5. Add the *showext.c* file to the project.
6. Select the Compile menu Build All option to build the file.

In this case, the *showext.c* program displays the value of the external variable *tip_count*. The program does not use the *show_title* function, although the program could have—simply by invoking *show_title*. However, the program's goal was to illustrate the use of the *extern* keyword.

Note: *To use externals within other compilers, refer to the compiler's on-line help documentation or the printed documentation that came with the compiler.*

UNDERSTANDING EXTERNAL STATIC 269

In Tip 267 you learned that the *extern* keyword tells the C compiler that you are referencing a global variable that a program in a different file defines. When the linker links your program modules, the linker will determine the variable's memory location. In Tip 268 you used the global variable *tip_count*, which was defined in the object file *external.obj*. Because the *showext.c* program referred to the variable using the *extern* keyword, the program could access the variable. Depending on your programs, there may be times when you use global variables in an object file that you do not want functions outside of the object file to access. In such cases, you simply precede the variable name with the *static* keyword:

```
static int variable_name;
```

The following file, *stextern.c*, declares two global variables, one named *tip_count* and one named *title*:

```
#include <stdio.h>

int tip_count = 1500;   // Global variable
static char title[] = "Jamsa\'s C/C++ Programmer\'s Bible";

void show_title(void)
  {
     printf(title);
  }
```

Compile the *stextern.c* file to create the object file *stextern.obj*. Next, create the following program, *nostatic.c*, which tries to use both global variables contained within the *stextern.obj* file:

```
#include <stdio.h>

void main(void)
 {
    extern int tip_count;
    extern char *title;
    void show_title(void);

    printf("The number of tips is %d\n", tip_count);
    printf("The book\'s title is %s\n", title);
    show_title();
 }
```

As you learned in Tip 268, to compile and link the program using *Turbo C++ Lite*, perform the following steps:

1. Select the Project menu Open Project option.
2. Change to the directory which contains the *nostatic.c* program and enter the project's name as *nostatic*. Click your mouse on OK to create the project.
3. Select the Project menu Add Item option.
4. Add the *extern2.obj* file to the project.
5. Add the *nostatic.c* file to the project.
6. Select the Compile menu Build All option to build the file.

When you compile and link the *nostatic.c* program, the linker should display a message stating that the compiler could not resolve the *title* variable. Because the *static* keyword precedes the declaration of the *title* variable, the variable is only known within the object file *extern2.obj*.

270 UNDERSTANDING THE VOLATILE KEYWORD

As the complexity of your programs increases, you might eventually write low-level functions and routines that access the PC's I/O ports or that service the PC's interrupt registers (also referred to simply as *interrupts*). When your programs perform such operations, using an interrupt or accessing a port might change your variables that correspond to specific memory locations or port addresses. Because both your program and many factors external to your program can change such variables, you must tell the compiler that the variable's value can change at any time. To inform the compiler that operations outside of the program might change a variable's value, use the *volatile* keyword, as shown here:

```
volatile int some_variable;
```

When the compiler encounters the *volatile* keyword, the compiler knows not to make assumptions about the variable's value at any time. For example, the compiler will not place the variable's value into a register for quick access. Doing so would run the risk that the register value is not the same as the variable's memory contents, which an interrupt (for example) might have changed after the variable's storage into the register, without the program's knowledge. Instead, when your program must access a variable's value, the compiler will specifically reference the variable's memory location.

Note: *You should generally declare **volatile** variables as global variables. In this way, programs and the outside operations reference memory locations contained within the program's data segment, as opposed to stack locations, which the program discards when the corresponding function ends.*

271 UNDERSTANDING THE CALL FRAME AND BASE POINTER

You have learned that when your program invokes a function, C pushes the return address and the function's parameters onto the stack. Within the stack, C refers to the saved function call information as a *call frame*. To help your functions quickly locate the call frame, C assigns the base pointer register (BP) to the address of the start of the frame.

C also places the function's local variables onto the stack (within the call frame). Figure 271 illustrates the contents of a simple call frame:

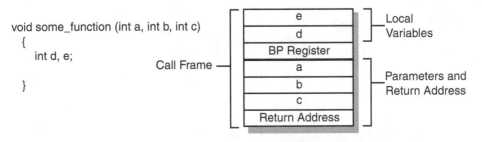

Figure 271 The information C places onto the stack for a function call constitutes a call frame.

When you write assembly language functions that you expect to call from within your C programs, you must understand the use and structure of the call frame so that your assembly language functions can access the parameter values stored within that call frame.

CALLING AN ASSEMBLY LANGUAGE FUNCTION 272

In Tip 236 you learned that your programs can call functions written in other programming languages, such as Pascal. In addition, your programs can call assembly language routines. The following assembly language routine, *swap_values*, exchanges the values of two variables passed to the function by reference (by address):

```
        .MODEL   small
        .CODE
        PUBLIC   _swap_values

_swap_values    PROC
        push     bp
        mov      bp,sp
        sub      sp,2
        push     si
        push     di

        mov      si,word ptr [bp+4]          ;Arg1
        mov      di,word ptr [bp+6]          ;Arg2

        mov      ax,word ptr [si]
        mov      word ptr [bp-2],ax

        mov      ax,word ptr [di]
        mov      word ptr [si],ax

        mov      ax,word ptr [bp-2]
        mov      word ptr [di],ax

        pop      di
        pop      si
        mov      sp,bp
        pop      bp
quit:            ret

_swap_values    ENDP
        END
```

The companion CD-ROM that accompanies this book contains the *swap.asm* file. If you are using Borland C++, assemble the file to create the object file *swap.obj*, as shown here:

```
C:\> TASM SWAP.ASM   <ENTER>
```

Next, create the following C program, *use_swap.c*, which uses the *swap_values* function:

```
#include <stdio.h>
void swap_values(int *, int *);
```

```
void main(void)
  {
    int a = 1, b = 2;

    printf("Original values a %d b %d\n", a, b);
    swap_values(&a, &b);
    printf("Swapped values a %d b %d\n", a, b);
  }
```

In this case, you wrote the function *swap_values* to support near pointers. If you change memory models, you must change the assembly language routine.

273 RETURNING A VALUE FROM AN ASSEMBLY LANGUAGE FUNCTION

In Tip 261 you learned how to call an assembly language function from within your C programs. In the *swap.asm* program, the function did not return a result. The following assembly language routine, *get_maximum*, however, returns the larger of two integer values:

```
            .MODEL small
            .CODE
            PUBLIC _get_maximum

_get_maximum    PROC
            push    bp
            mov     bp,sp

Arg1            equ     [bp+4]
Arg2            equ     [bp+6]

            mov     ax,Arg1        ;Move Arg1 into AX
            cmp     Arg2,ax        ;Compare Arg2 to Arg1
            jg      arg2_bigger    ;Jump if Arg2 is bigger
            jmp     finished

arg2_bigger:    mov     ax,Arg2

finished: pop     bp
            ret
_get_maximum    ENDP
            END
```

The companion CD-ROM that accompanies this book contains the *get_max.asm* file, which contains the *get_maximum* routine. As you can see, the assembly language routine places its result in the AX register. Later Tips explain the different registers in detail; for now, however, you can consider the AX register as similar to the BP register which the previous Tip explains. The following C program, *use_max.c*, invokes the assembly language function to determine the larger of two values:

```
#include <stdio.h>
extern int get_maximum(int, int);

void main(void)
  {
    int result;

    result = get_maximum(100, 200);
    printf("The larger value is %d\n", result);
  }
```

When the program calls the function, the C compiler will assign the value of the AX register as the function's result.

274 INTRODUCING FUNCTIONS THAT DO NOT RETURN VALUES

As the number of functions you create increases, you will eventually create a function that does not return a value. As you have learned, the C compiler, unless told otherwise, assumes that a function returns the type *int*. If your function does not return a value, you should declare the function as type *void*, as shown here:

```
void my_function(int age, char *name);
```

Should the program later try to use the function's return value, as shown here, the compiler will generate an error:

```
result = my_function(32, "Jamsa");
```

UNDERSTANDING FUNCTIONS THAT DO NOT USE PARAMETERS 275

As the number of programs and functions that you create increases, you might eventually create a function that does not use any parameters. When you define the function (and the function prototype), you should use the *void* keyword to inform the compiler (and other programmers) that the function does not use parameters:

```
int my_function(void);
```

Should the program later try to invoke the function with parameters, the compiler will generate an error.

UNDERSTANDING THE AUTO KEYWORD 276

As you examine C programs, you might find variable declarations that use the keyword *auto*, as shown here:

```
auto int counter;
auto int flags;
```

The *auto* keyword informs the compiler that the variable is local to the function and that the compiler should automatically create and destroy the variable. The compiler creates automatic variables by allocating stack space. Because variables are automatic by default, most programs omit the *auto* keyword. Within a function, the following variable declarations are identical:

```
auto int counter;
int counter;
```

UNDERSTANDING SCOPE 277

Within your programs, functions and variables have a *scope* that defines the areas within the program where their names have meaning. For example, consider the following program, *twocount.c*, which uses two variables named *count*:

```
#include <stdio.h>

void beeper(int beep_count)
  {
    int count;

    for (count = 1; count <= beep_count; count++)
      putchar(7);
  }

void main(void)
  {
    int count;

    for (count = 1; count <= 3; count++)
      {
        printf("About to beep %d times\n", count);
        beeper(count);
      }
  }
```

As you can see, the functions *beeper* and *main* both use variables named *count*. To C, however, both variables are distinct—each has a different scope. In the case of the function *beeper*, C only knows its *count* variable (that is, *count* has a defined scope) while the function is executing. Likewise, in the case of *main*, its *count* variable only has meaning while *main* is executing. As a result, the *for* loop that changes the *count* variable in the function *beeper* has no effect on the *count* variable within *main*.

When you discuss a variable's scope, you will often use the terms *local* and *global* variables. A local variable is one with scope restricted to a specific function. On the other hand, the entire program can know a global variable. In the case of the *twocount.c* program, each function defines each occurrence of the *count* variable as local.

278 UNDERSTANDING C'S CATEGORIES OF SCOPE

As you have learned, an identifier's *scope* (usually a variable or function name) is the part of the program within which the identifier has meaning (in other words, where the program can use the identifier). C defines four categories of scope: block, function, function prototype, and file. Additionally, C++ defines class scope. *Block scope* defines the bracketed region within which your program has defined a variable. Usually, block scope refers to a function. Local variables have block scope. As you learned in the "Getting Started with C" section of this book, however, you can declare variables after any open brace. The variable's scope exists up to the closing brace—meaning that a parameter with block scope may only have scope within an *if* conditional. Formal parameters have block scope, with the scope limited to the function defining the parameter. *Function scope* defines the region between a function's opening and closing brace. The only item with function scope is a label used by the *goto* statement. *Function prototype scope* specifies the region within the start and end of a function prototype. Identifiers that appear within a function prototype have meaning only within the function prototype, as shown here:

```
int some_function(int age, char *name);
```

File scope specifies a region from an identifier's declaration to the end of the source file. Global variables have file scope, which means only functions that physically follow the global variable declaration within the file can reference a global variable. In C++, *class scope* defines the named collection of methods and data structures that comprise the class.

279 UNDERSTANDING NAME SPACE AND IDENTIFIERS

As you have learned, *scope* defines the region of a program within which an identifier has meaning. Similarly, *name space* defines a region within which identifier names must be unique. In the simplest sense, an *identifier* is a name. C defines four classes of identifiers, as shown in the following list:

- *goto* label names: The label names a *goto* statement uses must be unique within a function.

- Structure, union, and enumeration tags: A *tag* is the name of a structure, union, or enumerated type. Tags must be unique within a block.

- Structure and union member names: The member names that appear within a structure or union must be unique. Different unions or structures can have the same member names.

- Variables, *typedef* identifiers, functions, and enumerated members: These identifiers must be unique within the scope (as explained in Tip 278) in which the identifier is defined.

280 UNDERSTANDING IDENTIFIER VISIBILITY

As you have learned, *scope* defines the program region within which an identifier has meaning. In a similar way, an identifier's *visibility* defines the region of code within which a program can access an identifier. Usually, an identifier's scope and visibility are the same. However, when your program declares an identifier with the same name within a block that appears inside of an existing identifier's scope, the compiler temporarily hides the outer identifier (in other words, the outer identifier loses visibility and the compiler does not recognize it). Consider the following program, *visible.c*, which uses two identifiers named *value*:

```
#include <stdio.h>
void main(void)
  {
    int value = 1500;
```

```
   if (value > 1499)
     {
       int value = 1;
       printf("Inner value is %d\n", value);
     }
   printf("Outer value is %d\n", value);
 }
```

When you compile and execute the *visible.c* program, your screen will display the following output:

```
Inner value is 1
Outer value is 1500
C:\>
```

When the program declares the variable *value* within the *if* statement, the variable declaration instructs the compiler to hide the outer occurrence of the variable with the same name. Outside of the block, however, the outer variable becomes visible to the compiler once again.

UNDERSTANDING DURATION 281

When you discuss variables, *duration* specifies the amount of time that an identifier possesses system-allocated memory. C supports three types of duration: *local*, *static*, and *dynamic*. Automatic variables created during a function invocation or variables defined within a block of statements have *local duration*. Your programs must always initialize local variables. If your program does not initialize a local variable, your program cannot predict the variable's contents. The compiler creates *static variables* as the program execution begins. Static variables usually correspond to global variables. Most C compilers initialize static variables to 0. The compiler allocates *dynamic variables* from the heap during the program's execution. In most cases, programs must initialize dynamic variables.

Note: Some run-time library functions will initialize dynamic memory locations to 0 (zero), while some will not.

FUNCTIONS THAT SUPPORT A VARYING NUMBER OF PARAMETERS 282

As you have learned, C maps the actual parameters that it passes to a function to the formal parameters defined in the function header. If the function expects three parameters, your function invocation should include three parameter values. If you consider functions such as *printf* or *scanf*, however, you will find that the functions support a varying number of parameters. For example, the following *printf* function calls are all valid:

```
printf("Jamsa\'s C/C++ Programmer\'s Bible");
printf("%d %d %d %d %d, 1, 2, 3, 4, 5);
printf("%f %s %s %d %x", salary, name, state, age, id);
```

As you will learn in Tip 283, you can use the macros *va_arg*, *va_end*, and *va_start* (defined in the header file *stdarg.h*) to direct your programs to create their own functions that support a varying number of parameters. The macros essentially pull parameters from the stack, one at a time, until the program reaches the last parameter. When you use these macros to get parameters, you must know each parameter's type. In the case of *printf*, the function uses the format specifiers (for example, *%d*, *%s*, and *%f*) to track the parameter types.

SUPPORTING A VARYING NUMBER OF PARAMETERS 283

In this Tip you will create a function called *add_values*, which adds up all the integer values the calling function passes to it. As shown here, the function supports a varying number of parameters. The value 0 within the function call indicates the last parameter (which does not affect the sum):

```
result = add_values(3,0);            // Returns 3
result = add_values(3,5,0);          // Returns 8
result = add_values(100,3,4,2,0);    // Returns 109
```

The following program, *addvalue.c*, contains and uses the *add_values* function:

```c
#include <stdio.h>
#include <stdarg.h>

int add_values(int value, ...)
  {
     va_list argument_ptr;
     int result = 0;

     if (value != 0)
       {
          result += value;
          va_start(argument_ptr, value);
          while ((value = va_arg(argument_ptr, int)) != 0)
            result += value;
          va_end(argument_ptr);
       }
     return(result);
  }

void main(void)
  {
     printf("Sum of 3 is %d\n", add_values(3, 0));
     printf("Sum of 3 + 5 is %d\n", add_values(3, 5, 0));
     printf("Sum of 3 + 5 + 8 is %d\n", add_values(3, 5, 8, 0));
     printf("Sum of 3 + 5 + 8 + 9 is %d\n", add_values(3, 5, 8 , 9, 0));
  }
```

The function *add_values* uses the *va_start* macro to assign a pointer (*argument_ptr*) to the first parameter on the stack. Next, the function uses the *va_arg* macro to get the values one at a time. The *va_arg* macro returns a value of the specified type and then increments the *argument_ptr* to point to the next argument. When the *argument_ptr* encounters the zero terminator, the function uses the *va_end* macro to assign a value to the *argument_ptr* that prevents the future use of the *argument_ptr* (until *va_start* reinitializes the *argument_ptr*). When you create functions that support a varying number of parameters, your functions must have a way to know the number of parameters and each parameter's type. In the case of *printf*, the format specifier defines the parameters and their types. In the case of *add_values*, the zero terminator marks the last parameter. Likewise, all the arguments passed to the function are the same type.

*Note: Note the use of the ellipses (...) within the **add_values** function header to indicate a variable number of parameters.*

284 How va_start, va_arg, and va_end Work

In Tip 283 you learned that you can use the *va_start*, *va_arg*, and *va_end* macros, defined within the header file *stdarg.h*, to create functions that support a varying number of parameters. To better understand how these macros work, consider the following function call to *add_values*:

```c
add_values(10, 20, 30, 0);
```

When the program makes the function call, the compiler will place the parameters onto the stack from right to left. Within the function, the *va_start* macro assigns a pointer to the first parameter, as shown in Figure 284.

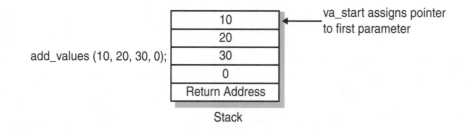

*Figure 284 Using **va_start** to assign a pointer to the first parameter.*

The *va_arg* macro returns the value pointed to by the argument pointer. To determine the value, the macro must know the parameter's type. A parameter of type *int*, for example, will use 16 bits, whereas a parameter of type *long* will use 32. After retrieving the parameter's value, the *va_arg* macro will increment the argument pointer so that it points to the next argument. To determine the number of bytes to add to the pointer, *va_arg* will again use the parameter's type. After the *va_arg* macro retrieves the last argument, the *va_end* macro will nullify the argument pointer's value.

CREATING FUNCTIONS THAT SUPPORT MANY PARAMETERS AND TYPES 285

In Tips 282 and 283 you learned how to create functions that support a variable number of parameters. Unfortunately, the *add_values* function you created supports only parameters of type *int*. The following program, *alltypes.c*, changes the *add_values* function to support values of all types. The function returns a value of type *float*. To help the function determine the parameter types, you pass to the function a format specifier similar to that which *printf* uses. For example, to add *three integer* values, use the following invocation:

```
result = add_values("%d %d %d", 1, 2, 3);
```

Likewise, to add three *floating-point* values, use the following invocation:

```
result = add_values("%f %f %f", 1.1, 2.2, 3.3);
```

Finally, to add *integer* and *floating-point* values, use the following invocation:

```
result = add_values("%f %d %f %d", 1.1, 2, 3.3, 4);
```

Using the format specifier, you eliminate the need to use the zero terminator. Additionally, the format specifier lets you determine how many bits each parameter uses, as shown here:

```c
#include <stdio.h>
#include <stdarg.h>
double add_values(char *str, ...)
{
    va_list marker;
    double result = 0.0;

    va_start(marker, str);                      // mark first additional argument
    while (*str)                                // examine each character in the string
      {
        if (*str == '%')                        // if not a %_ format specifier, skip it
          {
            switch (*(++str))
              {
                case 'd': result += va_arg(marker, int);
                          break;
                case 'f': result += va_arg(marker, double);
                          break;
              }
          }
        str++;
      }
   va_end(marker);
   return(result);
 }

void main(void)
 {
   double result;

   printf("Result %f\n", add_values("%f", 3.3));
   printf("Result %f\n", add_values("%f %f", 1.1, 2.2));
   printf("Result %f\n", add_values("%f %d %f", 1.1, 1, 2.2));
   printf("Result %f\n", add_values("%f %d %f %d", 1.1, 1, 2.2, 3));
 }
```

286 READING A CHARACTER FROM THE KEYBOARD

Even the simplest C programs must often read characters from the keyboard. The character may correspond to a menu option, a Yes or No response, or even one of many letters in a name. Programs often perform character input operations using the *getchar* macro. You will implement the *getchar* macro as shown here:

```
#include <stdio.h>

int getchar(void);
```

If successful, *getchar* returns the ASCII value for the read character. If an error occurs or *getchar* encounters an end of file (usually for redirected input), *getchar* returns *EOF*. The following program, *getchar.c*, uses *getchar* to read a Yes or No response from the keyboard:

```
#include <stdio.h>
#include <ctype.h>

void main(void)
  {
    int letter;
    printf("Type Y or N to continue and press Enter\n");
    do
      {
        letter = toupper(getchar());
      }
    while ((letter != 'Y') && (letter != 'N'));
    printf("You typed %c\n", ((letter == 'Y') ? 'Y': 'N'));
  }
```

As you can see, the program uses a *do while* loop to repeatedly invoke *getchar* until the user types either Y or N on the keyboard.

Note: To support I/O redirection, C actually defines the **getchar** *macro in terms of* **stdin** *(which corresponds to the keyboard by default).*

287 DISPLAYING A CHARACTER OF OUTPUT

In Tip 286 you learned how to use the *getchar* macro to read a character from the keyboard. In a similar way, C provides the *putchar* macro. The *putchar* macro writes a character to the screen (*stdout*). The format of the *putchar* macro is as follows:

```
#include <stdio.h>

int putchar(int letter);
```

If *putchar* succeeds, it returns the character written. If an error occurs, *putchar* returns *EOF*. The following program, *putchar.c*, uses *putchar* to display the letters of the alphabet:

```
#include <stdio.h>

void main(void)
  {
    int letter;
    for (letter = 'A'; letter <= 'Z'; letter++)
      putchar(letter);
  }
```

Note: Because C defines **putchar** *in terms of* **stdout**, *you can use the DOS output redirection operators to redirect the output of the* **putchar.c** *program to a file or printer.*

UNDERSTANDING BUFFERED INPUT

When your program uses buffered input, the operating system does not actually pass the letters the user types to the program until the user presses ENTER. In this way, the user can change characters as he or she types, using the BACKSPACE key to erase characters as needed. When the user presses ENTER, all the characters typed are available to the program. The *getchar* macro uses buffered input. If you use *getchar* to read a single character response, *getchar* does not read a character until the user presses ENTER. If the user types multiple characters, all the characters are available to *getchar* within the input buffer. The following program, *bufferio.c*, illustrates buffered input. Run the program and then type in a line of text. The characters you type will not be available to the program until you press ENTER. After you press ENTER, however, the program will read and display characters until it encounters the *newline* character (which the operating system creates when you press ENTER), as shown here:

```
#include <stdio.h>

void main(void)
  {
    int letter;
    do
      {
        letter = getchar();
        putchar(letter);
      }
    while (letter != '\n');
  }
```

When you run the *bufferio.c* program, experiment with the letters you input, using the BACKSPACE key to rub out letters, and so on. As you will find, the letters passed to the program correspond with your final text.

ASSIGNING KEYBOARD INPUT TO A STRING

The Strings section of this book looks at several different ways to manipulate strings. When you perform keyboard input, one of the most common operations your programs will perform is to assign the characters resulting from the keyboard input to a string. The following program, *fillstr.c*, uses the *getchar* macro to assign letters to the *string* variable. To assign characters, the program simply loops, assigning characters to the string elements until the program encounters the *newline* character. The program then assigns the *NULL* character (end of string) marker to the current string position, as shown here:

```
#include <stdio.h>

void main(void)
  {
    char string[128];
    int index = 0;
    int letter;
    printf("Type in a string and press Enter\n");
    while ((letter = getchar()) != '\n')
      string[index++] = letter;
    string[index] = NULL;
    printf("The string was: %s\n", string);
  }
```

COMBINING GETCHAR AND PUTCHAR

As you have learned, *getchar* lets you read a letter from the keyboard (*stdin*), while *putchar* lets you display a letter on the screen (*stdout*). Depending on your program's function, there may be times when you want to read and display characters. The following *do while* loop, for example, will read and display characters up to and including the *newline* character:

```
do
  {
     letter = getchar();
     putchar(letter);
  }
while (letter != '\n');
```

Because *getchar* and *putchar* both work with integer values, you can combine the previous statements, as shown here:

```
do
   putchar(letter = getchar());
while (letter != '\n');
```

In this case, *getchar* will assign the character typed to the *letter* variable. The *putchar* macro, in turn, will display the value assigned to *letter*.

291 REMEMBER, GETCHAR AND PUTCHAR ARE MACROS

As you create your programs, remember that *getchar* and *putchar* are macros, not functions. Therefore, some compilers will not let you leave spaces between their names and parentheses, as shown here:

```
letter = getchar();
putchar(letter);
```

If you examine the header file *stdio.h*, you will find the macro definitions for *getchar* and *putchar*. The I/O Redirection section of this book explains the *getchar* and *putchar* macro definitions in detail.

292 READING A CHARACTER USING DIRECT I/O

You learned in Tip 288 that when you perform keyboard input, your programs can perform direct or buffered input. When your programs use direct input operations, the characters users type at the keyboard are immediately available to the program (in other words, the operating system does not buffer the characters). If the user presses the BACK-SPACE key to erase a previous character, the program itself must handle the editing operation (erasing the previous character from the screen and removing the character from the buffer). The *getche* function lets your programs read a character from the keyboard using direct input. The format of the *getche* function is as follows:

```
#include <conio.h>
int getche(void);
```

The following program, *getche.c*, uses the *getche* function to read a Yes or No response from the keyboard:

```
#include <stdio.h>
#include <ctype.h>
#include <conio.h>

void main(void)
  {
    int letter;
    printf("Do you want to continue? (Y/N): ");
    do
      {
         letter = getche();
         letter = toupper(letter);
      }
    while ((letter != 'Y') && (letter != 'N'));

    if (letter == 'Y')
      printf("\nYour response was Yes\n");
    else
      printf("\nWhy not?\n");
  }
```

Unlike the program *getchar.c*, which requires the user to press ENTER to make the response available, the keys the user typed into the *getche.c* program are immediately available to the program.

DIRECT KEYBOARD INPUT WITHOUT CHARACTER DISPLAY 293

In Tip 292 you learned how to use the *getche* function to read characters from the keyboard as the user types the characters (using direct I/O). When you use *getche*, the program will display the letters the user types on the screen as the user types them. Depending on your program, there may be times when you want to read characters from the keyboard without displaying the characters on the screen. For example, if your program prompts the user for a password, the letters the user types should not appear on the screen for others to see. The *getch* function lets your programs read characters from the keyboard without displaying (echoing) the characters to the screen. The format of the *getch* function is as follows:

```
#include <conio.h>

int getch(void);
```

The following program, *getch.c*, uses the *getch* function to read characters from the keyboard. As the user types, the program uses *getch* to read each character, converts each character to uppercase, and then displays each character's uppercase equivalent on the screen. The following program, *getch.c*, shows how you can quickly implement such processing:

```
#include <stdio.h>
#include <conio.h>
#include <ctype.h>

void main(void)
 {
   int letter;

   printf("Type in a string of characters and press Enter\n");
   do
    {
      letter = getch();
      letter = toupper(letter);
      putch(letter);
    }
   while (letter != '\r');
 }
```

KNOWING WHEN TO USE '\R' AND '\N' 294

As you have learned, C uses the '\r' escape sequence to indicate a carriage return. Likewise, C uses '\n' to represent a *newline* (carriage return and linefeed). When your programs perform buffered input using *getchar*, C will convert the ENTER key to a carriage return and linefeed (*newline*) sequence. On the other hand, when you perform direct I/O using *getch* or *getche*, either function will return the ENTER key simply as a carriage return ('\r'). Therefore, you must test for the correct character within your programs, as shown here:

```
do
 {
   letter = getchar();
   putchar(letter);
 }
while (letter != '\n');
do
 {
   letter = getch();
   putchar(letter);
 }
while (letter != '\r');
```

295 Performing Direct Output

As you have learned, the functions *getch* and *getche* let your programs read characters directly from the keyboard, bypassing C's buffered (file system-based) input streams. In a similar way, your programs can perform fast screen output using the *putch* function, as shown here:

```
#include <conio.h>

int putch(int letter);
```

If successful, *putch* returns the letter it displayed. If an error occurs, *putch* returns *EOF*. To perform fast output, the *putch* function communicates with the BIOS video services or directly accesses the PC's video memory. Functions such as *putchar*, on the other hand, use the file system, which in turn calls the BIOS. The *putch* function does not convert a linefeed character into a carriage return and linefeed sequence. The following program, *putch.c*, uses *putch* and *putchar* to display the letters of the alphabet 1,001 times. The program then displays the amount of time each function required, as shown here:

```
#include <stdio.h>
#include <conio.h>
#include <time.h>

void main(void)
  {
    int letter;
    int count;

    time_t start_time, stop_time;
    time(&start_time);
    for (count = 0; count < 1000; count++)
     for (letter = 'A'; letter <= 'Z'; letter++)
      putchar(letter);
    time(&stop_time);
    printf("\n\nTime required for putchar %d seconds\n", stop_time-start_time);
    printf("Press any key...\n");
    getch();
    time(&start_time);
    for (count = 0; count < 1000; count++)
      for (letter = 'A'; letter <= 'Z'; letter++)
        putch(letter);
    time(&stop_time);
    printf("\n\nTime required for putch %d seconds\n", stop_time-start_time);
  }
```

296 Placing a Keystroke Back into the Keyboard Buffer

As you have learned, the *getch* function lets your programs read a character from the keyboard. Depending on how you write your program, there may be times when you read keystrokes up to a specific character and then process the keystrokes. When the processing completes, you read the remaining characters. When you write such code, there may be times when you want your program to "unread" a character. The *ungetch* function lets your programs "unread" a character. To do so, you will implement the *ungetch* function, as shown here:

```
#include <conio.h>

int ungetch(int character);
```

In addition, at times you may want to place a character into the keyboard buffer so that your program can reread the keystroke it just read. Using *ungetch,* your programs can do just that. The following program, *ungetch.c*, reads letters from the keyboard until it encounters a non-lowercase letter. The program then displays the letters and afterwards reads and displays any remaining characters on a different line:

```
#include <stdio.h>
#include <ctype.h>
#include <conio.h>
```

```
void main(void)
  {
    int letter;
    int done = 0;
    int uppercase_found = 0;

    do
     {
        letter = getch();
        if (islower(letter))
          putchar(letter);
        else
         {
            if (isupper(letter))
             {
                ungetch(letter);
                uppercase_found = 1;
                putchar('\n');
             }
            done = 1;
         }
     }
    while (! done);
    if (uppercase_found)
      do
       {
          letter = getch();
          putchar(letter);
       }
      while (letter != '\r');
  }
```

If you are reading characters using *getchar*, you can use the *ungetc* function to unread a character, as shown here:

```
ungetc(letter, stdin);
```

FAST FORMATTED OUTPUT USING CPRINTF 297

As you know, the *printf* function lets your programs perform formatted output. C actually defines the *printf* function in terms of the file handle *stdout*. As a result, you can redirect *printf's* output from the screen to a file or device. Because *printf* uses *stdout* to display characters, *printf* uses the C file system, which, in turn, uses the DOS functions. Each of the DOS functions, in turn, calls the BIOS. For faster formatted output, your programs can use the following function, *cprintf*, which works directly with the BIOS or your computer's video memory:

```
#include <conio.h>

int cprintf(const char *format[,arguments...]);
```

The following program, *cprintf.c*, writes the string "Jamsa's C/C++ Programmer's Bible" to your screen 1,001 times using *printf* and then *cprintf*. The program then displays a summary of the amount of time both functions required:

```
#include <stdio.h>
#include <conio.h>
#include <time.h>

void main(void)
  {
    int count;

    time_t start_time, stop_time;
    time(&start_time);
    for (count = 0; count < 1001; count++)
      printf("Jamsa\'s C/C++ Programmer\'s Bible\n");
    time(&stop_time);
    printf("\n\nTime required for printf %d seconds\n", stop_time-start_time);
    printf("Press any key...\n");
```

```
    getch();
    time(&start_time);
    for (count = 0; count < 1001; count++)
      cprintf("Jamsa\'s C/C++ Programmer\'s Bible\r\n");
    time(&stop_time);
    printf("\n\nTime required for cprintf %d seconds\n", stop_time-start_time);
}
```

*Note: The **cprintf** function does not convert the **newline** character into a carriage return linefeed sequence.*

298 FAST FORMATTED INPUT FROM THE KEYBOARD

In Tip 297 you learned that the *cprintf* lets your programs bypass the file system to perform fast output to the screen display. In a similar way, the *cscanf* function lets your programs perform fast formatted input from the keyboard, as shown here:

```
#include <conio.h>

int cscanf(char *format [,arguments]);
```

The following program, *cscanf.c*, prompts you for three integer values. The program then reads the values using *cscanf*:

```
#include <conio.h>

void main(void)
  {
    int a, b, c;

    cprintf("Type 3 integer values and press Enter\r\n");
    cscanf("%d %d %d", &a, &b, &c);
    cprintf("The values entered were %d %d %d\r\n", a, b, c);
  }
```

299 WRITING A CHARACTER STRING

As you have learned, the *printf* function lets your programs write formatted output to the screen display. Using *printf*, your programs can write strings, integers, floating-point numbers, or combinations of different values to the screen. When your programs only need to write a character string, however, you may be able to improve your program's performance by using the *puts* function instead of *printf*, as shown here:

```
#include <stdio.h>

int puts(const char *string);
```

The *puts* function writes a *NULL*-terminated string to the screen (actually to *stdout*). If *puts* succeeds, *puts* returns a non-negative value. If an error occurs, *puts* returns *EOF*. The *puts* function automatically writes a *newline* character at the end of the string. The following program, *puts.c*, uses *printf* and *puts* to output the string "Jamsa's C/C++ Programmer's Bible" 1,001 times. The program displays the amount of time each function required:

```
#include <stdio.h>
#include <conio.h>
#include <time.h>

void main(void)
  {
    int count;

    time_t start_time, stop_time;
    time(&start_time);
    for (count = 0; count < 1001; count++)
      printf("Jamsa\'s C/C++ Programmer\'s Bible\n");
    time(&stop_time);
    printf("\n\nTime required for printf %d seconds\n", stop_time-start_time);
    printf("Press any key...\n");
```

```
    getch();
    time(&start_time);
    for (count = 0; count < 1001; count++)
      puts("Jamsa\'s C/C++ Programmer\'s Bible");
    time(&stop_time);
    printf("\n\nTime required for puts %d seconds\n", stop_time-start_time);
  }
```

Note: *Because the* **puts** *function automatically appends a* **newline** *character, the character string the program instructs* **puts** *to display does not include the newline character.*

FASTER STRING OUTPUT USING DIRECT I/O $\quad$ C300

In Tip 299 you learned that the *puts* function lets your programs quickly output a character string. However, because C defines the *puts* function in terms of *stdout* (so it can support redirection), the function must use the file system. For faster string output to the screen, your programs might want to use the *cputs* function, as shown here:

```
#include <conio.h>

int cputs(const char string);
```

Like *puts*, the *cputs* function outputs a *NULL*-terminated string. Unlike *puts*, however, *cputs* does not automatically append a *newline* character. The following program, *cputs.c*, uses the *puts* and *cputs* functions to display the string "Jamsa's C/C++ Programmer's Bible" 1500 times. The program displays the amount of time each function required to generate the output:

```
#include <stdio.h>
#include <conio.h>
#include <time.h>

void main(void)
 {
   int count;

   time_t start_time, stop_time;
   time(&start_time);
   for (count = 0; count < 1500; count++)
     puts("Jamsa\'s C/C++ Programmer\'s Bible");
   time(&stop_time);
   printf("\n\nTime required for puts %d seconds\n", stop_time-start_time);
   printf("Press any key...\n");
   getch();
   time(&start_time);
   for (count = 0; count < 1500; count++)
     cputs("Jamsa\'s C/C++ Programmer\'s Bible\r\n");
   time(&stop_time);
   printf("\n\nTime required for cputs %d seconds\n", stop_time-start_time);
 }
```

READING A CHARACTER STRING FROM THE KEYBOARD $\quad$ C301

In Tip 299 you learned that C provides the *puts* function, which you can use within your programs to write a character string to the screen display. In a similar way, your programs can use the *gets* function to read a character string from the keyboard, as shown here:

```
#include <stdio.h>

char *gets(char *string);
```

If *gets* is successful, it will return a pointer to the character string. If an error occurs or if *gets* encounters the end of file marker, *gets* will return the *NULL* value. The *gets* function reads characters up to and including the *newline* character. However, *gets* replaces the *newline* character with *NULL*. The following program, *gets.c*, uses the *gets* function to read a string of characters from the keyboard:

```
#include <stdio.h>

void main(void)
  {
     char string[256];

     printf("Type in a string of characters and press Enter\n");
     gets(string);
     printf("The string was %s\n", string);
  }
```

Note: C actually defines *the gets* function in terms of *stdin* (which is by default the keyboard), which lets the function support I/O redirection.

302 PERFORMING FASTER KEYBOARD STRING INPUT

In Tip 301 you learned how your programs can use the *gets* function to read a character string from the keyboard. Because C defines *gets* in terms of *stdin*, *gets* must use the file system to perform its input operations. If you do not need support for I/O redirection, you can use the *cgets* function to read characters from the keyboard, thereby improving your program's performance. You will implement *cgets* as shown here:

```
#include <conio.h>

char *cgets(char *string);
```

If *cgets* successfully reads characters from the keyboard, *cgests* will return a pointer to the string beginning at *string[2]*. If an error occurs, *cgets* will return *NULL*. The *cgets* function behaves differently from the *gets* function Before you call *cgets* with a character string, you must first assign the maximum number of characters *cgets* will read to *string[0]*. When *cgets* returns, *string[1]* will contain a number count of characters *cgets* has read. The *NULL*-terminated character string actually begins at *string[2]*. The following program, *cgets.c*, illustrates how to use the *cgets* function:

```
#include <stdio.h>
#include <conio.h>

void main(void)
  {
     char buffer[256];

     buffer[0] = 253;   // Number of characters that can be read
     printf("Type in a string and press Enter\n");
     cgets(buffer);
     printf("\n\nThe number of characters read was %d\n", buffer[1]);
     printf("The string read: %s\n", &buffer[2]);
  }
```

To experiment with this program, reduce the number of characters *cgets* can read to 10. If the user tries to type more than 10 characters, the function will ignore the extra characters.

303 DISPLAYING OUTPUT IN COLOR

Using the *ansi.sys* device driver, your programs can display screen output in color. In addition, many C compilers provide text-based output functions that let you display color output. If you are using *Turbo C++ Lite*, Borland C++ or Microsoft C++, the *outtext* (called *_outtext* for Microsoft C++) function lets you display colored output. If you are using *Turbo C++ Lite* or Borland C++, you can only use the *outtext* function in graphics mode. The Microsoft *_outtext* function, on the other hand, works in either text or graphics mode. If you must perform colored output, refer to the documentation that accompanied your compiler for specifics on these functions. As you will find, the compilers provide functions that set text position, colors, and graphics modes. Because the ANSI output routines are compiler dependent, this book will not cover routines as Tips.

CLEARING THE SCREEN DISPLAY 304

Most C compilers do not provide a function that lets you clear the screen display. If you are using *Turbo C++ Lite*, Borland C, or Microsoft C, however, you can use the *clrscr* function to clear a text mode window's contents, as shown here:

```
#include <conio.h>
void clrscr(void);
```

The following program, *clrscr.c*, uses the *clrscr* function to clear the screen display:

```
#include <conio.h>
void main(void)
  {
    clrscr();
  }
```

ERASING TO THE END OF THE CURRENT LINE 305

As your programs perform screen I/O, there may be times when you want to erase the contents of a line from the current cursor position to the end of the line. To do so, your programs can use the *clreol* function, as shown here:

```
#include <conio.h>
void clreol(void);
```

The *clreol* function erases the remaining contents of the current line beyond the cursor without moving the cursor.

DELETING THE CURRENT SCREEN LINE 306

As your programs perform screen-based I/O, there may be times when you want to delete the current line's contents, moving all the output that follows up one line. In such cases, your programs can use the *delline* function, as shown here:

```
#include <conio.h>
void delline(void);
```

The following program, *delline.c*, fills the screen with 24 lines of text. When you press ENTER, the program will use *delline* to erase lines 12, 13, and 14, as shown here:

```
#include <conio.h>
void main(void)
  {
    int line;

    clrscr();
    for (line = 1; line < 25; line++)
     cprintf("This is line %d\r\n", line);
    cprintf("Press a key to Continue: ");
    getch();
    gotoxy(1, 12);
    for (line = 12; line < 15; line++)
      delline();
    gotoxy(1, 25);
  }
```

POSITIONING THE CURSOR FOR SCREEN OUTPUT 307

As you have learned, you can use the *ansi.sys* device driver to position the cursor for screen output operations. If you are working in a DOS environment, many C compilers provide the *gotoxy* function, which lets you position the cursor at a specific column and row intersection, as shown here:

```
#include <conio.h>

void gotoxy(int column, int row);
```

The *column* parameter specifies a column position (x) from 1 through 80. The *row* parameter specifies a row position (y) from 1 through 25. If either value is invalid, the compiler will ignore the *gotoxy* operation. The following program, *gotoxy.c*, uses the *gotoxy* function to display screen output at specific locations:

```
#include <conio.h>

void main(void)
  {
    clrscr();
    gotoxy(1, 5);
    cprintf("Output at row 5 column 1\n");
    gotoxy(20, 10);
    cprintf("Output at row 10 column 20\n");
  }
```

308 DETERMINING THE ROW AND COLUMN POSITION

In Tip 307 you learned how to use *gotoxy* to place the cursor at a specific row and column position. In many cases, your programs will want to know the current cursor position before performing a screen I/O operation. The functions *wherex* and *wherey* return the cursor's column and row, as shown here:

```
#include <conio.h>

int wherex(void);
int wherey(void);
```

The following program, *wherexy.c*, clears the screen, writes three lines of output, and then uses the *wherex* and *wherey* functions to determine the current cursor position:

```
#include <conio.h>

void main(void)
  {
    int row, column;

    clrscr();
    cprintf("This is line 1\r\n");
    cprintf("Line 2 is a little longer\r\n");
    cprintf("This is the last line");
    row = wherey();
    column = wherex();
    cprintf("\r\nThe cursor position was row %d column %d\n", row, column);
  }
```

309 INSERTING A BLANK LINE ON THE SCREEN

As your programs perform screen-based I/O operations, there may be times when you want to insert a blank line on the screen so that you can insert text in the middle of existing text. To do so, your programs can use the *insline* function, as shown here:

```
#include <conio.h>

void insline(void);
```

When you invoke the *insline* function, all text below the current cursor position moves down one line. The line at the bottom of the screen will scroll off the window. The following program, *insline.c*, writes 25 lines of text on the screen. The program then uses the *insline* function to insert text at line 12, as shown here:

```
#include <conio.h>

void main(void)
  {
    int line;
```

```
    clrscr();
    for (line = 1; line < 25; line++)
     cprintf("This is line %d\r\n", line);
    cprintf("Press a key to Continue: ");
    getch();
    gotoxy(1, 12);
    insline();
    cprintf("This is new text!!!");
    gotoxy(1, 25);
}
```

COPYING SCREEN TEXT TO A BUFFER 310

When your programs perform extensive screen I/O, there may be times when the program must copy the current screen contents to a buffer. To copy screen text, your programs can use the *gettext* function, as shown here:

```
#include <conio.h>

int gettext(int left, int top, int right, int bottom, void *buffer);
```

The *left* and *top* parameters specify the column and row positions of the upper-left corner of the screen region that you want to copy. Likewise, the *right* and *bottom* parameters specify the region's lower-right corner. The *gettext* function places the text and its attributes in the *buffer* parameter. The PC uses an attribute byte for every letter of text it displays on your screen. If you want to buffer 10 characters, for example, your buffer must be large enough to hold the 10 ASCII characters plus the 10 attribute bytes (20 bytes in length). The following program, *savescr.c*, saves the current text mode screen contents to the file *savescr.dat*:

```
#include <conio.h>
#include <io.h>
#include <fcntl.h>
#include <sys\stat.h>

void main(void)
 {
   char buffer[8000];
   int handle;

   if ((handle = creat("SAVESCR.DAT", S_IWRITE)) == -1)
     cprintf("Error opening SAVESCRN.DAT\r\n");
   else
     {
       gettext(1, 1, 80, 25, buffer);
       write(handle, buffer, sizeof(buffer));
       close(handle);
     }
}
```

*Note: In most cases, the current text attribute is 7. If you try to display the contents of the **savescr.dat** file using the **TYPE** command, your system will beep for every attribute value.*

WRITING A TEXT BUFFER AT A SPECIFIC SCREEN LOCATION 311

As you have learned, many DOS-based compilers provide functions that your programs can use to control video output. In Tip 310 you learned that your programs can use the *gettext* function to copy a range of screen characters (and their attributes) to a buffer. After you copy a text buffer, you can later copy it back to the screen using the *puttext* function, as shown here:

```
#include <conio.h>

int puttext(int left, int top, int right, int bottom, void *buffer);
```

The *left, top, right,* and *bottom* parameters specify the screen location to which you want the buffer's contents written. The *buffer* parameter contains the characters and attributes that *gettext* previously stored. The following program, *puttext.c*, moves the text "Jamsa's C/C++ Programmer's Bible" around your screen until you press any key:

```
#include <conio.h>
#include <io.h>
#include <fcntl.h>
#include <sys\stat.h>
#include <stdlib.h>
#include <dos.h>

void main(void)
 {
   char buffer[128];
   int row, column;

   clrscr();
   cprintf("Jamsa\'s C/C++ Programmer\'s Bible\r\n");
   gettext(1, 1, 23, 1, buffer);
   while (! kbhit())
    {
      clrscr();
      row = 1 + random(24);
      column = 1 + random(58);
      puttext(column, row, column+22, row, buffer);
      delay(2000);
    }
 }
```

312 DETERMINING TEXT MODE SETTINGS

As you have learned, many C compilers provide several text-based functions that your programs can use to control screen output operations. To help your programs determine the current screen settings, your programs can use the *gettextinfo* function, as shown here:

```
#include <conio.h>

void gettextinfo(struct text_info *data);
```

The data parameter is a pointer to a structure of type *text_info*, as shown here:

```
struct text_info
 {
   unsigned char winleft;           // Left column
   unsigned char wintop;            // Top row
   unsigned char winright;          // Right column
   unsigned char winbottom;         // Bottom row
   unsigned char attribute;         // Text attribute
   unsigned char normattr;          // Normal attribute
   unsigned char currmode;          // Current text mode
   unsigned char screenheight;      // In rows
   unsigned char screenwidth;       // In columns
   unsigned char curx;              // Cursor column
   unsigned char cury;              // Cursor row;
 };
```

The following program, *textinfo.c*, uses the *gettextinfo* function to display the current text settings:

```
#include <conio.h>

void main(void)
 {
   struct text_info text;

   gettextinfo(&text);
   cprintf("Screen coordinates %d,%d to %d,%d\r\n",
            text.wintop, text.winleft, text.winbottom, text.winright);
   cprintf("Text attribute %d Normal attribute %d\r\n", text.attribute,
            text.normattr);
   cprintf("Screen height %d width %d\r\n", text.screenheight, text.screenwidth);
   cprintf("Cursor position was row %d column %d\r\n", text.cury, text.curx);
 }
```

CONTROLLING SCREEN COLORS C313

As you have learned, your programs can use the *ansi.sys* device driver to display screen output in color. In addition, many DOS-based compilers provide the *textattr* function, which lets you select the foreground and background text colors:

```
#include <conio.h>
void textattr(int attribute);
```

The attribute parameter contains eight bits that specify the colors you desire. The least significant four bits specify the foreground color. The three bits that follow specify the background color, and the most significant bit controls blinking. To select a color, you must assign the desired color value to the correct bits. Table 313 specifies the color values.

Color Constant	Value	Use
BLACK	0	Foreground/background
BLUE	1	Foreground/background
GREEN	2	Foreground/background
CYAN	3	Foreground/background
RED	4	Foreground/background
MAGENTA	5	Foreground/background
BROWN	6	Foreground/background
LIGHTGRAY	7	Foreground/background
DARKGRAY	8	Foreground
LIGHTBLUE	9	Foreground
LIGHTGREEN	10	Foreground
LIGHTCYAN	11	Foreground
LIGHTRED	12	Foreground
LIGHTMAGENTA	13	Foreground
YELLOW	14	Foreground
WHITE	15	Foreground
BLINK	128	Foreground

Table 313 Color attribute parameters.

The following program, *textattr.c*, illustrates the available foreground colors:

```
#include <conio.h>
void main(void)
 {
  int color;

  for (color = 1; color < 16; color++)
   {
     textattr(color);
     cprintf("This is color %d\r\n", color);
   }
  textattr(128 + 15);
  cprintf("This is blinking\r\n");
 }
```

ASSIGNING BACKGROUND COLOR C314

As you learned in Tip 313, the *textattr* function lets your programs select foreground and background colors. To set the background color using *textattr*, your program must assign the color value you desire to bits 4 through 6 of the color value. To assign color value, your programs can use bitwise shift operations, or you can declare a structure with bit fields, as shown here:

```
struct TextColor {
  unsigned char foreground:4;
  unsigned char background:3;
  unsinged char blinking:1;
};
```

The following program, *setback.c*, uses the *TextColor* structure to set the current screen colors:

```
#include <conio.h>

void main(void)
 {
    union TextColor
     {
        struct
         {
            unsigned char foreground:4;
            unsigned char background:3;
            unsigned char blinking:1;
         } color_bits;
        unsigned char value;
     } colors;
    colors.color_bits.foreground = BLUE;
    colors.color_bits.background = RED;
    colors.color_bits.blinking = 1;
    textattr(colors.value);
    clrsqr();
    cprintf("This is the new text color\n");
 }
```

315 SETTING THE FOREGROUND COLOR USING TEXTCOLOR

As you have learned, many DOS-based compilers provide the *textattr* function, which lets you select your desired foreground and background colors. To simplify the process of assigning a foreground color, you might want to use the *textcolor* function, as shown here:

```
#include <conio.h>

void textcolor(int foregroundcolor);
```

The *foregroundcolor* parameter will specify one of the color values listed in Table 315.

Color Constant	Value	Color Constant	Value
BLACK	0	DARKGRAY	8
BLUE	1	LIGHTBLUE	9
GREEN	2	LIGHTGREEN	10
CYAN	3	LIGHTCYAN	11
RED	4	LIGHTRED	12
MAGENTA	5	LIGHTMAGENTA	13
BROWN	6	YELLOW	14
LIGHTGRAY	7	WHITE	15
		BLINK	128

Table 315 Valid foreground color values for **textcolor**.

The following program, *txtcolor.c*, illustrates how to use the *textcolor* function to set the foreground color:

```
#include <conio.h>
void main(void)
 {
  int color;

  for (color = 1; color < 16; color++)
   {
```

```
      textcolor(color);
      cprintf("This is color %d\r\n", color);
  }
  textcolor(128 + 15);
  cprintf("This is blinking\r\n");
}
```

SETTING THE BACKGROUND COLOR USING TEXTBACKGROUND 316

As you have learned, many DOS-based compilers provide the *textattr* function, which lets you select the foreground and background colors you want for text display. To simplify the process of assigning a background color, you can use the *textbackground* function, as shown here:

```
#include <conio.h>

void textbackground(int backgroundcolor);
```

The *backgroundcolor* parameter must specify one of the color values listed in Table 316.

Color Constant	Value	Color Constant	Value
BLACK	0	RED	4
BLUE	1	MAGENTA	5
GREEN	2	BROWN	6
CYAN	3	LIGHTGRAY	7

Table 316 Valid background color values.

The following program, *backgrnd.c*, uses the *textbackground* function to display the different background colors:

```
#include <conio.h>

void main(void)
  {
    int color;

    for (color = 0; color < 8; color++)
      {
        textbackground(color);
        cprintf("This is color %d\r\n", color);
        cprintf("Press any key to continue\r\n");
        getch();
      }
  }
```

CONTROLLING TEXT INTENSITY 317

As you have learned, many DOS-based compilers provide functions that let you control your screen output. When you use these functions to write text to the screen, you want to control the intensity (brightness) of information your programs write to the screen. To control intensity, you can use one of the following three functions to select the text output intensity:

```
#include <conio.h>

void highvideo(void);
void lowvideo(void);
void normvideo(void);
```

The functions control the intensity with which your screen will display text. The following program, *ntensity.c*, illustrates how to use these three functions:

```
#include <conio.h>

void main(void)
  {
```

```
    clrscr();
    highvideo();
    cprintf("This text is high video\r\n");
    lowvideo();
    cprintf("This text is low video\r\n");
    normvideo();
    cprintf("This text is normal video\r\n");
}
```

318 DETERMINING THE CURRENT TEXT MODE

As you have learned, many DOS-based compilers provide functions that your programs can use to control text-based output. When your programs perform screen output, they must know, and possibly change, the PC's current text mode. For example, a program that expects 80 columns will display inconsistent results on a screen that is in 40-column mode. To help your programs change the current text mode, your programs can use the *textmode* function, as shown here:

```
#include <conio.h>

void textmode(int desired_mode);
```

The *desired_mode* parameter specifies the text mode you desire. Table 318 lists the valid text modes.

Constant	Value	Text Mode
LASTMODE	-1	Previous mode
BW40	0	Black and white 40 column
C40	1	Color 40 column
BW80	2	Black and white 80 column
C80	3	Color 80 column
MONO	7	Monochrome 80 column
C4350	64	EGA 43 line or VGA 50 line

Table 318 Valid text mode operations.

The following statement, for example, will select a 43 mode on an EGA monitor or 50 line mode on a VGA monitor:

```
textmode(C4350);
```

Note: If you use **textmode** to change the current text mode, the change will remain in effect after your program ends.

319 MOVING SCREEN TEXT FROM ONE LOCATION TO ANOTHER

As you have learned, many DOS-based compilers provide functions that let you control your screen's text output. If your program performs extensive screen output, there may be times when you want to copy or move the text that appears on one section of your screen to another section. To copy screen text, your programs can use the *movetext* function, as shown here:

```
#include <conio.h>

int movetext(int left, int top, int right, int bottom,
  int destination_left, int destination_top);
```

The *left, top, right,* and *bottom* parameters describe a box which encloses the region of text that you want to move. The *destination_left* and *destination_top* parameters specify the desired location of the box's upper-left corner. The following program, *movetext.c*, writes five lines of text to the screen and then asks you to press a key. When you do, the program will then copy the text to a new location, as shown here:

```
#include <conio.h>

void main(void)
  {
    int i;
```

```
   clrscr();
   for (i = 1; i <= 5; i++)
     cprintf("This is line %d\r\n", i);
   cprintf("Press any key\n\r");
   getch();
   movetext(1, 1, 30, 6, 45, 18);
   gotoxy(1, 24);
 }
```

To move the text to the new location, as opposed to just copying the text to the new location, you must delete the original text after the program completes the *movetext* operation.

DEFINING A TEXT WINDOW 320

As you have learned, many DOS-based compilers provide functions that your programs can use to better control screen output. By default, these functions write their output to the entire screen. Depending on your program's purpose, there may be times when you want to restrict the program's output to a specific screen region. To do so, your programs can use the *window* function, as shown here:

```
#include <conio.h>

void window(int left, int top, int right, int bottom);
```

The *left, top, right,* and *bottom* parameters define the upper-left and lower-right corners of a screen region within which you want to write output. The following program, *window.c*, restricts the program's output to the top-left quarter of the screen:

```
#include <conio.h>

void main(void)
  {
    int i, j;

    window(1, 1, 40, 12);
    for (i = 0; i < 15; i++)
      {
        for (j = 0; j < 50; j++)
          cprintf("%d", j);
        cprintf("\r\n");
      }
  }
```

When program output reaches the right edge of the window, the output wraps to the next line. After the program ends, output operations will have access to the entire screen.

USING THE ABSOLUTE VALUE OF AN INTEGER EXPRESSION 321

The *absolute value* specifies the number-line distance of the value from 0. Absolute values are always positive. For example, the absolute value of 5 is 5. Likewise, the absolute value of –5 is 5. To help your programs determine an absolute value, C provides the *abs* function. The function *abs* returns the absolute value for an integer expression. You will construct the *abs* function as shown here:

```
#include <stdlib.h>

int abs(int expression);
```

The following program, *show_abs.c*, illustrates how to use the *abs* function:

```
#include <stdio.h>
#include <stdlib.h>

void main(void)
  {
    printf("The absolute value of %d is %d\n", 5, abs(5));
```

```
   printf("The absolute value of %d is %d\n", 0, abs(0));
   printf("The absolute value of %d is %d\n", -5, abs(-5));
}
```

When you compile and execute the *show_abs.c* program, your screen will display the following:

```
The absolute value of 5 is 5
The absolute value of 0 is 0
The absolute value of -5 is 5
C:\>
```

Note: Many C compilers also provide the function **labs**, which returns the absolute value for an expression of type **long int**.

322 USING THE ARCCOSINE

The arccosine is the ratio between the hypotenuse of a right triangle and the leg adjacent to a given acute angle. In other words, the arccosine is the geometric inverse of an angle's cosine. In other words, if *y* is the cosine of some angle theta, theta is the arccosine of *y*. To help your programs determine the arccosine, C provides the *acos* function. The *acos* function returns an angle's arccosine (0 through pi) specified in radians (as type *double*), as shown here:

```
#include <math.h>

double acos(double expression);
```

If the specified expression is not in the range –1.0 through 1.0, *acos* will set the global variable *errno* to *EDOM* and display a *DOMAIN* error to *stderr*. The following program, *showacos.c*, illustrates how to use the *acos* function:

```
#include <stdio.h>
#include <math.h>

void main(void)
  {
    double radians;

    for (radians = -0.5; radians <= 0.5; radians += 0.2)
      printf("%f %f\n", radians, acos(radians));
  }
```

Note: Many C compilers also provide the function **acosl**, which returns the arccosine value for a **long double** expression.

323 USING THE ARCSINE

The arcsine is the ratio between the hypotenuse of a right triangle and the leg opposite a given acute angle. In other words, the arcsine is the geometric inverse of an angle's sine. If *y* is the sine of some angle theta, then theta is the arcsine of *y*. To help your programs determine the arcsine, C provides the *acos* function. The *acos* function returns an angle's arcsine (–pi/2 through pi/2), specified in radians (as type *double*), as shown here:

```
#include <math.h>

double asin(double expression);
```

If *expression* is not in the range –1.0 through 1.0, then *asin* will set the global variable *errno* to *NAN* and display a *DOMAIN* error to *stderr*. The following program, *showasin.c*, illustrates how to use the *asin* function:

```
#include <stdio.h>
#include <math.h>

void main(void)
  {
    double radians;

    for (radians = -0.5; radians <= 0.5; radians += 0.2)
      printf("%f %f\n", radians, asin(radians));
  }
```

Note: Many C compilers also provide the function **asinl**, which returns the arcsine value for a **long double** expression.

USING THE ARCTANGENT $\qquad$ 324

The arctangent is the ratio between the leg adjacent to a given acute angle and the leg opposite that angle in a right triangle. In other words, the arctangent is the geometric inverse of an angle's tangent. If *y* is the tangent of some angle theta, theta is the arctangent of *y*. To help your programs determine the arctangent, C provides the *atan* function. The *atan* function returns an angle's arctangent (–pi/2 through pi/2), specified in radians (as type *double*), as shown here:

```
#include <math.h>

double atan(double expression);
```

The following program, *showatan.c*, illustrates how to use the *atan* function:

```
#include <stdio.h>
#include <math.h>

void main(void)
  {
    double radians;

    for (radians = -0.5; radians <= 0.5; radians += 0.2)
      printf("%f %f\n", radians, atan(radians));
  }
```

Note: *Many C compilers also provide the function* **atanl**, *which returns the arctangent value for a* **long double** *expression. Also, C provides the functions* **atan2** *and* **atan2l**, *which return the arctangent of* **y/x**.

OBTAINING A COMPLEX NUMBER'S ABSOLUTE VALUE $\qquad$ 325

As you have learned, a complex number contains a real and imaginary part. C functions represent complex numbers as a structure with an *x* and *y* member, as shown here:

```
struct complex
  {
    double x, y;
  };
```

When you work with complex numbers, there may be times when you must calculate the number's absolute value (its positive distance from zero). To let your program calculate a complex number's absolute value, C provides the *cabs* function, as shown here:

```
#include <math.h>

double cabs(struct complex value);
```

The *cabs* function is similar to taking the square root of the sum of the square of each complex number. In the following example, the *cabs* function will return $(10^2 + 5^2)^{1/2}$. The following program, *showcabs.c*, illustrates how to use the C language *cabs* function:

```
#include <stdio.h>
#include <math.h>

void main(void)
  {
    struct complex complex_number;

    complex_number.x = 10;
    complex_number.y = 5;
    printf("Absolute value of 10,5 is %f\n", cabs(complex_number));
  }
```

When you compile and execute the *showcabs.c* program, your screen will display the following output:

```
Absolute value of 10,5 is 11.180340
C:\>
```

Note: *Many C compilers also provide the function* **cabls**, *which returns an absolute value for* **long double** *complex numbers. The companion CD-ROM that accompanies this book includes a substantially longer program to test for the absolute value of a complex number, because the C++ implementation of complex numbers is substantially different than C's. The* **showcabs2.cpp** *program compiles in both the C and C++ environments.*

326 ROUNDING UP A FLOATING-POINT VALUE

When you work with floating-point numbers, there may be times when you must round up the value of a floating-point variable or expression to the next higher integer. For such cases, C provides the *ceil* function, as shown here:

```
#include <math.h>

double ceil(double value);
```

As you can see, *ceil* receives a parameter of type *double* and returns a value of type *double*. The following program, *showceil.c*, illustrates how to use the *ceil* function:

```
#include <stdio.h>
#include <math.h>

void main(void)
  {
    printf("The value %f ceil %f\n", 1.9, ceil(1.9));
    printf("The value %f ceil %f\n", 2.1, ceil(2.1));
  }
```

When you compile and execute the *showceil.c* program, your screen will display the following output:

```
The value 1.900000 ceil 2.000000
The value 2.100000 ceil 3.000000
C:\>
```

Note: *Many C compilers also provide the function* **ceill**, *which rounds up a value of type* **long double**.

327 USING THE COSINE OF AN ANGLE

For a triangle, the cosine of an angle is the ratio of the angle's adjacent edge to the hypotenuse. To help your programs determine the cosine, C provides the *cos* function. The *cos* function returns an angle's cosine, specified in radians (as type *double*), as shown here:

```
#include <math.h>

double cos(double expression);
```

The *cos* function returns a value in the range –1.0 through 1.0. The following program, *show_cos.c*, illustrates how to use the *cos* function:

```
#include <stdio.h>
#include <math.h>

void main(void)
  {
    printf("cosine of pi/2 is %6.4f\n", cos(3.14159/2.0));
    printf("cosine of pi is %6.4f\n", cos(3.14159));
  }
```

When you compile and execute the *show_cos.c* program, your screen will display the following output:

```
cosine of pi/2 is 0.0000
cosine of pi is -1.0000
C:\>
```

Note: *Many C compilers also provide the function* **cosl**, *which returns the cosine value for a* **long double** *expression.*

USING THE HYPERBOLIC COSINE OF AN ANGLE 328

The hyperbolic cosine of an angle is the cosine of a "circular-like" angle defined using ratios of hyperbolic radians. To help your programs determine the hyperbolic cosine, C provides the *cosh* function. The *cosh* function returns a "circular-like" angle's hyperbolic cosine, specified in radians (as type *double*), as shown here:

```
#include <math.h>

double cosh(double expression);
```

If overflow occurs, *cosh* will return the value *HUGE_VAL* (or *_LHUGE_VAL* for *coshl*) and set the global variable *errno* to *ERANGE*. The following program, *showcosh.c*, illustrates how to use the *cosh* function:

```
#include <stdio.h>
#include <math.h>

void main(void)
  {
    double radians;

    for (radians = -0.5; radians <= 0.5; radians += 0.2)
      printf("%f %f\n", radians, cosh(radians));
  }
```

*Note: Many C compilers also provide the function **coshl**, which returns the hyperbolic cosine value for a **long double** expression.*

USING THE SINE OF AN ANGLE 329

In a triangle, the sine of an angle is the ratio of the angle's opposite edge to the hypotenuse. To help your programs determine the sine, C provides the *sin* function. The *sin* function returns an angle's sine, specified in radians (as type *double*), as shown here:

```
#include <math.h>

double sin(double expression);
```

The following program, *show_sin.c*, illustrates how to use the *sin* function:

```
#include <stdio.h>
#include <math.h>

void main(void)
  {
    double radians;

    for (radians = 0.0; radians < 3.1; radians += 0.1)
      printf("Sine of %f is %f\n", radians, sin(radians));
  }
```

*Note: Many C compilers also provide the function **sinl**, which returns the sine value for a **long double** expression.*

USING THE HYPERBOLIC SINE OF AN ANGLE 330

The hyperbolic sine of an angle is the sine of a "circular-like" angle defined using ratios of hyperbolic radians. To help your programs determine the hyperbolic sine, C provides the *sinh* function. The *sinh* function returns a "circular-like" angle's hyperbolic sine, specified in radians (as type *double*), as shown here:

```
#include <math.h>

double sinh(double expression);
```

If overflow occurs, *sinh* will return the value *HUGE_VAL* (or *_LHUGE_VAL* for *sinhl*) and set the global variable *errno* to *ERANGE*. The following program, *showsinh.c*, illustrates how to use the *sinh* function:

```
#include <stdio.h>
#include <stdlib.h>
#include <math.h>

void main(void)
  {
    double radians;
    double result;

    for (radians = 0.0; radians < 3.1; radians += 0.1)
      if (((result = sinh(radians)) == HUGE_VAL) && (errno == ERANGE))
        printf("Overflow error\n");
      else
        printf("Sine of %f is %f\n", radians, result);
  }
```

*Note: Many C compilers also provide the function **sinhl**, which returns the hyperbolic sine value for a **long double** expression.*

331 USING THE TANGENT OF AN ANGLE

In a triangle, the tangent of an angle is the ratio of the angle's opposite edge to the adjacent edge. To help your programs determine the tangent, C provides the *tan* function. The function returns an angle's tangent, specified in radians (as type *double*), as shown here:

```
#include <math.h>

double tan(double expression);
```

The following program, *show_tan.c*, illustrates how to use the *tan* function:

```
#include <stdio.h>
#include <math.h>

void main(void)
  {
    double pi = 3.14159265;

    printf("Tangent of pi is %f\n", tan(pi));
    printf("Tangent of pi/4 is %f\n", tan(pi / 4.0));
  }
```

When you compile and execute the *show_tan.c* program, your screen will display the following output:

```
Tangent of pi is -0.000000
Tangent of pi/4 is 1.000000
C:\>
```

*Note: Many C compilers also provide the function **tanl**, which returns the tangent value for a **long double** expression.*

332 USING THE HYPERBOLIC TANGENT OF AN ANGLE

The hyperbolic tangent of an angle is the tangent of a "circular-like" angle defined using ratios of hyperbolic radians. To help your programs determine the hyperbolic tangent, C provides the *tanh* function. The *tanh* function returns an angle's hyperbolic tangent, specified in radians (as type *double*), as shown here:

```
#include <math.h>

double tanh(double expression);
```

*Note: Many C compilers also provide **tanhl**, which returns the hyperbolic tangent value for a **long double** expression.*

333 PERFORMING INTEGER DIVISION

As you have learned, C provides the division (/) and modulo (%) operators that let your programs perform a division or determine the remainder of a division operation. Similarly, C provides the function *div*, which divides a numerator value by a denominator, returning a structure of type *div_t* that contains the quotient and remainder, as shown here:

```
struct div_t
  {
    int quot;
    int rem;
  } div_t;
```

The *div* function works with integer values, as shown here:

```
#include <stdlib.h>

div_t div(int numerator, int denominator);
```

The following program, *div_rem.c*, illustrates how to use the *div* function:

```
#include <stdio.h>
#include <stdlib.h>

void main(void)
{
  div_t result;

  result = div(11, 3);
  printf("11 divided by 3 is %d Remainder %d\n", result.quot, result.rem);
}
```

When you compile and execute the *div_rem.c* program, your screen will display the following output:

```
11 divided by 3 is 3 Remainder 2
C:\>
```

Note: *Many C compilers also provide the function **ldiv**, which returns the quotient and remainder for **long** values.*

WORKING WITH AN EXPONENTIAL 334

When your programs perform complex mathematical operations, your programs will often need to calculate the exponential of e^x. In such cases, your programs can use the *exp* function, which returns a value of type *double*, as shown here:

```
#include <math.h>

double exp(double x);
```

The following program, *show_exp.c*, illustrates how to use the *exp* function:

```
#include <stdio.h>
#include <math.h>

void main(void)
{
  double value;

  for (value = 0.0; value <= 1.0; value += 0.1)
    printf("exp(%f) is %f\n", value, exp(value));
}
```

Note: *Many C compilers also provide the function **expl**, which works with values of type **long double**.*

USING THE ABSOLUTE VALUE OF A FLOATING-POINT EXPRESSION 335

As you have learned, the *absolute value* specifies a value's number line distance from zero. Absolute values are always positive. For example, the absolute value of 2.5 is 2.5. Likewise, the absolute value of –2.5 is 2.5. When you work with absolute values, there may be times when you must calculate the absolute value of a floating-point expression. For such cases, C provides the *fabs* function. The *fabs* function returns the absolute value for a floating-point number, as shown here:

```
#include <math.h>

float fabs(float expression);
```

The following program, *showfabs.c*, illustrates how to use the *fabs* function:

```
#include <stdio.h>
#include <math.h>

void main(void)
  {
    float value;

    for (value = -1.0; value <= 1.0; value += 0.1)
      printf("Value %f fabs %f\n", value, fabs(value));
  }
```

Note: Many C compilers also provide the function *fabsl*, which returns the absolute value for an expression of type *long double*.

336 USING THE FLOATING-POINT REMAINDER

In Tip 82 you learned how to use C's modulo operator (%) to get the remainder of an integer division. Depending on your program, there may be times when you want to know the remainder of a floating-point division. In such cases, your programs can use C's *fmod* function to divide two floating-point values. The *fmod* function will return the remainder as a floating-point value, as shown here:

```
#include <math.h>

double fmod(double x, double y);
```

As an example, if you invoke *fmod* with the values 10.0 and 3.0, *fmod* will return the value 1.0 (10 divided by 3 is 3 remainder 1). The following program, *showfmod.c*, illustrates how to use the *fmod* function:

```
#include <stdio.h>
#include <math.h>

void main(void)
  {
    double numerator = 10.0;
    double denominator = 3.0;

    printf("fmod(10, 3) is %f\n", fmod(numerator, denominator));
  }
```

When you compile and execute the *showfmod.c* program, your screen will display the following output:

```
fmod(10, 3) is 1.000000
C:\>
```

Note: Many C compilers also provide the function *fmodl*, which returns the fractional remainder of a *long double* value.

337 USING A FLOATING-POINT VALUE'S MANTISSA AND EXPONENT

When your programs work with floating-point values, the computer stores the values using a mantissa (whose value is between 0.5 and 1.0) and an exponent, as shown in Figure 337.

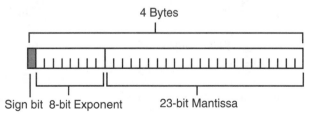

Figure 337 The computer stores floating-point values using a mantissa and exponent format.

To determine the stored value, the computer combines the mantissa and exponent, as shown here:

```
value = mantissa * (2 * exponent);
```

Usually, you do not need to be aware that the computer is using the mantissa and exponent. Depending on your program, however, there may be times when you want to know the mantissa and exponent values. For such cases, C provides the *frexp* function, which returns the mantissa and assigns the exponent to the variable *exponent*, which the calling function must pass to the *frexp* function by reference:

```
#include <math.h>

double frexp(double value, int *exponent);
```

The following program, *frexp.c*, illustrates how to use the *frexp* function:

```c
#include <stdio.h>
#include <math.h>

void main(void)
  {
    double value = 1.2345;
    double mantissa;
    int exponent;

    mantissa = frexp(value, &exponent);
    printf("Mantissa %f Exponent %d Value %f\n",
       mantissa, exponent, mantissa * pow(2.0, 1.0 * exponent));
  }
```

When you compile and execute the *frexp.c* program, your screen will display the following output:

```
Mantissa 0.617250 Exponent 1 Value 1.234500
c:\
```

Note: *Many C compilers also provide the function **frexpl**, which returns the exponent and mantissa of a **long double** value.*

CALCULATING THE RESULT OF X * 2E   338

In Tip 334 you learned how to use C's *exp* function to obtain the result ex. Depending on your programs, there may be times when you must calculate $x * 2e$. In such situations, you can use C's *ldexp* function, as shown here:

```
#include <math.h>

double ldexp(double value, int exponent);
```

The following program, *ldexp.c*, illustrates how to use the *ldexp* function:

```c
#include <stdio.h>
#include <math.h>

void main(void)
  {
    printf("3 *\' 2 raised to the 4\' is %f\n", ldexp(3.0, 4));
  }
```

When you compile and execute the *ldexp.c* program, your screen will display the following output:

```
3 * 2 raised to the 4 is 48.000000
C:\>
```

Note: *Many C compilers also provide the function **ldexpl** to support **long double** values.*

CALCULATING THE NATURAL LOGARITHM   339

The natural logarithm of a number is the power to which *e* must be raised to equal the given number. To help your programs determine the "natural log," C provides the *log* function, which returns the natural logarithm of a floating-point value:

```
#include <math.h>

double log(double value);
```

If the *value* parameter is less than 0, log will set the global variable *errno* to *ERANGE* and return the value *HUGE_VAL* (or *_LHUGE_VAL* for *logl*). The following program, *show_log.c*, illustrates how to use the *log* function:

```
#include <stdio.h>
#include <math.h>

void main(void)
  {
    printf("Natural log of 256.0 is %f\n", log(256.0));
  }
```

When you compile and execute the *show_log.c* program, your screen will display the following output:

```
Natural log of 256.0 is 5.545177
C:\>
```

Note: *Many C compilers also provide the function **logl**, which returns the natural logarithm of a **long double** expression.*

340 CALCULATING THE RESULT OF LOG10x

In Tip 339 you learned how to use C's *log* function to calculate a natural logarithm. As your programs perform mathematical operations, there may be times when you must determine the log to the base 10 of a value (commonly written as *log10x*). For such cases, C provides the *log10* function, as shown here:

```
#include <math.h>

double log10(double value);
```

If the *value* parameter is 0, *log10* will set the global variable *errno* to *EDOM* and return the value *HUGE_VAL* (or *_LHUGE_VAL* for *log10l*). The following program, *log_10.c*, illustrates how to use C's *log10* function:

```
#include <stdio.h>
#include <math.h>

void main(void)
  {
    printf("Log10 of 100 is %f\n", log10(100.0));
    printf("Log10 of 10000 is %f\n", log10(10000.0));
  }
```

When you compile and execute the *log_10.c* program, your screen will display the following output:

```
Log10 of 100 is 2.000000
Log10 of 10000 is 4.000000
C:\>
```

Note: *Many C compilers also provide the function **log10l**, which supports **long double** values.*

341 DETERMINING MAXIMUM AND MINIMUM VALUES

When your programs compare two numbers, there will be times when you will want to know the minimum or maximum of two values. For such cases, the header file *stdlib.h* provides the macros *min* and *max*. The following program, *min_max.c*, illustrates how to use these two macros:

```
#include <stdio.h>
#include <stdlib.h>

void main(void)
  {
    printf("Maximum of %f and %f is %f\n", 10.0, 25.0, max(10.0, 25.0));
    printf("Minimum of %f and %f is %f\n", 10.0, 25.0, min(10.0, 25.0));
  }
```

To better understand these two macros, consider the following implementations:

```
#define max(x,y)   (((x) > (y)) ? (x) : (y))
#define min(x,y)   (((x) < (y)) ? (x) : (y))
```

BREAKING A DOUBLE INTO ITS WHOLE AND REAL COMPONENTS   342

As you have learned, a floating-point value consists of two parts, an integer portion and a fractional portion. For example, given the number 12.345, the value 12 is the integer portion and 0.345 is the fractional portion. Depending on your program, there may be times when you will want to work with both a value's integer and fractional components, or with each component individually. For such cases, C provides the *modf* function, as shown here:

```
#include <math.h>

double modf(double value, double *integer_part);
```

The *modf* function returns the value's fractional portion and assigns the integer portion to the specified variable. The following program, *int_frac.c*, illustrates how to use the *modf* function:

```
#include <stdio.h>
#include <math.h>

void main(void)
  {
    double value = 1.2345;
    double int_part;
    double fraction;

    fraction = modf(value, &int_part);
    printf("Value %f Integer part %f Fraction %f\n", value, int_part, fraction);
  }
```

When you compile and execute the *int_frac.c* program, your screen will display the following output:

```
Value 1.234500 Integer part 1.000000 Fraction 0.234500
C:\>
```

*Note: Many C compilers also provide the function **modfl**, which returns the integer and fractional parts of a **long double** expression.*

CALCULATING THE RESULT OF X   343

Raising a value to a given power is one of the most common mathematical operations your programs will perform. C provides the function *pow*, which returns the result of a value raised to a given power, as shown here:

```
#include <math.h>

double pow(double value, double power);
```

If evaluating the *value* raised to the given *power* results in overflow, *pow* will assign the global variable *errno* the value *ERANGE* and return *HUGE_VAL* (or *_LHUGE_VAL* for *powl*) to the calling function. If the calling function passes a *value* parameter to *pow* which is less than 0 and the power is not a whole number, then *pow* will set the global variable *errno* to *EDOM*. The following program, *show_pow.c*, illustrates how to use C's *pow* function:

```
#include <stdio.h>
#include <math.h>

void main(void)
  {
    int power;

    for (power = -2; power <= 2; power++)
      printf("10 raised to %d is %f\n", power, pow(10.0, power));
  }
```

When you compile and execute the *show_pow.c* program, your screen will display the following output:

```
10 raised to -2 is 0.010000
10 raised to -1 is 0.100000
10 raised to 0 is 1.000000
10 raised to 1 is 10.000000
10 raised to 2 is 100.000000
C:\>
```

Note: *Many C compilers also provide the function* ***powl****, which supports values of type* ***long double****. Likewise, if you are working with complex values, the header file* ***complex.h*** *defines a function prototype for* ***pow*** *that works with complex numbers.*

344 CALCULATING THE RESULT OF 10^x

In Tip 343 you learned how to use the *pow* function to determine the result of a value raised to a given power. There may be times when your programs must calculate the result of 10^X. In such cases, you can use the *pow* function or, if your compiler supports it (as the *Turbo C++ Lite* compiler does), you can use C's *pow10*, as shown here:

```
#include <math.h>

double pow10(int power);
```

The following program, *pow10.c*, illustrates how to use the *pow10* function:

```
#include <stdio.h>
#include <math.h>

void main(void)
  {
    printf("10 raised to -1 is %f\n", pow10(-1));
    printf("10 raised to 0 is %f\n", pow10(0));
    printf("10 raised to 1 is %f\n", pow10(1));
    printf("10 raised to 2 is %f\n", pow10(2));
  }
```

When you compile and execute the *pow10.c* program, your screen will display the following output:

```
10 raised to -1 is 0.100000
10 raised to 0 is 1.000000
10 raised to 1 is 10.000000
10 raised to 2 is 100.000000
C:\>
```

Note: *Many C compilers also provide the function* ***pow10l****, which supports values of type* ***long double****.*

345 GENERATING A RANDOM NUMBER

Depending on your program, there may be times when you must generate one or more random numbers. For such cases, C provides two functions, *rand* and *random*, which both return integer random numbers, as shown here:

```
#include <stdlib.h>

int rand(void);
int random(int ceiling);
```

The first function, *rand*, returns an whole, random number in the range 0 through *RAND_MAX* (defined in *stdlib.h*). The second function, *random*, returns a random number in the range through *ceiling*, where *ceiling* is the maximum random number size, which the calling function passes to the *random* function. The following program, *random.c*, illustrates how to use both random-number generators:

```
#include <stdio.h>
#include <stdlib.h>

void main(void)
  {
    int i;
```

```
      printf("Values from rand\n");
      for (i = 0; i < 100; i++)
        printf("%d ", rand());

      printf("Values from random(100))\n");
      for (i = 0; i < 100; i++)
        printf("%d ", random(100));
  }
```

MAPPING RANDOM VALUES TO A SPECIFIC RANGE

In Tip 345, you learned that the C functions *rand* and *random* return random numbers. When your program generates random numbers, there may be times when your program must map the values to a specific range. If you are working with integer values, you can use the *random* function by using a parameter to specify the highest value in the range of random numbers. If you are working with floating-point values, however, such as values in the range 0.0 through 1.0, you can divide the number by a constant to derive a random floating-point number. To map a random integer series to a floating-point number series, simply divide the random number by the random number's upper bound, as shown here:

```
random(100)/100
```

The previous example yields a random value in the range 0.01-0.99. If your program requires more digits in the random floating-point number, you can generate a random number through 1000 and divide by 1000, as shown here:

```
random(1000)/1000
```

The previous example yields a random value in the range 0.001-0.999. If your program requires more precision in your random numbers, simply increase the maximum random integer size and the constant by which you divide *random's* result. The following program, *map_rand.c*, maps random numbers to the range 0.0 through 1.0 and integer values to the range –5 though 5:

```
#include <stdio.h>
#include <stdlib.h>

void main(void)
  {
    int i;

    printf("Values from random\n");
    for (i = 0; i < 10; i++)
      printf("%f\n", random(100)/100);
    printf("Values from random(-5) to random(5)\n");
    for (i = 0; i < 100; i++)
      printf("%d\n", random(10)-5);
  }
```

SEEDING THE RANDOM NUMBER GENERATOR

Tip 345 presented C's *rand* and *random* functions that you will use within your programs to generate random numbers. When you work with random numbers, there will be times when you will want to control the series of numbers that the random number generator creates (so that you can test your program's processing with the same set of numbers). There will also be times when you will want the generator to create actual numbers at random. The process of assigning the random number generator's starting number is called *seeding the generator*. To help you seed the random number generators, C provides two functions, *randomize* and *srand*, as shown here:

```
#include <stdlib.h>

void randomize(void);
void srand(unsigned seed);
```

The first function, *randomize*, uses the PC's clock to produce a random seed. On the other hand, the second function, *srand*, lets you specify the starting value of the random number generator. Your programs can use *srand* to control the range of numbers the random number generator creates. The following program, *randseed.c*, illustrates how to use the *srand* and *randomize* functions:

```c
#include <stdio.h>
#include <time.h>
#include <stdlib.h>

void main(void)
  {
    int i;

    srand(100);
    printf("Values from rand\n");
    for (i = 0; i < 5; i++)
      printf("%d ", rand());
    printf("\nSame 5 numbers\n");
    srand(100);
    for (i = 0; i < 5; i++)
      printf("%d ", rand());
    randomize();
    printf("\nDifferent 5 numbers\n");
    for (i = 0; i < 5; i++)
      printf("%d ", rand());
  }
```

348 CALCULATING A VALUE'S SQUARE ROOT

When your programs calculate mathematical expressions, they often must perform square root operations. To help your programs perform square root operations, C provides the *sqrt* function, as shown here:

```c
#include <math.h>

double sqrt(double value);
```

The *sqrt* function only works with positive values. If your program invokes *sqrt* with a negative value, *sqrt* will set the global variable *errno* to *EDOM*. The following program, *sqrt.c*, illustrates how to use the *sqrt* function:

```c
#include <stdio.h>
#include <math.h>

void main(void)
  {
    double value;

    for (value = 0.0; value < 10.0; value += 0.1)
      printf("Value %f sqrt %f\n", value, sqrt(value));
  }
```

Note: *Many C compilers also provide the function **sqrtl**, which returns the square root of a **long double** value.*

349 CREATING A CUSTOMIZED MATH ERROR HANDLER

Several functions presented in this section detect range and overflow errors. By default, when such errors occur, the functions invoke a special function named *matherr*, which performs additional processing, such as assigning the global variable *errno* a specific error number. As it turns out, if your programs define their own *matherr* function, the C math routines will invoke your custom handler. When the math routines invoke your *matherr* function, they will pass to *matherr* a pointer to a variable of type *exception*, as shown here:

```c
struct exception
  {
    int type;
    char *function;
    double arg1, arg2, retval;
  };
```

The *type* member contains a constant that describe the error's type. Table 349 describes the error values.

Error Value	Meaning
DOMAIN	An argument is not in the domain of values the function supports
OVERFLOW	An argument produces a result that overflows the resulting type
SING	An argument produces a result in a singularity
TLOSS	An argument produces a result in which all the digits of precision are lost
UNDERFLOW	An argument produces a result that overflows the resulting type

Table 349 *C constants that describe mathematical errors.*

The *function* member contains the name of the routine that experienced the error. The members *arg1* and *arg2* contain the parameters that the function experiencing the error passed to *matherr*, while *retval* contains a default return value (which you can assign). If *matherr* cannot determine the specific cause of the error, *matherr* will display a generic error message on the screen. The following program, *matherr.c*, illustrates how to use a custom error handler:

```c
#include <stdio.h>
#include <math.h>

void main(void)
 {
   printf("Sqrt of -1 is %f\n", sqrt(-1.0));
 }

int matherr(struct exception *error)
 {
   switch (error->type)
    {
      case DOMAIN:      printf("Domain error\n");
                        break;
      case PLOSS:       printf("Partial precision loss error\n");
                        break;
      case OVERFLOW:    printf("Overflow error\n");
                        break;
      case SING:        printf("Error in singularity\n");
                        break;
      case TLOSS:       printf("Total precision loss error\n");
                        break;
      case UNDERFLOW:   printf("Underflow error\n");
                        break;
    };
   printf("Error occurred in %s values %f\n", error->name, error->arg1);
   error->retval = 1;
   return(1);
 }
```

Note: *The* **matherr** *function only catches domain and overflow errors. To detect divide-by-zero errors, use* **signal**. *Many C compilers also support the function* **matherrl**, *which supports arguments of type* **long double**.

DETERMINING THE CURRENT DISK DRIVE
350

If your programs work in the DOS environment, there will be many times when they must determine the current disk drive. In such cases, your programs can use the *getdisk* function, as shown here:

```c
#include <dir.h>

int getdisk(void);
```

The function returns a disk drive number, where 1 is drive A, 2 is drive B, and so on. The following program, *getdrive.c*, uses the *_dos_getdrive* function to display the current disk drive letter:

```c
#include <stdio.h>
#include <dir.h>
```

```
void main(void)
  {
    printf("The current drive is %c\n", getdisk() + 'A');
  }
```

Note: *The companion CD-ROM that accompanies this book includes the* **win_getd.c** *file, which performs the same task as the* **getdrive.c** *program but works only under Windows 95 or Windows NT.*

351 SELECTING THE CURRENT DRIVE

In Tip 350 you learned how to use the *getdisk* function to determine the current disk drive in a DOS-based environment. Just as there may be times when your programs must determine the current disk drive, at other times your programs must select a specific disk drive. In such cases, your programs can use the function *setdisk*, as shown here:

```
#include <dir.h>

int setdisk(int drive);
```

The *drive* parameter is an integer value that specifies the desired drive, where 0 is drive A, 1 is drive B, and so on. The function returns the number of disk drives present in the system. The following program, *select_c.c*, uses the *setdisk* function to select drive C as the current drive. The program also displays a count of the number of available drives (as set by the LASTDRIVE entry in the *config.sys* file):

```
#include <stdio.h>
#include <dir.h>

void main(void)
  {
    int drive_count;

    drive_count = setdisk(3);
    printf("The number of available drives is %d\n", drive_count);
  }
```

Note: *The companion CD-ROM that accompanies this book includes the* **win_setd.cpp** *file, which performs the same task as the* **select_c.c** *program, but works only under Windows 95 or Windows NT.*

352 DETERMINING AVAILABLE DISK SPACE

When your programs store considerable amounts of information onto a disk—whether the disk is a floppy disk, hard disk, or other type—each program should keep track of the available disk space to reduce the possibility of running out of room during a critical disk operation. If you are working in a DOS-based system, your programs can use the *getdfree* function. The *getdfree* function returns a structure of type *dfree*, as shown here:

```
struct dfree
  {
    unsigned df_avail;              // Available clusters
    unsigned df_total;              // Total clusters
    unsigned df_bsec;              // Bytes per sector
    unsigned df_sclus;            // Sectors per cluster
  };
```

The format of the *getdfree* function is as follows:

```
#include <dos.h>

void getdfree(unsigned char drive, struct dfree *dtable);
```

The *drive* parameter specifies the desired drive, where 1 is drive A, 2 is drive B, and so on. The following program, *diskfree.c*, uses the *getdfree* function to obtain specifics about the current disk drive:

```
#include <stdio.h>
#include <dos.h>
```

```
void main(void)
{
  struct dfree diskinfo;
  long disk_space;

  getdfree(3, &diskinfo);
  disk_space = (long) diskinfo.df_avail *
               (long) diskinfo.df_bsec *
               (long) diskinfo.df_sclus;
  printf("Available disk space %ld\n", disk_space);
}
```

Note: *The companion CD-ROM that accompanies this book includes the* **win_free.cpp** *file, which performs the same task as the* **diskfree.c** *program, but works only under Windows 95 or Windows NT.*

WATCHING OUT FOR DBLSPACE

Some Tips in this section show you ways to perform absolute disk read and write operations that work with a disk's sectors. Before your programs perform low-level disk I/O operations, make sure that the disk you are going to read is not a compressed disk with contents that *dblspace* or another third-party disk utility has previously compressed. Compressed disks store information on a sector-by-sector basis. If you write a compressed disk sector, you run considerable risk of corrupting the compressed disk—losing the information it contains. As a rule, most programs do not need to perform such low-level disk read and write operations. If you are writing a disk utility program such as *undelete*, make sure that you know how to test for and work with compressed disks before you begin.

READING FILE ALLOCATION TABLE INFORMATION

If you are working in a DOS-based system, the file allocation table tracks which parts of your disk are in use, which parts are damaged, and which parts are available (for file and program storage). If your programs perform low-level disk operations, there may be times when you must know information such as the disk's type, bytes per sector, number sectors per cluster, and the number of clusters on the disk. In such cases, your programs can use the *getfat* or *getfatd* functions, as shown here:

```
#include <dos.h>

void getfat(unsigned char drive, struct fatinfo *fat);
void getfatd(struct fatinfo *fat);
```

The *getfat* function lets you specify the desired drive, whereas *getfatd* returns the information for the current drive. To specify a disk drive letter to the *getfat* function, specify a number value where 1 is drive A, 2 is drive B, 3 is drive C, and so on. The *getfat* and *getfatd* functions assign the information to a structure of type *fatinfo*, as shown here:

```
struct fatinfo
{
  char fi_sclus;        // sectors per cluster
  char fi_fatid;        // disk type
  unsigned fi_nclus;    // clusters per disk
  int fi_bysec;         // bytes per sector
};
```

The following program, *getfatd.c*, uses the *getfatd* function to display information about the current disk drive:

```
#include <stdio.h>
#include <dos.h>

void main(void)
{
  struct fatinfo fat;

  getfatd(&fat);

  printf("Sectors per cluster %d\n", fat.fi_sclus);
  printf("Clusters per disk %u\n", fat.fi_nclus);
```

```
    printf("Bytes per cluster %d\n", fat.fi_bysec);
    printf("Disk type %x\n", fat.fi_fatid & 0xFF);
}
```

Note: *If your computer is running Windows NT and you have partitioned the drive as an NT File System (NTFS) drive, there is no FAT table for you to access. To learn more about NTFS, visit the Yale Computer Science Department's Web site at* **http://pclt.cis.yale.edu/pclt/BOOT/IFS.HTM.**

355 UNDERSTANDING THE DISK ID

In Tip 354 you used the *getfat* and *getfatd* functions to get information about the current disk drive. As you found, these functions returned a byte called the *fi_fatid*, which contains a representation of the DOS disk ID. Table 355 specifies the possible values for *fi_fatid*.

Value (Hex)	Disk Type
F0H	3 1/2 inch 1.44Mb or 2.88Mb
	Zip Disk
F8H	Hard Disk
	CD-ROM Drive
F9H	3 1/2 inch 720Kb or 5 1/4 inch 1.2Mb
FAH	5 1/4 inch 320Kb
FCH	5 1/4 inch 180Kb
FDH	5 1/4 inch 360Kb
FEH	5 1/4 inch 160Kb
FFH	5 1/4 inch 320Kb

Table 355 Disk ID values DOS returns.

Note: *The companion CD-ROM that accompanies this book includes the* **win_did.cpp** *file, which lists disk IDs under Windows 95 or Windows NT and outputs them to the screen.*

356 PERFORMING AN ABSOLUTE SECTOR READ OR WRITE

If you work in a DOS-based environment, DOS lets you perform absolute disk read and write operations at the sector level. Normally, your programs use the DOS services to perform these operations. However, to make these operations easier to perform, many C compilers provide the *absread* and *abswrite* functions, as shown here:

```
#include <dos.h>

int absread(int drive, int number_of_sectors, long starting_sector, void *buffer);
int abswrite(int drive, int number_of_sectors, long starting_sector, void *buffer);
```

The *drive* parameter specifies the disk drive you want to read, where 0 is drive A, 1 is drive B, and so on. The *number_of_sectors* parameter specifies the number of sectors you want to read or write, beginning at the sector the *starting_sector* parameter specifies. Finally, the *buffer* parameter is a pointer to the buffer into which information is read or from which the output is written. If the functions succeed, they return the value 0. If an error occurs, the functions return the value –1. The following program, *chk_disk.c*, reads every sector on drive C. If the program experiences errors reading a sector, it will display the sector number:

```
#include <stdio.h>
#include <dos.h>
#include <alloc.h>

void main(void)
  {
```

```
struct fatinfo fat;
long sector, total_sectors;
void *buffer;

getfat(3, &fat);
total_sectors = fat.fi_nclus * fat.fi_sclus;
if ((buffer = malloc(fat.fi_bysec)) == NULL)
  printf("Error allocating sector buffer\n");
else
   for (sector = 0; sector < total_sectors; sector++)
     if (absread(2, 1, sector, buffer) == -1)
      {
        printf("\n\007Error reading sector %ld press Enter\n", sector);
        getchar();
      }
     else
        printf("Reading sector %ld\r", sector);
}
```

Note: While you can perform absolute sector read and writes in Windows, the way Windows writes information to the disk makes absolute read and writes both dangerous and inconsistent. You should avoid absolute disk activities in Windows and process your disk reads and writes through the Windows Application Programming Interface (API).

PERFORMING BIOS-BASED DISK I/O 357

When your programs perform file operations, they use the DOS system services to manipulate files. The DOS services, in turn, call other DOS services to read and write logical disk sectors. To perform the actual disk I/O operations, the DOS services then call BIOS disk services. If you write disk utility programs, for example, your programs may need to perform low-level disk I/O operations. In such cases, your programs can use the *biosdisk* function, as shown here:

```
#include <bios.h>

int biosdisk(int operation, int drive, int head, int track, int sector,
  int sector_count, void *buffer);
```

The *drive* parameter specifies the drive number, where 0 is drive A, 1 is drive B, and so on. For a hard disk, 0x80 is the first hard drive, 0x81 is the second drive, and so on. The *head, track, sector,* and *sector_count* parameters specify the physical disk sectors that you want to read or write. The *buffer* parameter is a pointer to the buffer into which *biosdisk* reads the data or from which *biosdisk* writes the data. Finally, the *operation* parameter specifies the desired function. Table 357.1 lists the valid operations.

Operation	Function
0	Reset the disk system
1	Return the status of the last disk operation
2	Read the specified number of sectors
3	Write the specified number of sectors
4	Verify the specified number of sectors
5	Format the specified track—buffer contains a table of bad locations
6	Format the specified track, setting bad sectors
7	Format the drive beginning at the specified track
8	Return the drive parameters in the first four bytes of buffer
9	Initialize the drive
10	Perform a long read—512 sector bytes plus four extra
11	Perform a long write—512 sector bytes plus four extra

*Table 357.1 Valid **biosdisk** operations. (continued on following page)*

Operation	Function
12	Perform a disk seek
13	Alternate disk reset
14	Read sector buffer
15	Write sector buffer
16	Test drive ready
17	Recalibrate the drive
18	Perform the controller RAM diagnostic
19	Perform the drive diagnostic
20	Perform the controller internal diagnostic

*Table 357.1 Valid **biosdisk** operations. (continued from previous page)*

If successful, the function returns the value 0. If an error occurs, the return value of the function specifies the error. Table 357.2 lists the error values.

Error Value	Error
0	Successful
1	Invalid command
2	Address mark not found
3	Write-protected disk
4	Sector not found
5	Hard disk reset failed
6	Disk change line
7	Drive parameter activity failed
8	DMA overrun
9	DMA across 64Kb boundary
10	Bad sector
11	Bad track
12	Unsupported track
16	CRC/ECC read error
17	CRC/ECC corrected data
32	Controller failure
64	Seek failed
128	No response
170	Hard disk not ready
187	Undefined error
204	Write fault
224	Status error
255	Sense operation failed

*Table 357.2 Error status values **biosdisk** returns.*

Note: *Many compilers also provide a function named **_bios_disk**, which performs processing identical to **biosdisk**, with the exception that your programs pass to the function a structure of type **diskinfo_t**, which contains the **drive**, **head**, **track**, **sector**, and **sector count** values.*

Note: *While you can use **bios_disk** to perform BIOS-based disk I/O under Windows, the methods Windows uses to write information to the disk makes BIOS-based disk I/O both dangerous and inconsistent. You should avoid BIOS-based disk I/O in Windows, and process your disk reads and writes through the Windows Application Programming Interface (API).*

TESTING A FLOPPY DRIVE'S READINESS

In Tip 357 you learned how to use the *biosdisk* function to invoke BIOS disk services. A useful operation the *biosdisk* function can perform is to test whether a floppy disk contains a disk and is ready for access. The following program, *test_a.c*, uses the *biosdisk* function to check the floppy disk:

```
#include <stdio.h>
#include <bios.h>

void main(void)
  {
    char buffer[8192];

    // Try reading head 1, track 1, sector 1
    if (biosdisk(2, 0, 1, 1, 1, 1, buffer))
      printf("Error accessing drive\n");
    else
      printf("Drive ready\n");
  }
```

Note: *The companion CD-ROM that accompanies this book includes the **win_a.cpp** file, which performs the same task as the **test_a.c** program, but works only under Windows 95 or Windows NT.*

OPENING A FILE USING FOPEN

Many C programs you create will store and retrieve information in a file. Before your programs can read information from or write information to a file, the program must open the file. The *fopen* function lets your programs open a file. The format of *fopen* is as follows:

```
#include <stdio.h>

FILE *fopen(const char *filename, const char *mode);
```

The *filename* parameter is a character string that contains the name of the desired file, such as "*c:\datafile.dat*". The *mode* parameter specifies how you want to use the file—to read, write, or append. Table 359 describes the mode values *fopen* supports.

Mode	Meaning
a	Opens the file for append operations—if the file does not exist, the operating system creates the file
r	Opens an existing file for read operations
w	Opens a new file for output—if a file with the same name exists, the operating system overwrites the file
r+	Opens an existing file for reading and writing
w+	Opens a new file for reading and writing—if a file with the same name exists, the operating system overwrites the file
a+	Opens a file for append and read operations—if the file does not exist, the operating system creates the file

*Table 359 Mode values **fopen** supports.*

The *fopen* function returns a pointer (called a *file pointer*) to a structure of type *FILE* that the header file *stdio.h* defines. Your program will use the file pointer for its input and output operations. If the *fopen* function cannot open the specified file, it returns the value *NULL*. Your programs should always test *fopen's* return value to make sure it successfully opened the file, as shown here:

```
if ((fp = fopen("FILENAME.EXT", "r")) != NULL)
  {
    // File successfully opened
  }
```

```
    else
      {
        // Error opening the file
      }
```

Within your program, you must declare the file pointer variable as follows:

```
void main(void)
   {
        FILE *fp;   // Pointer to a structure of type FILE
```

Many programs open one file for input and another for output. In such cases, you would declare two file pointers, as shown here:

```
FILE *input, *output;
```

Many Tips in this section use *fopen* to open a file for read, write, or append operations.

360 UNDERSTANDING THE FILE STRUCTURE

As you have learned, when your programs perform file input and output operations, they normally declare file pointers using the *FILE* structure, as shown here:

```
FILE *input, *output;
```

If you examine the header file *stdio.h*, you will find the definition of the *FILE* structure. In the case of *Turbo C++ Lite*, the structure takes the following form:

```
typedef struct
   {
      short level;              // fill/empty level of buffer
      unsigned flags;           // File status flags
      char fd;                  // File descriptor
      unsigned char hold;       // Ungetc char if no buffer
      short bsize;              // Buffer size
      unsigned char *buffer;    // Data transfer buffer
      unsigned char *curp;      // Current active pointer
      unsigned istemp;          // Temporary file indicator
      short token;              // Used for validity checking
   } FILE;                      // This is the FILE object
```

The *FILE* structure contains the low-level *file descriptor* the operating system uses to access the file, the file's buffer size and location, the character buffer *unget* uses, a flag that indicates whether the file is a temporary file, and other flag variables. In addition, the *FILE* structure stores the file pointer that keeps track of your current location within the file.

If you are working in the DOS environment, most compilers define a fixed size array (usually 20) of file pointers that hold the information for each file your program opens. If your program must open more than 20 files, you must refer to the documentation that accompanied your compiler for the steps you must perform to change the file pointer array size.

361 CLOSING AN OPEN FILE

Just as your programs must open a file before they use it, your programs should also close the file when they no longer need it. Closing a file directs the operating system to flush all the disk buffers associated with the file and to free up system resources the file consumed, such as the file pointer data. The C *fclose* function closes the file associated with the specified file pointer, as shown here:

```
#include <stdio.h>

int fclose(FILE *file_pointer);
```

If *fclose* is successful, it will return the value 0. If an error occurs, *fclose* returns the constant *EOF*, as shown here:

```
if (fclose(fp) == EOF)
  printf("Error closing the data file\n");
```

As you examine C programs, you will find that most programs do not test *fopen*'s return status value, as shown here:

```
fclose(fp);
```

In most cases, should a file close operation experience an error, the program can do very little to correct the situation. However, if you are working with critical data files, you should display an error message to the user so the user can examine the file's contents.

Note: *If you do not invoke the* **fclose** *function, C will close your open files when the program ends.*

READING AND WRITING FILE INFORMATION ONE CHARACTER AT A TIME 362

When your programs perform file input and output operations, your programs can read and write data one character at a time or one line at a time. For character input and output operations, your programs can use the *fgetc* and *fputc* functions, whose formats are shown here:

```
#include <stdio.h>

int fgetc(FILE *input_pointer);
int fputc(int character, FILE *output_pointer);
```

The *fgetc* function reads the current character from the specified input file. If the file pointer has reached the end of the file, *fgetc* returns the constant *EOF*. The *fputc* function writes a character to the current file pointer location within the specified output file. If an error occurs, *fputc* returns the constant *EOF*. The following program, *confcopy.c*, uses *fgetc* and *fputc* to copy the contents of the root directory file *config.sys* to a file named *config.tst*:

```
#include <stdio.h>

void main(void)
  {
    FILE *input, *output;
    int letter;

    if ((input = fopen("\\CONFIG.SYS", "r")) == NULL)
      printf("Error opening \\CONFIG.SYS\n");
    else if ((output = fopen("\\CONFIG.TST", "w")) == NULL)
      printf("Error opening \\CONFIG.TST\n");
    else
      {
        // Read and write each character in the file
        while ((letter = fgetc(input)) != EOF)
          fputc(letter, output);
        fclose(input);        // Close the input file
        fclose(output);       // Close the output file
      }
  }
```

UNDERSTANDING THE FILE POINTER'S POSITION POINTER 363

Tip 360 presented the *FILE* structure. As you learned, one of the structure's fields holds a *position pointer* to the current location within the file. When you first open a file for read or write operations, the operating system sets the position pointer to the start of the file. Each time you read or write a character, the position pointer advances one character. If you read a line of text from the file, the position pointer advances to the start of the next line. Using the position pointer, the file input and output functions can always keep track of the current location within the file. When you open a file in append mode, the operating system sets the position pointer to the very end of the file. In later Tips you will learn how to change the position pointer to specific file locations using the *fseek* and *fsetpos* functions. Table 363 specifies the location at which *fopen* places the position pointer when you open the file in read, write, and append modes.

Open Mode	File Pointer Position
a	Immediately after the last character in the file
r	At the start of the file
w	At the start of the file

*Table 363 The file position pointer settings that result from a call to **fopen**.*

364 DETERMINING THE CURRENT FILE POSITION

In Tip 363 you learned how C tracks the current position in files open for input or output operations. Depending on your program, there may be times when you must determine the position pointer's value. In such cases, your programs can use the *ftell* function, as shown here:

```
#include <stdio.h>
long int ftell(FILE *file_pointer);
```

The *ftell* function returns a long integer value that specifies the byte offset of the current position in the specified file. The following program, *show_pos.c*, uses the *ftell* to display position pointer information. The program begins by opening the root directory file *config.sys* in read mode. The program then uses *ftell* to display the current position. Next, the program reads and displays the file's contents. After finding the end of the file, the program again uses *ftell* to display the current position, as shown here:

```
#include <stdio.h>

void main(void)
 {
   FILE *input;
   int letter;

   if ((input = fopen("\\CONFIG.SYS", "r")) == NULL)
     printf("Error opening \\CONFIG.SYS\n");
   else
     {
       printf("Current position is byte %d\n\n", ftell(input));
         // Read and write each character in the file
       while ((letter = fgetc(input)) != EOF)
         fputc(letter, stdout);
       printf("\nCurrent position is byte %d\n", ftell(input));
       fclose(input);       // Close the input file
     }
 }
```

365 UNDERSTANDING FILE STREAMS

Many books and magazines refer to C's file pointers as *pointers to file streams*. Unlike many other programming languages, C does not assume that files contain information in a specific format. Instead, C considers all files as nothing more than a collection of bytes. As you read a file, you read one byte after another, in other words, a *stream* of bytes. Your programs or functions, such as *fgets*, are left to interpret the bytes. For example, *fgets* considers the linefeed character as the end of one line and the start of another. The *fgets* function makes this character interpretation by itself. That is, C itself does not interpret the bytes. As you write programs and functions that manipulate files, think of the files as nothing more than a collection of bytes.

366 UNDERSTANDING FILE TRANSLATIONS

The C file manipulation functions, such as *fgets* and *fputs*, can interpret files in one of two ways: *text* and *binary* mode. By default, the *fgets* and *fputs* functions use text mode. In text mode, functions such as *fputs*, which write information to a file, convert the linefeed character to a carriage return linefeed combination. During an input operation, functions such as *fgets* convert the carriage return linefeed combination to a single linefeed character. In binary mode, on the other hand, the functions do not perform these character translations. To help you determine the current translation mode, many DOS- and Windows-based compilers provide the global variable *_fmode*, which contains one of the values listed in Table 366.

Constant	Description
O_TEXT	Text mode translations
O_BINARY	Binary mode translations

Table 366 The constant values for _fmode.

By default, the value of *_fmode* under both DOS and Windows is *O_TEXT*. The following program, *fmode.c*, displays the current value of the *_fmode* variable:

```
#include <stdio.h>
#include <fcntl.h>   // Contains the _fmode declaration

void main(void)
 {
   if (_fmode == O_TEXT)
     printf("Text mode translations\n");
   else
     printf("Binary mode translations\n");
 }
```

UNDERSTANDING THE CONFIG.SYS FILES= ENTRY   367

If you are working in a DOS-based environment, the FILES entry in the *config.sys* file specifies the number of files that the system can open at one time (in a Windows-based environment, Windows limits the number of open files based on the system's available memory, disk space, other resource usage, and so on). As briefly discussed in the "Files, Directories, and Disks" section of this book, DOS uses the first five file handles for *stdin, stdout, stderr, stdaux,* and *stdprn*. By default, DOS provides support for eight file handles. Because this number is too few for all but the simplest programs, most users increase the number of available handles to 20 or 30, as shown here:

```
FILES=30
```

The FILES entry defines the number of files DOS can open—not the number each program running under DOS can open. If you are running memory-resident programs, for example, the programs can have open files about which you are not aware. If you set the FILES entry to a large number of handles (DOS supports up to 255 handles), it does not mean that your C programs can open that many files. As it turns out, there are two problems with opening a large number of files within your C programs. First, most C compilers restrict the size of the file-pointer array to 20. Before you can open more than 20 files, you must change the array size. Second, as you will learn, DOS restricts the number of files a program can open to 20. Before you can open more than 20 files, you must use a DOS system service to request DOS to support more than 20 open files for the current program.

Note: *Tip 369 explains file handles.*

USING LOW-LEVEL AND HIGH-LEVEL FILE I/O   368

When your C programs work with files, they can perform two types of input and output operations: *low-level* and *high-level* file I/O. All the Tips presented to this point have used C's high-level (or stream-based) capabilities, such as *fopen, fgets,* and *fputs*. When you use C's high-level file I/O functions, they in turn, use operating system services that are based on *file handles*. The C run-time library provides low-level functions that your programs can use. Instead of working with a stream pointer, the low-level functions use *file descriptors*. Table 368 briefly describes several of C's most commonly used low-level functions.

Function Name	Purpose
close	Closes the file associated with the specified file handle, flushing the file's buffers
creat	Creates a file for output operations, returning a file handle
open	Opens an existing file for input or output, returning a file handle
read	Reads a specified number of bytes from the file associated with a given file handle
write	Writes a specified number of bytes to the file associated with a given handle

Table 368 *C's common low-level file functions.*

When you write your programs, your choice of using low-level or high-level functions depends upon your personal preference. However, keep in mind that most programmers have a better understanding of C's high-level file manipulation functions. As a result, if you use the high-level functions such as *fopen* and *fgets*, more programmers will readily understand your program code.

Note: *The Windows I/O section of this book discusses low-level and high-level file I/O under Windows in detail.*

369 UNDERSTANDING FILE HANDLES

As you know, the FILES entry in the *config.sys* file lets you specify the number of file handles DOS supports. In short, a *file handle* is an integer value that uniquely defines an open file. When you use C's low-level file I/O functions, you will declare your program's file handles as type *int*, as shown here:

```
int input_handle, output_handle;
```

The functions *open* and *creat* return file descriptors or the value –1 if the function cannot open the file:

```
int new_file, old_file;

new_file = creat("FILENAME.NEW", S_IWRITE); // Create a new file for output
old_file = open("FILENAME.OLD", O_RDONLY); // Open an existing file for reading
```

DOS assigns each file you open or create a unique file handle. The handle's value is actually an index into the process file table, within which DOS keeps track of the program's open files.

370 UNDERSTANDING THE PROCESS FILE TABLE

When you run a program in the DOS environment, DOS keeps track of the program's open files using a *process file table*. Within the program segment prefix, DOS stores a far pointer to a table that describes the program's open files. Actually, the table contains entries into a second table, the *system file table*, within which DOS tracks all open files. Figure 370 illustrates the relationship between the file handle, process file table, and system file table.

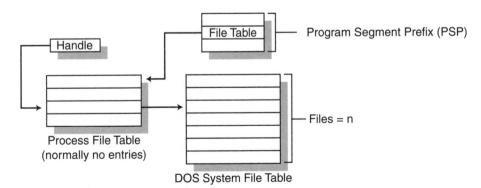

Figure 370 *The relationship between a file handle, process file table, and system file table.*

Under Windows, the Windows Task Manager maintains the list of all open processes, and Windows uses the DOS system file table to maintain the list of all open files. The companion CD-ROM that accompanies this book includes the program *Task_Man.cpp*, which lists all currently open programs on the system.

VIEWING THE PROCESS FILE TABLE ENTRIES 371

As Tip 370 describes, DOS keeps track of a program's open files using a process file table. At offset 18H, within the program segment prefix, is an array of integer values. The values that comprise this array specify indexes into the DOS system file table. If a value is not in use, the operating system sets it to FFH (decimal 255). The following program, *filetabl.c*, will display the values in the process file table. Remember, the table contains integer values that serve as indexes into the system file table:

```c
#include <stdio.h>
#include <dos.h>
#include <stdlib.h>

void main(void)
   {
     struct fcbs
       {
         char drive;
         char filename[8];
         char extension[3];
         int current_block;
         int record_size;
       };
     typedef struct fcbs fcb;
     struct program_segment_prefix
       {
         char near *int20;
         char near *next_paragraph_segment;
         char reserved_1;
         char dos_dispatcher[5];
         char far *terminate_vector;
         char far *ctrlc_vector;
         char far *critical_error_vector;
         char near *parent_psp;
         unsigned char file_table[20];
         char near *environment_block_segment;
         char far *stack_storage;
         int  handles_available;
         char far *file_table_address;
         char far *shares_previous_psp;
         char reserved_2[20];
         char dos_int21_retf[3];
         char reserved_3[9];
         fcb fcb1;
         fcb fcb2;
         char reserved_4[4];
         char command_tail[128];
       } far *psp;
     int i;

     psp = (struct program_segment_prefix far *) ((long) _psp << 16);
     for (i = 0; i < 20; i++)
       printf("Entry %d contains %x\n", i, psp->file_table[i]);
   }
```

When you compile and execute the *filetabl.c* program, you will find that the first five entries in the process file table are in use. These entries correspond to *stdin, stdout, stderr, stdaux,* and *stdprn*. Edit this program and open one or more files before displaying the file table entries, and you will find more entries within the process file table.

372 UNDERSTANDING THE SYSTEM FILE TABLE

File handles are index values into the process file table, which in turn points to the system file table. The system file table stores information about every file that either DOS, a device driver, a memory-resident program, or your program has open. Figure 372 illustrates the contents of the system file table.

00H	Far Pointer to Next Table
04H	Number of Entries in This Table
06H	Handles to This Entry
08H	File Open Mode
0AH	File Attribute
0BH	Device Local\Remote
0DH	Driver Header or DPB
12H	Starting Cluster
14H	Time Stamp
16H	Date Stamp
18H	File Size
1CH	Current Pointer Offset
20H	Relative Cluster
22H	Directory Entry Sector
26H	Directory Entry Offset
27H	Filename.Ext
34H	Reserved
44H	

Figure 372 *The contents of the DOS system file table.*

DOS actually divides the system table into two sections. The first section contains five entries. The second section provides enough space for the number of entries your FILES entry specifies in the *config.sys* file (minus five—the entries that reside in the table's first section).

373 DISPLAYING THE SYSTEM FILE TABLE

DOS stores information about every open file within the system file table. Using the DOS list of lists, discussed in the DOS and BIOS section of this book, the following program, *systable.c*, displays the system file table entries:

```c
#include <stdio.h>
#include <dos.h>
#include <stdlib.h>

void main(void)
  {
    union REGS inregs, outregs;
    struct SREGS segs;
    int i, j;
    int structure_size;
    struct SystemTableEntry
      {
        struct SystemTableEntry far *next; // Next SFT entry
        unsigned file_count;               // Files in table
        unsigned handle_count;             // Handles to this file
        unsigned open_mode;                // File open mode
        char file_attribute;               // Attribute byte
        unsigned local_remote;             // Bit 15 set means remote
        unsigned far *DPD;                 // Drive parameter block
        unsigned starting_cluster;
        unsigned time_stamp;
        unsigned date_stamp;
        long file_size;
        long current_offset;
        unsigned relative_cluster;
        long directory_sector_number;
```

```
        char directory_entry_offset;
        char filename_ext[11];    // No period, space padded
                                  // Ignore SHARE fields for example
    } far *table_ptr, far *file;
long far *system_table;

    // Get DOS version
inregs.x.ax = 0x3001;
intdos (&inregs, &outregs);
if (outregs.h.al < 3)
    {
        printf ("This program requires DOS version 3 or later\n");
        exit (1);
    }
else if (outregs.h.al == 3)
    structure_size = 0x35;
else if (outregs.h.al >= 4)
    structure_size = 0x3B;
    // Get the list of lists pointer
inregs.h.ah = 0x52;
intdosx (&inregs, &outregs, &segs);
    // The pointer to the system file table is at offset 4
system_table = MK_FP(segs.es, outregs.x.bx + 4);
table_ptr = (struct SystemTableEntry far *) *system_table;
do {
    printf ("%d entries in table\n", table_ptr->file_count);
    for (i = 0; i < table_ptr->file_count; i++)
      {
        file = MK_FP(FP_SEG(table_ptr), FP_OFF(table_ptr) +
          (i * structure_size));
        if (file->handle_count)
          {
            for (j = 0; j < 8; j++)
              if (file->filename_ext[j] != ' ')
                putchar(file->filename_ext[j]);
            else
              break;
            if (file->filename_ext[8] != ' ')
              putchar('.');
            for (j = 8; j < 11; j++)
              if (file->filename_ext[j] != ' ')
                putchar(file->filename_ext[j]);
            printf ("   %ld bytes %x attribute %d references\n",
              file->file_size, file->file_attribute,
              file->handle_count);
          }
      }
    table_ptr = table_ptr->next;
} while (FP_OFF(table_ptr) != 0xFFFF);
}
```

When you run the *systable.c* program from the DOS prompt, its output probably is not very exciting. However, if you have Windows available, start Windows and use the MSDOS icon to open a DOS window. From within the DOS window, run the *systable* program. You might also want to edit the program and use *fopen* to open one or more files before displaying the system file table contents.

DERIVING FILE HANDLES FROM STREAM POINTERS 374

Tip 360 presented the *FILE* structure defined in the header file *stdio.h*. You have learned that when you perform high-level file operations using *fopen* or *fgets*, you declare stream pointers in terms of the *FILE* structure, as shown here:

```
FILE *input, *output;
```

The C functions later convert the stream pointers to file handles to perform the actual I/O operation. To better understand the relationship between stream pointers and file handles, consider the following program, *handles.c,* which opens the root directory file *config.sys* and then displays the file descriptor for the file, as well as the predefined file handles *stdin, stdout, stderr, stdaux,* and *stdprn*:

```
#include <stdio.h>

void main(void)
  {
    FILE *input;

    if ((input = fopen("\\CONFIG.SYS", "r")) == NULL)
      printf("Error opening \\CONFIG.SYS\n");
    else
      {
        printf("Handle for CONFIG.SYS %d\n", input->fd);
        printf("Handle for stdin %d\n", stdin->fd);
        printf("Handle for stdout %d\n", stdout->fd);
        printf("Handle for stderr %d\n", stderr->fd);
        printf("Handle for stdaux %d\n", stdaux->fd);
        printf("Handle for stdprn %d\n", stdprn->fd);
        fclose(input);
      }
  }
```

When you compile and execute the *handles.c* program, your screen will display the handle values 0 through 5.

375 PERFORMING FORMATTED FILE OUTPUT

Several Tips in this section present ways that your programs can write output to a file. In many cases, your programs must perform formatted file output. For example, if you are creating an inventory report, you will want to line up columns, work with text and numbers, and so on. In this book's Getting Started section, you learned how to use the *printf* function to perform formatted I/O to the screen display. In a similar way, C provides the *fprintf* function, which uses format specifiers to write formatted file output, as shown here:

```
#include <stdio.h>

int fprintf(FILE *file_pointer, const char *format_specifier, [argument[,...]]);
```

The following program, *fprintf.c*, uses *fprintf* to write formatted output to a file named *fprintf.dat*:

```
#include <stdio.h>

void main(void)
  {
    FILE *fp;

    int pages = 800;
    float price = 49.95;

    if (fp = fopen("FPRINTF.DAT", "w"))
      {
        fprintf(fp, "Book Title: Jamsa\'s C/C++ Programmer\'s Bible\n");
        fprintf(fp, "Pages: %d\n", pages);
        fprintf(fp, "Price: $%5.2f\n", price);
        fclose(fp);
      }
    else
      printf("Error opening FPRINTF.DAT\n");
  }
```

376 RENAMING A FILE

As your programs work with files, there may be times when you must rename or move a file. For such cases, C provides the *rename* function. The format of the *rename* function is as follows:

```
#include <stdio.h>

int rename(const char *old_name, const char *new_name);
```

If *rename* successfully renames or moves a file, the function will return the value 0. If an error occurs, *rename* will return a non-zero value and assign to the global variable *errno* one of the error status values listed in Table 376.

Value	Meaning
EACCES	Access denied
ENOENT	File not found
EXDEV	Cannot move from one disk to another

Table 376 *The error status values for* **rename**.

The following program, *my_ren.c*, uses the *rename* function to create a program that can rename or move the file specified in the command line:

```
#include <stdio.h>

void main(int argc, char *argv[])
  {
  if (argc < 3)
    printf("Must specify a source and target filename\n");
  else if (rename(argv[1], argv[2]))
    printf("Error renaming file\n");
  }
```

Note: *Tip 1472 details how you will rename a file using the Windows API.*

DELETING A FILE

377

When your programs work with files, there will be many times when you must delete one or more files. In such cases, your programs can use C's *remove* function. The format of the *remove* function is as follows:

```
#include <stdio.h>

int remove(const char *filename);
```

If the function successfully removes the file, it returns the value 0. If an error occurs, *remove* returns the value –1 and assigns to the global value *errno* one of the values listed in Table 377.

Value	Meaning
EACCES	Access denied
ENOENT	File not found

Table 377 *The errors C's* **remove** *function returns.*

The following program, *my_del.c*, uses the *remove* function to delete all the files specified in the command line:

```
#include <stdio.h>

void main(int argc, char *argv[])
  {
    while (*++argv)
      if (remove(*argv))
        printf("Error removing %s\n", *argv);
  }
```

In addition to the *remove* function, most C compilers support the *unlink* function, which also deletes a file:

```
#include <io.h>

int unlink(const char *filename);
```

If *unlink* successfully deletes the file, it returns the value 0. If an error occurs, *unlink* returns the error status –1, assigning to the global variable *errno* the error status constants listed in Table 377. The following program, *unlink.c*, uses the *unlink* function to delete the files specified in the program's command line:

```
#include <stdio.h>

void main(int argc, char *argv[])
  {
    while (*++argv)
      if (unlink(*argv))
        printf("Error removing %s\n", *argv);
  }
```

Note: *Tip 1473 details how you will delete a file using the Windows API.*

378 DETERMINING HOW A PROGRAM CAN ACCESS A FILE

When your program works with files, there may be times when you must determine whether your program can access a specific file as required. The C function *access checks* whether a file exists as specified and whether you can open the file as required. The format of the *access* function is as follows:

```
#include <io.h>

int access(const char *filename, int access_mode);
```

The *access_mode* parameter specifies how your program needs to use the file, as shown in Table 378.1.

Value	Meaning
0	Checks if the file exists
2	Checks if the file can be written to
4	Checks if the file can be read
6	Checks if the program has read and write permission for the file

*Table 378.1 The values for the **access_mode** parameter.*

If the program can access the file as specified, *access* returns the value 0. If an error occurs, *access* returns the value −1 and assigns the global variable *errno* one of the error values listed in Table 378.2.

Value	Meaning
EACCES	Access denied
ENOENT	File not found

*Table 378.2 The error values for the **access** function.*

The following program, *access.c*, uses the *access* function to determine how your program can access the file specified in the program's command line:

```
#include <stdio.h>
#include <io.h>

void main (int argc, char *argv[])
  {
    int access_mode;

    access_mode = access(argv[1], 0);

    if (access_mode)
      printf("File %s does not exist\n");
    else
      {
        access_mode = access(argv[1], 2);
        if (access_mode)
          printf("File cannot be written\n");
        else
          printf("File can be written\n");
        access_mode = access(argv[1], 4);
        if (access_mode)
          printf("File cannot be read\n");
```

```
      else
        printf("File can be read\n");
      access_mode = access(argv[1], 6);
      if (access_mode)
        printf("File cannot be read/written\n");
      else
        printf("File can be read/written\n");
    }
  }
```

Note: *Tip 1462 details how you will use file attributes under Windows to determine how a program can access a file.*

SETTING A FILE'S ACCESS MODE 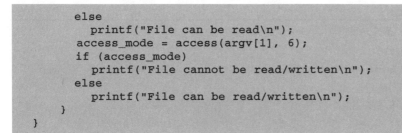379

When your programs work with files, there will be times when you want to change a program's read and write access. For example, assume that you have an important data file. To protect the file when the program is not in use, you might set the file to read-only access. In this way, the user cannot accidentally delete the file. When the program starts, you can change the file to read and write access, as required. For such cases, your programs can use C's *chmod* function, as shown here:

```
#include <sys\stat.h>
#include <io.h>

int chmod(const char *filename, int access_mode);
```

The file header file *sys\stat.h* defines the access mode constants listed in Table 379.1.

Value	Meaning
S_IWRITE	Write permission is authorized
S_IREAD	Read permission is authorized

Table 379.1 *The access mode constants for* ***chmod****.*

To provide read and write access, perform a *bitwise OR* of the two constants (*S_IWRITE | S_IREAD*). If *chmod* successfully changes the file's attributes, it returns the value 0. If an error occurs, *chmod* returns the value –1 and sets the global variable *errno* to one of the error status values listed in Table 379.2.

Value	Meaning
ENOENT	File not found
EACCES	Permission denied

Table 379.2 *The error values* ***chmod*** *returns.*

The following program, *readonly.c*, sets the file specified in the command line to read-only access:

```
#include <stdio.h>
#include <sys\stat.h>
#include <io.h>

void main(int argc, char *argv[])
  {
    if (chmod(argv[1], S_IREAD))
      printf("Error setting %s\n", argv[1]);
  }
```

Note: *Tip 1463 details how you will use file attributes under Windows to change how a program can access a file.*

GAINING BETTER CONTROL OF FILE ATTRIBUTES 380

In Tip 379 you learned how to use C's *chmod* function to set a file's read and write attributes. When you use the DOS operating system, you can work with the attributes shown in Table 380.1.

Value	Meaning
FA_ARCH	Archive attribute
FA_DIREC	Directory attribute
FA_HIDDEN	Hidden attribute
FA_LABEL	Disk volume label
FA_RDONLY	Read-only attribute
FA_SYSTEM	System attribute

Table 380.1 The attributes you can use with files within the DOS operating system.

Note: *Some compilers name these constants differently. Examine the include file **dos.h**, provided with your compiler, for the correct constant names.*

To help you work with these attributes, some C compilers provide the _chmod function, whose format is shown here (remember, parameters shown within brackets are optional):

```
#include <dos.h>
#include <io.h>

int _chmod(const char *filename, int operation [,int attribute]);
```

The operation tells _chmod if you want to set or get the attribute's setting. If the calling function sets the operation to 0, _chmod returns the file's current attributes. If the calling function sets the operation 1, _chmod sets the specified attribute. The left and right brackets, therefore, indicate that the *attributes* parameter is optional. If _chmod is successful, it returns the file's current attributes. If an error occurs, _chmod returns the value –1 and assigns the global variable *errno* one of the following values shown in Table 380.2.

Value	Meaning
ENOENT	File not found
EACCES	Permission denied

Table 380.2 The errors _chmod returns.

The following program, *tellattr.c*, uses _chmod to display a file's current attributes:

```
#include <stdio.h>
#include <dos.h>
#include <io.h>

void main(int argc, char *argv[])
  {
    int attributes;

    if ((attributes = _chmod(argv[1], 0)) == -1)
      printf("Error accessing %s\n", argv[1]);
    else
      {
          if (attributes & FA_ARCH)
            printf("Archive ");
          if (attributes & FA_DIREC)
            printf("Directory ");
          if (attributes & FA_HIDDEN)
            printf("Hidden ");
          if (attributes & FA_LABEL)
            printf("Volume label ");
          if (attributes & FA_RDONLY)
            printf("Readonly ");
          if (attributes & FA_SYSTEM)
            printf("System ");
      }
  }
```

Many C compilers also provide the functions *_dos_getfilefattr* and *_dos_setfileattr*, which let you get or set a file's DOS attributes, as shown here:

```
#include <dos.h>

int _dos_getfileattr(const char *filename, unsigned *attributes);
int _dos_setfileattr(const char *filename, unsigned attributes);
```

The *_dos_getfilefattr* and *_dos_setfileattr* functions use the attribute constants detailed in Table 380.3.

Value	Meaning
_A_ARCH	Archive attribute
_A_HIDDEN	Hidden attribute
_A_NORMAL	Normal attribute
_A_RDONLY	Read-only attribute
_A_SUBDIR	Directory attribute
_A_SYSTEM	System attribute
_A_VOLID	Disk volume label

Table 380.3 *The attribute constants the _dos_getfilefattr and _dos_setfileattr functions use.*

If the *_dos_getfileattr* and *_dos_setfileattr* functions succeed, the functions return the value 0. If an error occurs, the functions return the value −1 and assign the global variable *errno* the value *ENOENT* (file not found).

As a rule, your programs should only manipulate the archive, read-only, and hidden file attributes, reserving the other attributes for use by DOS. If you only change the read-only attribute, use the *chmod* function presented in Tip 379 to increase your program's portability.

Note: Tip 1463 details how you will use file attributes under Windows to change how a program can access a file.

TESTING FOR A FILE STREAM ERROR 381

When your programs perform file I/O operations, they should always test the return values of functions such as *fopen, fputs, fgets*, and so on to verify that the operations succeeded. To help your programs perform such testing, C provides the *ferror* macro, which examines an I/O stream for a read or write error. If an error has occurred, *ferror* returns a true value. If no error has occurred, *ferror* returns false, as shown here:

```
#include <stdio.h>

int ferror(FILE *stream);
```

After a file I/O error occurs, the *ferror* macro will remain true until your programs invoke the *clearerr* macro for the given stream:

```
#include <stdio.h>

void clearerr(FILE *stream);
```

The following program, *ferror.c*, reads and displays a file's contents to the screen. After each I/O operation, the program tests for an error. If an error occurs, the program ends, displaying an error message to *stderr*:

```
#include <stdio.h>
#include <stdlib.h>

void main(int argc, char *argv[])
 {
   FILE *fp;
   char line[256];

   if (fp = fopen(argv[1], "r"))
     {
        while (fgets(line, sizeof(line), fp))
          {
             if (ferror(fp))
               {
```

```
                    fprintf(stderr, "Error reading from %s\n", argv[1]);
                    exit(1);
                }
            else
                {
                    fputs(line, stdout);
                    if (ferror(fp))
                        {
                            fprintf(stderr, "Error writing to stdout\n");
                            exit(1);
                        }
                }
            }
        }
    else
        printf("Error opening %s\n", argv[1]);
}
```

382 DETERMINING A FILE'S SIZE

As your programs perform file I/O operations, at times you must determine a file's size in bytes. For such cases, you can use C's *filelength* function. The *filelength* function returns a *long* value. You must pass the program a file handle, not a file pointer, as shown here:

```
#include <io.h>

long filelength(int file_handle);
```

If *filelength* succeeds, it returns the file size in bytes. If an error occurs, *filelength* returns the value –1 and sets the global variable *errno* to *EBADF* (bad file number). The following program, *filelen.c*, will display the size of a given file to the screen:

```
#include <stdio.h>
#include <io.h>
#include <fcntl.h>
#include <sys\stat.h>

void main(int argc, char *argv[])
 {
   int file_handle;
   long file_size;

   if ((file_handle = open(argv[1], O_RDONLY)) == -1)
     printf("Error opening the file %d\n", argv[1]);
   else
     {
        file_size = filelength(file_handle);
        printf("The file size in bytes is %ld\n", file_size);
        close(file_handle);
     }
}
```

Note: *Tip 1463 details how you will determine a file's size using the Windows API.*

383 FLUSHING AN I/O STREAM

To improve your program performance, the C run-time library normally buffers your file output until it has a complete buffer (usually a disk sector) to write to disk, or until you close the file. In this way, the run-time library reduces the number of slow disk I/O operations. Unfortunately, when your programs use such a buffer, they leave the door open for the possibility of losing data. When your program performs a function such as *fputs* to write output and the function does not return an error, the program assumes the operating system has correctly recorded the data to the disk. In reality, however, the data still may reside in your computer's memory. If the user should turn off the computer, the user will lose the data. If you have a program for which you must ensure that all data writes to the disk, you can use *fflush* to direct the run-time library to write the data from its buffer in memory to disk. The format of the *fflush* function is as follows:

```
#include <stdio.h>

int fflush(FILE *file_stream);
```

If *fflush* succeeds, it returns the value 0. If an error occurs, *fflush* returns the constant *EOF*. The following statements illustrate how you can use *fflush* to empty the file buffer to disk following each output operation:

```
while (fgets(line, sizeof(line), input_file))
   {
     fputs(line, output_file);
     fflush(output_file);
   }
```

Note: *When you use the **fflush** function, you direct the C run-time library to invoke an operating system service to write the data to disk. If the operating system performs its own buffering (called a **disk cache**), the operating system may place your data into its memory buffer, as opposed to disk. Depending on the disk-caching software, you may be able to invoke another system service to flush the output.*

Closing All Open Files in One Step 384

As discussed in Tip 361, before your programs end you should use the *fclose* function to close your open files. Assume that you have a function that performs a critical operation. If the function experiences an error, the program should immediately end. Unfortunately, the function might not be aware of the open files. In such cases, your program can use C's *fcloseall* function to close all open files, as shown here:

```
#include <stdio.h>

int fcloseall(void);
```

If *fcloseall* succeeds, it returns the number of files it successfully closed. If an error occurs, *fcloseall* returns the *EOF* constant. The following statements illustrate how you might use *fcloseall*:

```
if (error_status == CRITICAL)
   {
     fprintf(stderr, "Critical device error\n");
     fcloseall();
     exit(1);
   }
```

Getting a File Stream's File Handle 385

As discussed in Tip 360, when your programs perform file operations, they can perform high-level operations using file streams (*FILE *stream*). You can also use low-level file handles (*int handle*). As you have learned, several of C's run-time library functions require file handles. If your program uses file streams, you can close the file and reopen it using a file handle, or you can obtain a file handle using C's *fileno* function, as shown here:

```
#include <stdio.h>

int fileno(FILE *stream);
```

The following program, *fileno.c*, uses the *fileno* function to get the file handle for an open file stream:

```
#include <stdio.h>
#include <io.h>

void main(int argc, char *argv[])
  {
     FILE *stream;
     int handle;
     long file_length;
```

```
    if (stream = fopen(argv[1], "r"))
      {
          // Some statements
          handle = fileno(stream);
          file_length = filelength(handle);
          printf("The file length is %ld\n", file_length);
          fclose(stream);
      }
    else
      printf("Error opening %s\n", argv[1]);
 }
```

386 CREATING A TEMPORARY FILENAME USING P_TMPDIR

As your programs perform file I/O operations, your programs often must open one or more temporary files or write output to a nonexistent file on disk. In such cases, the difficulty then becomes determining a unique filename so that the program does not overwrite an existing file. To help your programs generate unique filenames, you can use the *tmpnam* function, as shown here:

```
#include <stdio.h>

char *tmpnam(char *buffer);
```

If your program passes a buffer to *tmpnam*, the function will assign the temporary name to the buffer. If you invoke *tmpnam* with *NULL*, *tmpnam* will allocate memory for the filename, returning to the program a pointer to the start of the filename. The *tmpnam* function examines the *P_tmpdir* entry in the *stdio.h* header file. If *P_tmpdir* is defined, *tmpnam* creates the unique filename in the corresponding directory. Otherwise, *tmpnam* will create the file in the current directory. Note that *tmpnam* does not actually create the file, but rather, it returns a filename that your program can use with *fopen* or *open*. The following program, *tmpnam.c*, illustrates the use of the *tmpname* function:

```
#include <stdio.h>

void main(void)
 {
    char buffer[64];
    int counter;

    for (counter = 0; counter < 5; counter++)
       printf("Temporary filename %s\n", tmpnam(buffer));
 }
```

Note: *The companion CD-ROM that accompanies this book includes the program **mak_temp.cpp**, which creates a temporary file with the Windows API.*

387 CREATING A TEMPORARY FILENAME USING TMP OR TEMP

As your programs perform file I/O operations, your programs often must open one or more temporary files or write output to a nonexistent file on disk. In such cases, the difficulty then becomes determining a unique filename so that the program does not overwrite an existing file. To help your programs generate a unique filename, you can use the *tempnam* function, as shown here:

```
#include <stdio.h>
char *tempnam(char *buffer, char *prefix);
```

If your program passes a buffer to *tempnam*, the function assigns the temporary name to the buffer. If you invoke *tempnam* with *NULL*, *tempnam* allocates memory for the filename, returning to the program a pointer to the start of the filename. The *prefix* parameter lets you define a set of characters that you want *tempnam* to place at the start of each filename. The *tempnam* function examines the environment entries to determine if a TMP or TEMP entry exists. If TMP or TEMP is defined, *tempnam* will create the unique filename in the corresponding directory. Otherwise, *tempnam* creates the file in the current directory. Note that *tempnam* does not actually create the file, but rather, it returns a filename that your program can use with *fopen* or *open*. The following program, *tempnam.c*, illustrates the use of the *tempnam* function:

```
#include <stdio.h>
void main(void)
  {
    char buffer[64];
    int counter;
    printf("Temporary filename %s\n", tempnam(buffer, "Bible"));
  }
```

CREATING A TRULY TEMPORARY FILE 388

In Tips 386 and 387 you learned how to use the *tmpnam* and *tempnam* functions to generate temporary filenames. As you learned, *tmpnam* and *tempnam* do not actually create a file, rather they simply return a filename not currently in use. In addition, C also provides a function named *tmpfile* that determines a unique filename and then opens the file, returning a file pointer to the program. You will implement the *tmpfile* function as shown here:

```
#include <stdio.h>
FILE *tmpfile(void);
```

If *tmpfile* succeeds, it opens the file in read and write mode, returning a file pointer. If an error occurs, *tmpfile* returns *NULL*. The file *tmpfile* returns is a temporary file. When your program ends (or calls *rmtmp*), the operating system deletes the file and discards its contents. The following statements illustrate how your program might use the *tmpfile* function:

```
FILE *temp_file;
if (temp_file = tmpfile())
  {
     // Temporary file successfully opened
     // Statements that use the file
  }
else
  printf("Error opening temporary file\n");
```

REMOVING TEMPORARY FILES 389

In Tip 388 you learned that the *tmpfile* function lets your programs create a temporary file with contents that exist only for the duration of the program's execution. Depending on your programs, you may want to discard temporary files before the program ends. In such cases, your program can use the *rmtmp* function, whose format is shown here:

```
#include <stdio.h>
int rmtmp(void);
```

If *rmtmp* succeeds, it returns the number of files it successfully closed and deleted.

SEARCHING THE COMMAND PATH FOR A FILE 390

When you work within the DOS environment, the PATH command defines the directories that DOS searches for EXE, COM, and BAT files when you execute an external command. Because the subdirectories defined in the PATH normally contain your most commonly used commands, there may be times when you want a program to search the PATH subdirectory entries for a data file. For such cases, some compilers provide the *searchpath* function. You invoke the function with the desired filename. If *searchpath* successfully locates the file, it returns a complete pathname to the file that your programs can use within *fopen*. If *searchpath* does not find the file, it returns *NULL*, as shown here:

```
#include <dir.h>
char *searchpath(const char *filename);
```

The following program, *srchpath.c*, illustrates the use of the *searchpath* function to search for the specified filename:

```
#include <stdio.h>
#include <dir.h>

void main (int argc, char *argv[])
  {
    char *path;

    if (path = searchpath(argv[1]))
      printf("Pathname: %s\n", path);
    else
      printf("File not found\n");
  }
```

Note: The searchpath function searches the current directory for the specified file before searching the command path subdirectories.

391 SEARCHING AN ENVIRONMENT ENTRY'S SUBDIRECTORY LIST FOR A FILE

In Tip 390 you used the *searchpath* function to search directories in the command path for a specified file. In a similar way, you may want to search the directories specified in a different environment entry for a file. For example, many C compilers define *LIB* and *INCLUDE* entries that specify the location of library files (with the *.lib* extension) and header files (with the *.h* extension). To search the directories the *LIB* and *INCLUDE* entries specify, you can use the *_searchenv* function, as shown here:

```
#include <dos.h>

char *_searchenv(const char *filename, const char *environment_entry, *pathname);
```

The *_searchenv* function searches the directories specified in the *environment_entry* for the specified filename. If *_searchenv* finds the filename, *_searchenv* assigns the file's pathname to the pathname character string buffer, returning a pointer to the pathname. If *_searchenv* does not find the file, *_searchenv* returns *NULL*. The following program, *srch_env.c*, uses the *_searchenv* function to search the subdirectories specified in the *LIB* entry for a specified file:

```
#include <stdio.h>
#include <stdlib.h>

void main (int argc, char *argv[])
  {
    char path[128];

    _searchenv(argv[1], "LIB", path);
    if (path[0])
      printf("Pathname: %s\n", path);
    else
      printf("File not found\n");
  }
```

Note: The _searchenv function searches the current directory for the specified file before searching the environment entry's subdirectories.

Note: In Tips 1474 through 1476 you will learn how to use the Windows API to find files on your system.

392 OPENING FILES IN THE TEMP DIRECTORY

As you know, many programs create their temporary files in the subdirectory that the TEMP environment entry specifies within the *config.sys* file. Within your programs, you can easily create your own files within the directory the TEMP entry names, using the *getenv* function. The following statements illustrate how your programs can open a file named *tempdata.dat* within the temporary directory:

```
char pathname[_MAX_PATH];
strcpy(pathname, getenv("TEMP"));

if (pathname[0])
  strcat(pathname, "\\TEMPDATA.DAT");
```

```
else
   strcat(pathname, "TEMPDATA.DAT");
if (fp = fopen(pathname, "w"))
```

In this code fragment, if the TEMP entry exists, the program opens the file in the corresponding subdirectory. If there is no TEMP entry, the program opens the file in the current directory. Note that the code fragment assumes that the TEMP variable does not contain a value that ends with a backslash. Ideally, your programs will test TEMP's current value and process accordingly.

MINIMIZING FILE I/O OPERATIONS 393

Compared to the fast electronic speed of your computer's CPU and memory, the mechanical disk is very slow. As a result, you should try to minimize the number of disk I/O operations your programs must perform. With respect to file operations, the file that is open probably consumes the most time. Therefore, you should always examine your programs to make sure you do not open and close a file unnecessarily or repeatedly open a file from within a loop. For example, consider the following statements:

```
while (menu_choice != QUIT)
  {
    if (fp = fopen("DATABASE.DAT", "r"))
      {
        // Get customer name
        get_customer(name);
        // Search file for customer info
        search_customer_info(name, fp, data_buffer);
        fclose(fp);
      }
    else
      {
        file_open_error("Aborting...");
      }
    menu_choice = get_menu_choice();
  }
```

The statements repeatedly loop, getting customer information until the user selects the QUIT option. Note that the *fopen* function call occurs within the loop. Therefore, the program repeatedly performs the slow disk I/O operation. To improve the system's performance, the program should pull the *fopen* outside of the loop. If the *search_customer* function must start at the beginning of the file, the program can rewind the file, as shown here:

```
if (fp = fopen("DATABASE.DAT", "r"))
   file_open_error("Aborting...");
while (menu_choice != QUIT)
  {
    // Get customer name
    get_customer(name);
    rewind(fp);
    // Search file for customer info
    search_customer_info(name, fp, data_buffer);
    menu_choice = get_menu_choice();
  }
fclose(fp);
```

WRITING CODE THAT USES BACKSLASHES IN DIRECTORY NAMES 394

Several Tips presented in this section work with directory names. For example, the *chdir* function lets your programs select a specific directory. When your program specifies a directory name as a constant value, make sure you use double backslashes (\\) within pathnames, as required. The following *chdir* function call, for example, tries to select the subdirectory DOS:

```
status = chdir("\DOS");
```

When you use a backslash character within a C string, remember that C treats the backslash character as a special symbol. When the C compiler encounters the backslash, it checks the character that follows to determine if it is a special symbol and, if so, replaces the character with the correct ASCII counterparts. If the character that follows the backslash is not a special symbol, the C compiler ignores the backslash character. Therefore, the previous *chdir* function would try to select the directory DOS as opposed to \\DOS. The correct function invocation in this case would be as follows:

```
status = chdir("\\DOS");
```

395 CHANGING THE CURRENT DIRECTORY

As your programs execute, there may be times when your programs must change the current directory. To help you perform such operations, most C compilers provide the *chdir* function. The *chdir* function is very similar to the DOS CHDIR command: if you invoke the function with a string that does not contain a disk drive letter, *chdir* looks for the directory on the current drive. The following function call, for example, selects the directory *data* on drive C:

```
status = chdir("C:\\DATA");   // Note the use of \\
```

In a similar way, the following command selects the directory *tclite* on the current drive:

```
status = chdir("\\TCLITE");
```

If the *chdir* function succeeds, it returns the value 0. If the directory does not exist, *chdir* returns the value −1 and sets the global variable *errno* to the constant *ENOENT*. The following program, *newchdir.c*, implements the DOS CHDIR command:

```
#include <stdio.h>
#include <stdlib.h>
#include <dir.h>
#include <errno.h>
void main(int argc, char *argv[])
  {
    char directory[MAXPATH];
    if (argc == 1)                          // Display the current directory
      {
        getcwd(directory, MAXPATH);
        puts(directory);
      }
    else if ((chdir(argv[1])) && (errno == ENOENT))
      puts("Invalid directory");
  }
```

*Note: Some compilers define the symbol _MAX_PATH in the **direct.h** (or **dir.h**) include file, as opposed to using **MAXPATH**.*

Note: Tip 1468 explains in detail changing directories under Windows.

396 CREATING A DIRECTORY

As your programs execute, they may need to create a directory. To help your programs do so, most C compilers provide a *mkdir* function. The *mkdir* function is very similar to the DOS MKDIR command. If you invoke the function with a string that does not contain a disk drive letter, *mkdir* creates the directory on the current drive. The following function call, for example, creates the directory DATA on drive C:

```
status = mkdir("C:\\DATA");   // Note the use of \\
```

In a similar way, the following command creates the directory TEMPDATA on the current drive, in the current directory:

```
status = mkdir("TEMPDATA");
```

If the *mkdir* function succeeds, it returns the value 0. If *mkdir* cannot create the directory, it returns the value −1.

Note: Tip 1467 explains creating directories under Windows in detail.

REMOVING A DIRECTORY

As your programs execute, they may need to create or remove a directory. To help your programs remove a directory, most C compilers provide a *rmdir* function. The *rmdir* function is very similar to the DOS RMDIR command. If you invoke the function with a string that does not contain a disk drive letter, *rmdir* creates the directory on the current drive. The following function call, for example, removes the directory DATA from drive C:

```
status = rmdir("C:\\DATA");  // Note the use of \\
```

In a similar way, the following command removes the directory TEMPDATA from the current drive and directory:

```
status = rmdir("TEMPDATA");
```

If the *rmdir* function succeeds, it returns the value 0. If the directory does not exist or *rmdir* cannot remove it, *rmdir* returns the value –1 and assigns the global variable *errno* one of the values listed in Table 397.

Value	Meaning
EACCES	Access denied
ENOENT	No such directory

*Table 397 The error values for **mkdir**.*

Note: *Tip 1470 explains in detail removing directories under Windows.*

REMOVING A DIRECTORY TREE

In MS-DOS version 6, Microsoft introduced the DELTREE command. DELTREE lets you, in one step, delete a directory, its files, and any subdirectories within the directory. If you do not use DOS version 6, you can create your own DELTREE command using the program *deltree.c*, as shown here:

```c
#include <dos.h>
#include <stdio.h>
#include <stdlib.h>
#include <dir.h>
#include <alloc.h>
#include <string.h>

void main(int argc, char **argv)
 {
   void delete_tree(void);
   char buffer[128];
   char drive[MAXDRIVE], directory[MAXDIR], filename[MAXFILE], ext[MAXEXT];

   if (argc < 2)
     {
        printf ("Syntax error\n");
        exit(0);
     }
   fnsplit (argv[1], drive, directory, filename, ext);
   getcwd (buffer, sizeof(buffer));
   if (drive[0] == NULL)
     {
        fnsplit (buffer, drive, directory, filename, ext);
        strcpy (buffer, directory);
        strcat (buffer, filename);
        strcat (buffer, ext);
     }
   else
     {
        printf ("Do not specify drive letter\n");
        exit (1);
     }
   if (strcmpi(buffer, argv[1]) == 0)
     {
```

```
            printf ("Cannot delete current directory\n");
            exit (1);
        }
      getcwd (directory, 64);
      if (chdir (argv[1]))
        printf ("Invalid directory %s\n", argv[1]);
      else
        delete_tree ();
      chdir (directory);
      rmdir (argv[1]);
}

union REGS inregs, outregs;
struct SREGS segs;

void delete_tree(void)
  {
    struct ffblk fileinfo;
    int result;
    char far *farbuff;
    unsigned dta_seg, dta_ofs;

    result = findfirst("*.*", &fileinfo, 16);
    inregs.h.ah = 0x2f;
    intdosx (&inregs, &outregs, &segs);
    dta_seg = segs.es;
    dta_ofs = outregs.x.bx;
    while (! result)
      {
        if ((fileinfo.ff_attrib & 16) && (fileinfo.ff_name[0] != '.'))
          {
            inregs.h.ah = 0x1A;
            inregs.x.dx = FP_SEG(farbuff);
            segread(&segs);
            intdosx (&inregs, &outregs, &segs);
            chdir (fileinfo.ff_name);
            delete_tree();
            chdir ("..");
            inregs.h.ah = 0x1A;
            inregs.x.dx = dta_ofs;
            segs.ds = dta_seg;
            rmdir (fileinfo.ff_name);
          }
        else if (fileinfo.ff_name[0] != '.')
          {
            remove (fileinfo.ff_name);
          }
        result = findnext (&fileinfo);
      }
}
```

Note: *The companion CD-ROM that accompanies this book includes the **win_dtre.cpp** file, which performs the same task as the **deltree.c** program but works only under Windows 95 or Windows NT.*

399 BUILDING A FULL PATHNAME

When your programs work with files and directories, you might need to know the file's complete (full) pathname. For example, if the current directory is *data* and the current drive is C, the full name of the file *report.dat* is *c:\data\report.dat*. To help you resolve a file's full name (that is, combine its components), some C compilers provide a function named *fnmerge*. The function uses five parameters: a buffer within which the function places the full pathname, the drive name, the directory name, the file name, and the extension, as shown here:

```
#include <dir.h>

void fnmerge (char *buffer, const char *drive, const char *dir,
              const char *filename, const char *extension);
```

If the value of the *buffer* parameter is *NULL*, *fnmerge* will allocate the memory used to hold the full pathname. If *fnmerge* successfully resolves the filename, it will return a pointer to the buffer. If an error occurs, the function returns *NULL*. The following program, *fullname.c*, illustrates the use of the *fnmerge* function:

```
#include <string.h>
#include <stdio.h>
#include <dir.h>

void main(void)
 {
    char s[MAXPATH];
    char drive[MAXDRIVE];
    char dir[MAXDIR];
    char file[MAXFILE];
    char ext[MAXEXT];

    getcwd(s,MAXPATH);
    strcat(s,"\\");
    fnsplit(s,drive,dir,file,ext);
    strcpy(file,"DATA");
    strcpy(ext,".TXT");
    fnmerge(s,drive,dir,file,ext);
    puts(s);
 }
```

Note: *Some compilers use the include file* **direct.h**, *as opposed to* **dir.h**.

PARSING A DIRECTORY PATH

400

As your programs work with files and directories, you may need to parse a pathname into a disk drive letter, subdirectory path, filename, and extension. To help you parse a pathname (that is, separate it into its components), some C compilers provide the *_splitpath* function. The format of the function call is as follows:

```
include <dir.h>

int fnsplit (const char *path, const char *drive, const char *directory,
             const char *filename, const char *ext);
```

The following program, *split.c*, illustrates the use of the *fnsplit* function:

```
#include <stdio.h>
#include <dir.h>
#include <stdlib.h>

void main(void)
  {
    char *path_1 = "C:\\SUBDIR\\FILENAME.EXT";
    char *path_2 = "SUBDIR\\FILENAME.EXT";
    char *path_3 = "FILENAME.EXE";
    char subdir[MAXDIR];
    char drive[MAXDRIVE];
    char filename[MAXFILE];
    char extension[MAXEXT];
    int flags;                              // holds the fnsplit return value

    flags = fnsplit(path_1, drive, subdir, filename, extension);
    printf ("Splitting %s\n", path_1);
    printf ("Drive %s Subdir %s Filename %s Extension %s\n",
      drive, subdir, filename, extension);
    flags = fnsplit(path_2, drive, subdir, filename, extension);
    printf ("Splitting %s\n", path_2);
    printf ("Drive %s Subdir %s Filename %s Extension %s\n",
      drive, subdir, filename, extension);
    flags = fnsplit(path_3, drive, subdir, filename, extension);
    printf ("Splitting %s\n", path_3);
    printf ("Drive %s Subdir %s Filename %s Extension %s\n",
      drive, subdir, filename, extension);
  }
```

Note the use of the constants to define the proper buffer sizes. When you compile and execute the *split.c* program, your screen will display the following:

```
Splitting C:\SUBDIR\FILENAME.EXE
Drive C: Subdir \SUBDIR\ Filename FILENAME Extension .EXE
Splitting \SUBDIR\FILENAME.EXE
Drive   Subdir \SUBDIR\ Filename FILENAME Extension .EXE
Splitting FILENAME.EXE
Drive   Subdir  Filename FILENAME Extension .EXE
C:\>
```

401 BUILDING A PATHNAME

As you work with files and directories within your programs, at times you may want to combine a disk drive letter, subdirectory, filename, and extension into a complete pathname. To help you perform such operations, some C compilers provide the *fnmerge* function. The format of the *fnmerge* function is as follows:

```
fnmerge(pathname, drive, subdir, filename, ext);
```

The following program, *makepath.c*, illustrates how to use the *fnmerge* function:

```c
#include <stdio.h>
#include <stdlib.h>
#include <dir.h>

void main (void)
  {
    char pathname[MAXPATH];

    char *drive = "C:";
    char *subdir = "\\SUBDIR";
    char *filename = "FILENAME";
    char *extension = "EXT";

    fnmerge(pathname, drive, subdir, filename, extension);

    printf("The complete pathname is %s\n", pathname);
  }
```

When you compile and execute the *makepath.c* program, your screen will display the following output:

```
The complete pathname is C:\SUBDIR\FILENAME.EXT
C:\>
```

402 OPENING AND CLOSING A FILE USING LOW-LEVEL FUNCTIONS

C supports high-level file I/O operations that work with file streams and low-level operations that work with byte ranges. When your programs perform low-level I/O, you can open an existing file using the *open* function. To close the file later, you use *close*, as shown here:

```c
#include <fcntl.h>
#include <sys\stat.h>

int open(const char *path, int access_mode [,creation_mode]);
int close(int handle);
```

If *open* successfully opens the file, it returns a handle to the file. If an error occurs, *open* returns −1 and sets the global variable *errno* to one of the values listed in Table 402.1.

Value	Meaning
ENOENT	No such file or directory entry
EMFILE	Too many open files
EACCES	Access permission denied
EINVACC	Invalid access code

*Table 402.1 Error status codes **open** assigns to **errno**.*

The *path* parameter is a character string that contains the name of the desired file. The *access_mode* parameter specifies how you want to use the file. The *access_mode* value can be a combination (use a *bitwise OR*) of the values listed in Table 402.2.

Access Mode	Meaning
O_RDONLY	Read-only access
O_WRONLY	Write-only access
O_RDWR	Read and write access
O_NDELAY	Delay value UNIX uses
O_APPEND	Positions pointer for append operations
O_TRUNC	Truncates an existing file's contents
O_EXCL	If *O_CREAT* is specified and the file already exists, *open* returns an error
O_BINARY	Open file in binary mode
O_TEXT	Open file in text mode

*Table 402.2 The possible values for the **access_mode** parameter when you use it with **open**.*

By default, *open* will not create an output file if the file does not exist. If you want *open* to create files, you must include the *O_CREAT* flag along with the desired access modes (for example, *O_CREAT | O_TEXT*). If you specify *O_CREAT*, you can use the *creation_mode* parameter to specify the mode with which you want to create the file. The *creation_mode* parameter can use a combination of the values that Table 402.3 specifies.

Creation Mode	Meaning
S_IWRITE	Create for write operations
S_IREAD	Create for read operations

*Table 402.3 The possible values for the **creation_mode** parameter that **open** uses.*

The following statement illustrates how to use *open* to open the root directory file *config.sys* for read-only operations:

```
if ((handle = open("\\CONFIG.SYS", O_RDONLY)) == -1)
   printf("Error opening the file \\CONFIG.SYS\n");
else
   // Statements
```

If you want to open the file *output.dat* for write operations and you want *open* to create a file that does not yet exist, use *open* as follows:

```
if ((handle = open("\\CONFIG.SYS", O_RDONLY | O_CREAT, S_IWRITE)) == -1)
   printf("Error opening the file \\CONFIG.SYS\n");
else
   // Statements
```

When you finish using a file, you should close it using the *close* function, as shown here:

```
close(handle);
```

CREATING A FILE   403

In Tip 402 you learned that by default, the *open* function does not create a file if the file does not exist. As you also learned, however, you can direct *open* to create a file when you specify *O_CREAT* in the access mode. If you are using an older compiler, the *open* function might not support *O_CREAT*. As a result, you may need to use the *creat* function, as shown here:

```
#include <sys\stat.h>

int creat(const char *path, int creation_mode);
```

As before, the path parameter specifies the file you want to create. The *creation_mode* parameter can contain a combination of the values listed in Table 403.

Mode	Meaning
S_IWRITE	Create for write operations
S_IREAD	Create for read operations

*Table 403 The possible values for the **creation_mode** parameter.*

If *creat* succeeds, it will return a handle to the file. If an error occurs, *creat* will return the value −1 and assign an error status value to the global variable *errno*. The mode of translation (binary or text) that *creat* uses depends on the setting of the *_fmode* global variable. If a file with the specified name already exists, *creat* will truncate the file's contents. The following statement illustrates how to use *creat* to create the file *output.dat*:

```
if ((handle = creat("OUTPUT.DAT", S_IWRITE)) == -1)
  printf("Error creating file\n");
else
  // Statements
```

Note: *If you want it to be obvious to another programmer that you are creating a file, you might want to use the **creat** function, as opposed to using **open** with the **O_CREAT** flag set.*

404 PERFORMING LOW-LEVEL READ AND WRITE OPERATIONS

When you use file handles to perform low-level file I/O operations, you open and close files using the *open* and *close* functions. In a similar way, you read and write files using the *read* and *write* functions, as shown here:

```
#include <io.h>

int read(int handle, void *buffer, unsigned length);
int write(int handle, void *buffer, unsigned length);
```

The *handle* parameter is the handle the *open* or *creat* functions return. The *buffer* parameter is either the data buffer into which the *read* function reads information or from which the *write* function writes data. The *length* parameter specifies the number of bytes *read* or *write* will transfer (the maximum is 65,534). If *read* succeeds, it returns the number of bytes read. If *read* encounters the end of the file, *read* returns 0. On an error, *read* returns −1 and sets the global variable *errno* to one of the values listed in Table 404.

Value	Meaning
EACCES	Invalid access
EBADF	Invalid file handle

*Table 404 The possible error values **read** returns.*

If *write* is successful, it returns the number of bytes written. If an error occurs, *write* returns the value −1 and assigns the global variable *errno* one of the values previously shown. The following loop illustrates how you might use *read* and *write* to copy the contents of one file to another:

```
while ((bytes_read = read(input, buffer, sizeof(buffer))
    write(output, buffer, bytes_read);
```

405 TESTING FOR THE END OF A FILE

In Tip 404 you learned that the *read* function returns the value 0 when it encounters *EOF*. Depending on your program, at times you may want to test for the end of file before performing a specific operation. When you use file handles, the *eof* function returns the value 1 if the file pointer has reached the end of the file, 0 if the pointer is not at the end of the file, and −1 if the file handle is invalid:

```
#include <io.h.>

int eof(int handle);
```

The following statements modify the code shown in Tip 404 to use *eof* to test for the end of the input file:

```
while (! eof(input))
  {
    bytes_read = read(input, buffer, sizeof(buffer));
    write(output, buffer, bytes_read);
  }
```

PUTTING THE LOW-LEVEL FILE ROUTINES TO WORK C406

Several Tips in this section discuss C's low-level file I/O routines. To help you better understand each routine's use, consider the following program, *lowcopy.c*, which uses the *read* and *write* functions to copy the contents of the first file specified in the command line to the second:

```
#include <stdio.h>
#include <io.h>
#include <fcntl.h>
#include <sys\types.h>
#include <sys\stat.h>

void main(int argc, char *argv[])
  {
    int source, target; // file handles
    char buffer[1024];   // I/O buffer
    int bytes_read;

    if (argc < 3)
      fprintf(stderr, "Must specify source and target files\n");
    else if ((source = open(argv[1], O_BINARY | O_RDONLY)) == -1)
      fprintf(stderr, "Error opening %s\n", argv[1]);
    else if ((target = open(argv[2], O_WRONLY | O_BINARY | O_TRUNC |
              O_CREAT, S_IWRITE)) == -1)
       fprintf(stderr, "Error opening %s\n", argv[2]);
    else
      {
        while (!eof(source))
         {
           if ((bytes_read = read(source, buffer, sizeof(buffer)))<= 0)
            fprintf(stderr, "Error reading from source file");
           else if (write(target, buffer, bytes_read) != bytes_read)
            fprintf(stderr, "Error writing to target file");
         }
        close(source);
        close(target);
      }
  }
```

SPECIFYING THE MODE FOR A FILE-HANDLE TRANSLATION C407

As you have learned, C translates a file's contents using either binary or text translation. Unless you specify otherwise, C uses the setting in the *_fmode* global variable to determine the translation type, either *O_BINARY* or *O_TEXT*. When you open or create a file using C's low-level routines, you can specify the file's translation mode. In some cases, your program must specify the translation mode after you open the file. To specify the mode, you can use the *setmode* function, as shown here:

```
#include <fcntl.h>

int setmode(int handle, int translation_mode);
```

If *setmode* succeeds, it returns the previous translation mode. If an error occurs, *setmode* returns –1 and sets the global variable *errno* to *EINVAL* (invalid argument). The following statement, for example, sets the file associated with the handle *output* to text translation:

```
if ((old_mode = setmode(output, O_TEXT)) == -1)
  printf("Error changing file mode\n");
```

408 POSITIONING THE FILE POINTER USING LSEEK

As you work with C's low-level file I/O functions, you may want to position the file pointer to a specific location within the file before you perform a read or write operation. To do so, you can use the *lseek* function, as shown here:

```
#include <io.h>

long lseek(int handle, long offset, int relative_to)
```

The *handle* parameter specifies the file pointer you want to position. The *offset* and *relative_to* parameters combine to specify the desired position. The *offset* parameter contains the byte offset into the file. The *relative_to* parameter specifies the location in the file from which the *lseek* function should apply the *offset*. Table 408 specifies the values you can use for the *relative_to* parameter.

Constant	Meaning
SEEK_CUR	From the current file position
SEEK_SET	From the beginning of the file
SEEK_END	From the end of the file

Table 408 *File positions from which the **lseek** function can apply an offset.*

To position the file pointer at the end of a file, for example, you can use *lseek* as follows:

```
lseek(handle, 0, SEEK_END);   // At end of file
```

If successful, *lseek* will return the value 0. If an error occurs, *lseek* will return a non-zero value.

409 OPENING MORE THAN 20 FILES

As you have learned, a file handle is an integer value that identifies an open file. Actually, a file handle is an index into the process file table, which contains entries for up to 20 files. If your DOS-based program must open more than 20 files, the easiest way you can do so is to use the DOS file services. To begin, your program must request support for more than 20 files. You can do this by using the DOS *INT 21H function 67H* to increase the number of file handles. DOS will then allocate a table large enough to hold the number of handles specified (up to 255 minus the number of handles currently in use). Next, your program should open the files using the DOS services, as opposed to the C run-time library. In this way, your program can bypass the compiler's file limit. The following code fragment increases the number of file handles to 75:

```
inregs.h.ah = 0x67;
inregs.x.bx = 75;    // Number of handles
intdos(&inregs, &outregs);

if (outregs.x.ax)
  printf("Error allocating handles\n");
```

Note: *The number of available file handles is only an issue in a DOS environment or a DOS window. Windows determines the limit on the number of files that you can open at a single time based on your current memory, hard drive free space, and other Windows-specific considerations.*

410 USING DOS-BASED FILE SERVICES

As the DOS and BIOS section of this book details, DOS provides a collection of file services that let you open, read, write, and close files. To make these services easier to use from within C, many C compilers provide the functions listed in Table 410.

Function	Purpose
_dos_creat	Creates a file, returning a file handle
_dos_close	Closes a specified file
_dos_open	Opens a file, returning a file handle
_dos_read	Reads the specified number of bytes from a file
_dos_write	Writes the specified number of bytes to a file

Table 410 Functions that use the DOS file system services.

To help you better understand file services, consider the following program, *doscopy.c*, which copies the contents of the first file specified in the command line to the second file specified in the command line:

```c
#include <stdio.h>
#include <dos.h>
#include <fcntl.h>

void main(int argc, char *argv[])
 {
    char buffer[1024];
    int input, output;                  // file handles
    unsigned bytes_read, bytes_written;  // actual number of bytes transferred

    if (argc < 3)
      fprintf(stderr, "Must specify source and target file\n");
    else if (_dos_open (argv[1], O_RDONLY, &input))
      fprintf(stderr, "Error opening source file\n");
    else if (_dos_creat (argv[2], 0, &output))
      fprintf(stderr, "Error opening target file\n");
    else
     {
       while (!_dos_read(input, buffer, sizeof(buffer), &bytes_read))
        {
          if (bytes_read == 0)
             break;
          _dos_write(output, buffer, bytes_read, &bytes_written);
        }
       _dos_close(input);
       _dos_close(output);
     }
 }
```

Note: *Although the DOS-based file routines are very similar to C's low-level file functions, you will increase your programs' portability by using C's **open**, **read**, and **write** functions, as opposed to the DOS-based functions. Most C compilers support C's low-level functions.*

Note: *When you program in Windows, you will use the Windows API functions rather than the DOS-based file routines to manage files. Tips 1450 through 1478 detail many Windows File API functions.*

OBTAINING A FILE'S DATE AND TIME STAMP
411

When you perform a directory listing, the DOS DIR command will display each file's name, extension, size, and the date and time the file was created or last changed. The date and time DOS stores for the file is called the file's *date and time stamp*. DOS only changes the date and time stamp when you make changes to the file. Some operating systems, on the other hand, track the date and time the file was created or last modified, as well as the date and time the file was last used (read). The operating systems refer to this second date and time stamp as the *last access time*. Depending on your program's purpose, there may be times when you must know a file's date and time stamp. Therefore, most compilers provide the *_dos_getftime* function, as shown here:

```c
#include <dos.h>

unsigned _dos_getftime(int handle, unsigned *datefield, unsigned *timefield);
```

If the function successfully gets the file's date and time stamp, the function returns the value 0. If an error occurs, the function returns a non-zero value and assigns the global variable *errno* the value *EBADF* (invalid handle). The *handle* parameter is an open file handle to the desired file. The *datefield* and *timefield* parameters are pointers to unsigned integer values with bit meanings, as listed in Tables 411.1 and 411.2, respectively.

Date Bits	Meaning
0–4	Day from 1 through 31
5–8	Month from 1 through 12
9–15	Years since 1980

*Table 411.1 The components of the **datefield** parameter.*

Time Bits	Meaning
0–4	Seconds divided by 2 (1 through 30)
5–10	Minutes from 1 through 60
11–15	Hours from 1 through 12

*Table 411.2 The components of the **timefield** parameter.*

The following program, *filedt.c*, uses the *_dos_getftime* function to display the date and time stamp of the file specified in the command line:

```
#include <stdio.h>
#include <dos.h>
#include <fcntl.h>

void main(int argc, char *argv[])
 {
    unsigned date, time;
    int handle;

    if (_dos_open(argv[1], O_RDONLY, &handle))
       fprintf(stderr, "Error opening source file\n");
    else
     {
       if (_dos_getftime(handle, &date, &time))
          printf("Error getting date/time stamp\n");
       else
          printf("%s last modified %02d-%02d-%d %02d:%02d:%02d\n",
                  argv[1],
                  (date & 0x1E0) >> 5,   /* month */
                  (date & 0x1F),         /* day */
                  (date >> 9) + 1980,    /* year */
                  (time >> 11),          /* hours */
                  (time & 0x7E0) >> 5,   /* minutes */
                  (time & 0x1F) * 2);    /* seconds */
       _dos_close(handle);
     }
 }
```

As you can see, the program uses C's bitwise operators to extract the *date* and *time* fields. You learned how to perform similar processing using structure bit fields in Tip 380.

Note: Tip 1465 details how you will obtain a file's date and time stamp within Windows.

412 OBTAINING A FILE'S DATE AND TIME USING BIT FIELDS

In Tip 411 you used the function *_dos_getftime* to obtain a file's date and time stamp. As you learned, the *_dos_getftime* function encodes the *date* and *time* fields as bits within two unsigned values. To extract the field values, the program *filedt.c* uses C's bitwise operators. To make your program easier to understand, you might consider using *bit* fields within a structure. To do so, you can use the following program, *dtbits.c*:

```
#include <stdio.h>
#include <dos.h>
#include <fcntl.h>

void main(int argc, char *argv[])
  {
     struct Date
       {
          unsigned int day:5;
          unsigned int month:4;
          unsigned int years:7;
       } date;
     struct Time
       {
          unsigned seconds:5;
          unsigned minutes:6;
          unsigned hours:5;
       } time;
     int handle;

     if (_dos_open(argv[1], O_RDONLY, &handle))
        fprintf(stderr, "Error opening source file\n");
     else
       {
         if (_dos_getftime(handle, &date, &time))
            printf("Error getting date and time stamp\n");
         else
            printf("%s last modified %02d-%02d-%d %02d:%02d:%02d\n",
                   argv[1],
                   date.month,            // month
                   date.day,              // day
                   date.years + 1980,     // year
                   time.hours,            // hours
                   time.minutes,          // minutes
                   time.seconds * 2);     // seconds
          _dos_close(handle);
       }
  }
```

By using *bit* fields, the program eliminates the need for other programmers to understand the complicated bitwise operations that occurred in the *filedt.c* program.

Note: Tip 1465 details how you will obtain a file's date and time stamp within Windows.

SETTING A FILE'S DATE AND TIME STAMP 413

In Tips 411 and 412, you used the *_dos_getftime* function to obtain a file's date and time stamp. Depending on your program, you may need to set a file's date and time stamp. For such cases, many C compilers provide the *_dos_setftime* function, as shown here:

```
#include <dos.h>

unsigned _dos_setftime(int handle, unsigned date, unsigned time);
```

If the function succeeds, it returns the value 0. If an error occurs, the function returns a non-zero value. The *handle* parameter is a handle to an open file. The *date* and *time* parameters contain the bit-encoded date and time values (similar to those shown in Tip 411). The following program, *july4_97.c*, sets the date and time stamp of the file the command line specifies to noon, July 4, 1997:

```
#include <stdio.h>
#include <dos.h>
#include <fcntl.h>

void main(int argc, char *argv[])
  {
     union
       {
```

```
        struct Date
           {
               unsigned int day:5;
               unsigned int month:4;
               unsigned int years:7;
           } bits;
        unsigned value;
     } date;
  union
   {
       struct Time
          {
             unsigned seconds:5;
             unsigned minutes:6;
             unsigned hours:5;
           } bits;
        unsigned value;
    } time;
  int handle;

  if (_dos_open(argv[1], O_RDONLY, &handle))
      fprintf(stderr, "Error opening source file\n");
  else
   {
      date.bits.day = 4;
      date.bits.month = 7;
      date.bits.years = 17;   // 1980 + 17
      time.bits.hours = 12;
      time.bits.minutes = 0;
      time.bits.seconds = 0;
      if (_dos_setftime(handle, date.value, time.value))
        printf("Error setting date/time stamp\n");
      _dos_close(handle);
   }
}
```

The *july4_97.c* program uses *bit* fields to simplify the assignment of the date and time bits. However, the *_dos_setftime* function requires parameters of type *unsigned int*. Because the bits must be viewed in two different ways, they are excellent candidates for a *union*. Tip 481 discusses unions in detail.

Note: Tip 1465 details how you will set a file's date and time stamp within Windows.

414 SETTING A FILE DATE AND TIME STAMP TO THE CURRENT DATE AND TIME

Several Tips in this book show ways to set a file's date and time stamp. When you want to set a file's date and time stamp to the current date and time, you can do so quickly with the *utime* function, as shown here:

```
#include <utime.h>
int utime(char *path, struct utimbuf *date_time);
```

The *path* parameter is a character string that specifies the name and directory of the file you want. The *date_time* parameter is a structure that contains the date and time the file was last changed and last accessed, as shown here:

```
struct utimbuf
  {
     time_t actime;     // Last access
     time_t modtime;    // Last modification
  };
```

If you are working in the DOS environment, DOS uses only the modification time. If you invoke the *utime* function with *date_time* set to *NULL*, the function sets the date and time stamp to the current date and time. If the function succeeds, it will return 0. If an error occurs, the function will return –1 and set the global variable *errno*. The following program, *utime.c*, uses the *utime* function to set the date and time stamp of the file specified to the current date and time:

```
#include <stdio.h>
#include <utime.h>

void main(int argc, char **argv)
 {
    if (utime(argv[1], (struct utimbuf *) NULL))
      printf("Error setting date and time\n");
    else
      printf("Date and time stamp set\n");
 }
```

Note: Tip 1465 details how you will set a file's date and time stamp within Windows.

Reading and Writing Data One Word at a Time   415

As you have learned, the *getc* and *putc* functions let you read and write file information one byte at a time. Depending on your file's contents, at times you may want to read and write data one word at a time. To help you do so, most C compilers provide the *getw* and *putw* functions, as shown here:

```
#include <stdio.h>

int getw(FILE *stream);
int putw(int word, FILE *stream);
```

If *getw* succeeds, it will return the integer value read from the file. If an error occurs or *getw* encounters the end of file, *getw* will return *EOF*. If *putw* succeeds, it will return the integer value which *putw* wrote to the file. If an error occurs, *putw* will return *EOF*. The following program, *putwgetw.c*, uses the function *putw* to write the values 1 to 100 to a file. *Putwgetw.c* then opens the same file and reads the values using *getw*, as shown here:

```
#include <stdio.h>
#include <stdlib.h>

void main(void)
 {
   FILE *fp;
   int word;
   if ((fp = fopen("DATA.DAT", "wb")) == NULL)
    {
       printf("Error opening DATA.DAT for output\n");
       exit(1);
    }
   else
    {
       for (word = 1; word <= 100; word++)
         putw(word, fp);
       fclose(fp);
    }
   if ((fp = fopen("DATA.DAT", "rb")) == NULL)
    {
       printf("Error opening DATA.DAT for input\n");
       exit(1);
    }
   else
    {
      do
       {
          word = getw(fp);
          if ((word == EOF) && (feof(fp)))
            break;
          else
            printf("%d ", word);
       }
      while (1);
      fclose(fp);
    }
 }
```

416 CHANGING A FILE'S SIZE

As you work with files, there may be times when you must allocate a large amount of disk space for a file or when you want to truncate a file's size. For such cases, your programs can use the *chsize* function, as shown here:

```
#include <io.h>

int chsize(int handle, long size);
```

The *handle* parameter is the file handle that *open* or *creat* previously returned to the program. The *size* parameter specifies the desired file size. If *chsize* succeeds, it will return the value 0. If an error occurs, *chsize* will return the value −1 and set the global variable *errno* to one of the values listed in Table 416.

Value	Meaning
EACCES	Invalid access
EBADF	Invalid file handle
ENOSPC	Insufficient space (Unix)

*Table 416 Error values **chsize** returns.*

If you increase a file's size, then *chsize* will fill the new file space with *NULL* characters. The following program, *chsize.c*, creates a file named *100zeros.dat* and then uses the *chsize* function to zero-fill the file's first 100 bytes:

```
#include <stdio.h>
#include <io.h>
#include <fcntl.h>
#include <sys\types.h>
#include <sys\stat.h>

void main(void)
 {
   int handle;

   if ((handle = creat("100ZEROS.DAT", S_IWRITE)) == -1)
      fprintf(stderr, "Error opening 100ZEROS.DAT");
   else
    {
      if (chsize(handle, 100L))
        printf("Error changing file size\n");
      close(handle);
    }
 }
```

417 CONTROLLING READ AND WRITE FILE-OPEN OPERATIONS

As you have learned, when you open a file, whether you are using *open*, *creat*, or *fopen*, you must specify whether you want to access the file in read, write, or read and write mode. The *umask* function lets you control how the program later opens files. The format of the *umask* function is as follows:

```
#include <io.h>

unsigned umask(unsigned access_mode);
```

The *access_mode* parameter specifies the modes you want to prevent files from using. Valid values for the *access_mode* parameter are shown in Table 417.

Access Mode	Meaning
S_IWRITE	Prevents write access
S_IREAD	Prevents read access
S_IWRITE | S_IREAD	Prevents read and write access

*Table 417 The valid values for the **access_mode** parameter of the **umask** function.*

As an example, if you want to prevent a program from opening files with write access, then you would use *umask* as follows:

```
old_mode = umask(S_IWRITE);
```

As shown here, the function returns the previous setting. The following program, *umask.c*, uses the *umask* function to set the access mode to *S_IWRITE*, which will clear the file's write-access bit (making the file read-only). The program then creates and writes output to the file *output.dat*. After the program closes the file, it tries to open *output.dat* for write access. Because *umask* previously set the file to read-only, the open operation fails, as shown here:

```
#include <stdio.h>
#include <io.h>
#include <fcntl.h>
#include <sys\stat.h>
#include <stdlib.h>

void main(void)
  {
    int output;
    int old_setting;

    old_setting = umask(S_IWRITE);
    if ((output = creat("OUTPUT.DAT", S_IWRITE)) == -1)
      {
         fprintf(stderr, "Error creating OUTPUT.DAT\n");
         exit(1);
      }
    else
      {
        if (write(output, "Test", 4) == -1)
          fprintf(stderr, "Cannot write to file\n");
        else
          printf("File successfully written to\n");
        close(output);
      }
    if ((output = open("OUTPUT.DAT", O_WRONLY)) == -1)
      fprintf(stderr, "Error opening OUTPUT.DAT for output\n");
    else
      printf("File successfully opened for write access\n");
  }
```

Note: *To remove the file **output.dat** from your disk, you must issue the command **ATTRIB -R output.dat** and then delete the file.*

ASSIGNING A FILE BUFFER 418

In the Keyboard section of this book you will learn that C provides I/O functions that perform buffered and direct I/O. For buffered I/O operations, data writes to or reads into a buffer before becoming available to your program. File operations, for example, use buffered I/O. When your programs perform direct I/O, on the other hand, the data is immediately available to your programs without being placed in an intermediate buffer. You can often use direct I/O to gain direct access to the keyboard. Usually, C automatically allocates a buffer for file streams. However, you can use the *setbuf* function to specify your own buffer, as shown here:

```
#include <stdio.h>
void setbuf(FILE *stream, char *buffer);
```

The *stream* parameter corresponds to the open file to which you want to assign the new buffer. The *buffer* parameter is a pointer to the desired buffer. If the *buffer* parameter contains *NULL*, the open file that *stream* specifies will not buffer the data. The following program, *setbuf.c*, uses the *setbuf* function to change the buffer that C assigns to the *stdout* file handle. The program then writes output to *stdout*. However, because the program is placing the data in a large buffer, the data will not appear on your screen until a three-second delay passes. The program then fills the buffer one character at a time, delaying ten milliseconds between characters. When the buffer becomes full, it flushes (writes) to the screen, as shown here:

```
#include <stdio.h>
#include <dos.h>
#include <conio.h>

void main(void)
  {
    char buffer[512];
    int letter;

    setbuf(stdout, buffer);
    puts("First line of output");
    puts("Second line of output");
    puts("Third line of output");
    delay(3000);
    printf("About to fill buffer\n");
    fflush(stdout);
    for (letter = 0; letter < 513; letter++)
      {
        putchar('A');
        delay(10);
      }
  }
```

419 ALLOCATING A FILE BUFFER

In Tip 418 you learned how to use the *setbuf* function to assign a buffer to a file. When you use *setbuf*, you must specify the desired buffer. In a similar way, many C compilers provide the *setvbuf* function, which allocates a buffer (using *malloc*) of the desired size and then assigns the buffer to the specified file. In addition, *setbuf* lets you specify the buffering you desire, as shown here:

```
#include <stdio.h>
int setvbuf(FILE *stream, char *buffer, int buffer_type, size_t buffer_size);
```

The *stream* parameter is a pointer to an open file. The *buffer* parameter is a pointer to the buffer into which C buffers your data. If the *buffer* parameter is *NULL*, the *setvbuf* function will allocate the buffer for you. The *buffer_type* parameter lets you control the buffer type. Finally, the *buffer_size* parameter lets you specify a buffer size up to 32,767 bytes. If *setvbuf* succeeds, it returns 0. If an error occurs (such as insufficient memory), *setvbuf* returns a non-zero value. Table 419 lists the valid values for the *buffer_type* parameter.

Buffer Type	Buffering
_IOFBF	Full buffering. When the buffer is empty, the next read operation will try to fill the buffer. For output, the buffer must be full before *setvbuf* writes data to the disk.
_IOLBF	Line buffering. When the buffer is empty, the next read operation will try to fill the buffer. For output, *setvbuf* writes the buffer to disk when the buffer is full or when *setvbuf* encounters the *newline* character.
_IONBF	Unbuffered. The program will perform direct I/O.

Table 419 Valid buffering types setvbuf uses.

The following program, *setvbuf.c*, uses *setvbuf* to allocate an 8Kb buffer for full buffering:

```
#include <stdio.h>
#include <dos.h>
#include <conio.h>

void main(void)
  {
    char line[512];
    char *buffer;
    FILE *input;

    if ((input = fopen("\\AUTOEXEC.BAT", "r")) == NULL)
      printf("Error opening \\AUTOEXEC.BAT\n");
```

```
      else
        {
          if (setvbuf(input, buffer, _IOFBF, 8192))
            printf("Error changing file buffer\n");
          else
            while (fgets(line, sizeof(line), input))
              fputs(line, stdout);
          fclose(input);
        }
    }
```

CREATING A UNIQUE FILENAME USING MKTEMP   420

As you work with files, the ability to create a unique filename for temporary files is very important. Some of the Tips in this section demonstrate ways to create random filenames. In many cases, you will want to create a unique filename, but you will also want the filename to follow a specific format that will relate it to the application. For example, for an accounting program you might want all your filenames to begin with the letters *ACCNTG*. To help you control the creation of unique filenames, many C compilers provide the *mktemp* function, as shown here:

```
#include <dir.h>

char *mktemp(char *template);
```

The *template* is a pointer to a character string that contains six characters followed by six Xs and a *NULL*. In the case of the accounting example, the template would be a pointer to "ACCNTGXXXXXX". The *mktemp* function replaces the Xs with two filename characters, a period, and three characters for the extension. If *mktemp* succeeds, it will return a pointer to the template string. If an error occurs, the function will return *NULL*. Because *mktemp* appends letters to the *template* parameter, you must ensure that you allocate 13 or more character positions within the string. The following program, *mktemp.c*, illustrates how to use the *mktemp* function:

```
#include <stdio.h>
#include <dir.h>

void main(void)
  {
     char name_a[13] = "ACCTNGXXXXXX";
     char name_b[13] = "COMPUTXXXXXX";
     char name_c[13] = "PCCHIPXXXXXX";

     if (mktemp(name_a))
       puts(name_a);
     if (mktemp(name_b))
       puts(name_b);
     if (mktemp(name_c))
       puts(name_c);
  }
```

When you compile and execute the *mktemp.c* program, your screen will display the following:

```
ACCTNGAA.AAA
COMPUTAA.AAA
PCCHIPAA.AAA
C:\>
```

READING AND WRITING STRUCTURES   421

The Structures section of this book presents many programs that work with structures. When your programs work with structures, there will be many times when your programs must store the structure data onto either a floppy disk or the computer's hard drive and then later read the data. As a rule, when you must read or write a structure, you can treat the structure as a long byte range. For example, the following program, *dtout.c*, uses C's *write* function to write the current system date and time to the file *datetime.dat*:

```
#include <stdio.h>
#include <dos.h>
#include <io.h>
#include <sys\stat.h>

void main(void)
{
   struct date curr_date;
   struct time curr_time;
   int handle;

   getdate(&curr_date);
   gettime(&curr_time);
   if ((handle = creat("DATETIME.OUT", S_IWRITE)) == -1)
     fprintf(stderr, "Error opening file DATETIME.OUT\n");
   else
     {
        write(handle, &curr_date, sizeof(curr_date));
        write(handle, &curr_time, sizeof(curr_time));
        close(handle);
     }
}
```

As you can see, to write the structure the program simply passes the structure's address. In a similar way, the following program, *dtin.c*, uses the *read* function to read the date and time structures:

```
#include <stdio.h>
#include <dos.h>
#include <io.h>
#include <fcntl.h>

void main(void)
{
   struct date curr_date;
   struct time curr_time;
   int handle;

   if ((handle = open("DATETIME.OUT", O_RDONLY)) == -1)
     fprintf(stderr, "Error opening file DATETIME.OUT\n");
   else
     {
        read(handle, &curr_date, sizeof(curr_date));
        read(handle, &curr_time, sizeof(curr_time));
        close(handle);
        printf("Date: %02d-%02d-%02d\n", curr_date.da_mon,
               curr_date.da_day, curr_date.da_year);
        printf("Time: %02d:%02d\n", curr_time.ti_hour, curr_time.ti_min);
     }
}
```

422 READING STRUCTURE DATA FROM A FILE STREAM

In Tip 421 you learned how to use C's *read* and *write* functions to perform file I/O operations that use structures. If your programs use file streams, as opposed to file handles, for file I/O you can perform similar processing using the *fread* and *fwrite* functions, as shown here:

```
#include <stdio.h>

size_t fread(void *buffer, size_t buffer_size, size_t element_count, FILE *stream);
size_t fwrite(void *buffer, size_t buffer_size, size_t element_count, FILE *stream);
```

The *buffer* parameter contains a pointer to the data you want to output. The *buffer_size* parameter specifies the data's size in bytes. The *element_count* parameter specifies the number of structures that you are writing, and the *stream* parameter is a pointer to an open file stream. If the functions succeed, they will return the number of items read or written. If an error occurs or either function encounters the end of file, both functions will return 0. The following program, *dtoutf.c*, uses the *fwrite* function to write the current date and time structures to a file:

```
#include <stdio.h>
#include <dos.h>

void main(void)
  {
     struct date curr_date;
     struct time curr_time;
     FILE *output;

     getdate(&curr_date);
     gettime(&curr_time);
     if ((output = fopen("DATETIME.OUT", "w")) == NULL)
       fprintf(stderr, "Error opening file DATETIME.OUT\n");
     else
       {
          fwrite(&curr_date, sizeof(curr_date), 1, output);
          fwrite(&curr_time, sizeof(curr_time), 1, output);
          fclose(output);
       }
  }
```

Likewise, the program *dtinf.c* uses the *fread* function to read the structure values, as shown here:

```
#include <stdio.h>
#include <dos.h>

void main(void)
  {
     struct date curr_date;
     struct time curr_time;
     FILE *input;

     if ((input = fopen("DATETIME.OUT", "r")) == NULL)
       fprintf(stderr, "Error opening file DATETIME.OUT\n");
     else
       {
          fread(&curr_date, sizeof(curr_date), 1, input);
          fread(&curr_time, sizeof(curr_time), 1, input);
          fclose(input);
          printf("Date: %02d-%02d-%02d\n", curr_date.da_mon,
                  curr_date.da_day, curr_date.da_year);
          printf("Time: %02d:%02d\n", curr_time.ti_hour, curr_time.ti_min);
       }
  }
```

DUPLICATING A FILE HANDLE 423

Several Tips in this section present functions that work with file handles. Depending on your programs, there may be times when you want to duplicate a handle's value. For example, if your program performs critical I/O operations, you might want to duplicate a file handle and then close the new copied handle in order to flush the file's output to disk. Because the first file handle remains open, you do not have the overhead of reopening the file after the flush operation, as shown here:

```
#include <io.h>

int dup(int handle);
```

The *handle* parameter is the open file handle that you want to duplicate. If *dup* successfully duplicates the handle, it will return a non-negative value. If an error occurs, *dup* will return –1. The following program, *dup.c*, illustrates how you might use the *dup* function to flush a file's buffers:

```
#include <stdio.h>
#include <fcntl.h>
#include <io.h>
#include <sys\stat.h>

void main(void)
  {
```

```
    int handle;
    int duplicate_handle;
    char title[] = "Jamsa\'s C/C++ Programmer\'s Bible!";
    char section[] = "Files";

    if ((handle = open("OUTPUT.TST", O_WRONLY | O_CREAT, S_IWRITE)) == -1)
      printf("Error opening OUTPUT.TST\n");
    else
     {
       if ((duplicate_handle = dup(handle)) == -1)
         printf("Error duplicating handle\n");
       else
         {
           write(handle, title, sizeof(title));
           close(duplicate_handle);                    // Flush the buffer
           write(handle, section, sizeof(section));
           close(handle);
         }
     }
 }
```

424 FORCING A FILE HANDLE'S SETTING

In Tip 423 you learned how to use the *dup* command to make a duplicate copy of a file handle's contents. There may be times when you want to change an open file handle's setting and assign the value of a different handle. When performing change and assign operations with files, you can use *dup2*, as shown here:

```
#include <io.h>

int dup2(int source_handle, int target_handle);
```

The *target_handle* parameter is the file handle whose value you want to update. If the function successfully assigns the handle, it will return the value 0. If an error occurs, the function will return –1. The *source_handle* parameter is the file handle whose value you want to assign to the target. The following program, *dup2.c*, uses the *dup2* function to assign the value of the *stderr* function to *stdout*. In this way, users cannot redirect the program's output from the screen display:

```
#include <stdio.h>
#include <io.h>

void main(void)
 {
   dup2(2, 1);  // stdout is handle 1 stderr is handle 2
   printf("This message cannot be redirected!\n");
 }
```

425 ASSOCIATING A FILE HANDLE WITH A STREAM

Many Tips in this section present functions that work with either file streams or file handles. Depending on your program, there may be times when you are working with a file handle and want to use a function that corresponds to a file stream. In such cases, your programs can use the *fdopen* function to associate a file handle with a file stream, as shown here:

```
#include <stdio.h>

FILE *fdopen(int handle, char *access_mode);
```

The *handle* parameter is the handle of an open file that you want to associate with a file stream. The *access_mode* parameter is a pointer to a character string that specifies how you plan to use the file stream. The *access_mode* value must be one of the mode values you would usually use with *fopen*. If the function succeeds, it returns the stream pointer. If an error occurs, the function returns *NULL*. The following statement, for example, associates the file handle *input* with the file pointer *fpin* for read access:

```
if ((fp = fdopen(input, "r")) == NULL)
   printf("Error associating file\n");
else
```

```
{
    gets(string, sizeof(string), fpin);
    fclose(fpin);
}
```

UNDERSTANDING FILE SHARING 426

If you are working in a network environment and have installed the DOS SHARE command, you can write programs that let more than one program access different parts of the same file at the same time. For example, consider a program that lets multiple users assign seats in an airplane. When one user wants to assign a specific seat, the program locks that seat so another user will not also assign it. After the program assigns the seat, the user unlocks the seat.

When you share files in this way, you must first use the *sopen* function to open the file for sharing. Next, when your program wants to access a range of bytes in the file, the program tries to lock the data. If no one else is currently using (locking) the data, then the program's lock succeeds. After the program finishes with the data, it can unlock the range of bytes in the file.

When a program locks a range of bytes within a file, the program can assign a lock that will let other users access the data in specific ways. For example, the program might let another file read the locked range or it might let other programs read and write the same byte range. Several of the following Tips discuss C run-time library functions that support file sharing and locking.

OPENING A FILE FOR SHARED ACCESS 427

In Tip 426 you learned that you can use the DOS SHARE command to open files for multiple programs to use at the same time. To open a file for shared use, your programs must use the *sopen* function, as shown here:

```
#include <share.h>
int sopen(char *pathname, int access_mode, int share_flag[, int create_mode]);
```

The *pathname*, *access_mode*, and *create_mode* parameters are similar to those the *open* function uses. The *share_flag* parameter specifies how different programs can share the file. If *sopen* successfully opens the file, it will return a file handle. If an error occurs, *sopen* will return –1. Table 427 lists the valid values for the *share_flag* parameter.

Share Flag	Sharing Allowed
SH_COMPAT	Allows compatible sharing
SH_DENYRW	Prevents read and write access
SH_DENYWR	Prevents write access
SH_DENYRD	Prevents read access
SH_DENYNONE	Allows all access (read and write)
SH_DENYNO	Allows all access (read and write)

*Table 427 Shared access modes **sopen** supports.*

The following program, *sopen.c*, opens the file specified in the command line for shared read access. The file then waits for you to press a key before reading and displaying the file's contents, as shown here:

```
#include <stdio.h>
#include <share.h>
#include <io.h>
#include <fcntl.h>
void main(int argc, char *argv[])
  {
    int handle, bytes_read;
    char buffer[256];
```

```
if ((handle = sopen(argv[1], O_RDONLY, SH_DENYWR)) == -1)
  printf("Error opening the file %s\n", argv[1]);
else
  {
    printf("Press Enter to continue\n");
    getchar();
    while (bytes_read = read(handle, buffer, sizeof(buffer)))
      write(1, buffer, bytes_read);  // 1 is stdout
    close(handle);
  }
}
```

To better understand how the *sopen.c* program works, invoke the SHARE command. Next, start Windows and create a DOS window within which you run the program using the filename *sopen.c* as the shared file. When the program prompts you to press a key, open a second DOS window and use TYPE to display the file's contents. As TYPE displays the *sopen.c* file's contents, two programs have the file open at the same time. Close the window and return to the first window. Press ENTER to display the file's contents. Experiment with the *sopen.c* program by chaining the shared modes. Repeat the process of trying to access the file using two programs.

428 LOCKING A FILE'S CONTENTS

As you have learned, when you share a file's contents, there may be times when you want to lock a range of bytes within a file to prevent another program from changing them. To lock a specific range of bytes within a file, your programs can use the *lock* function, as shown here:

```
#include <io.h>

int lock(int handle, long start_position, long byte_count);
```

The *handle* parameter is a handle that corresponds to a file that *sopen* opened for sharing. The *start_position* parameter specifies the starting offset of the range of bytes you want to lock within the file. The *byte_count* parameter specifies the number of bytes you want to lock. If the *lock* function successfully locks the range of bytes, it will return the value 0. If an error occurs, the function will return –1. You must have the DOS SHARE command installed for the *lock* function to work.

After you lock a range of bytes, other programs will try three times to read or write the locked range. If after the third try the program cannot read the data, then the *read* or *write* function will return an error. The following program, *lockauto.c*, locks the first five bytes of the root directory file *autoexec.bat* and then waits for you to press a key:

```
#include <stdio.h>
#include <io.h>
#include <share.h>
#include <fcntl.h>

void main(void)
  {
    int handle;

    if ((handle = sopen("\\AUTOEXEC.BAT", O_RDONLY, SH_DENYNO)) == -1)
      printf("Error opening AUTOEXEC.BAT\n");
    else
      {
        lock(handle, 0L, 5L);
        printf("File locked--press Enter to continue\n");
        getchar();
        close(handle);
      }
  }
```

Next, the following program, *tryauto.c*, tries to read the file *autoexec.bat* one byte at a time. If an error occurs while it reads the file, then the program will display an error message, as shown here:

```c
#include <stdio.h>
#include <io.h>
#include <share.h>
#include <fcntl.h>

void main(void)
 {
   int handle;
   int offset = 0;
   int bytes_read;
   char buffer[128];

   if ((handle = sopen("\\AUTOEXEC.BAT", O_BINARY | O_RDONLY, SH_DENYNO)) == -1)
     printf("Error opening AUTOEXEC.BAT\n");
   else
    {
      while (bytes_read = read(handle, buffer, 1))
       {
         if (bytes_read == -1)
           printf("Error reading offset %d\n", offset);
         else
           write(1, buffer, bytes_read);
         offset++;
         lseek(handle, offset, SEEK_SET);
       }
      close(handle);
    }
 }
```

GAINING FINER FILE-LOCKING CONTROL 429

In Tip 428 you learned how to use the *lock* function to lock a range of bytes within a file. When you use the *lock* function, the operation either succeeds or immediately fails. If you want finer control of the lock operation, you can use the *locking* function, as shown here:

```c
#include <io.h>
#include <sys\locking.h>

int locking(int handle, int lock_command, long byte_count);
```

The *handle* parameter is the handle associated with the file you want to lock. The *lock_command* parameter specifies the desired locking operation. The *byte_count* parameter specifies the number of bytes you want to lock. The start of the region depends on the file's current position pointer. If you want to lock a specific region, you can first use the *lseek* function to position the file pointer. Table 429.1 specifies the possible values for *lock_command*.

Lock Command	Meaning
LK_LOCK	Locks the specified region. If the lock does not succeed, *locking* will try once every second for ten seconds to apply the lock.
LK_RLCK	Performs the same functions as *LK_LOCK*.
LK_NBLCK	Locks the specified region. If the lock does not succeed, *locking* will immediately return an error.
LK_UNLCK	Unlocks a previously locked region.

*Table 429.1 Commands the **locking** function uses.*

If the *locking* function successfully locks the file, it will return the value 0. If an error occurs, the *locking* function will return the value −1 and set the global variable *errno* to one of the values specified in Table 429.2.

Error Status	Meaning
EBADF	Invalid file handle
EACCESS	File already locked or unlocked

*Table 429.2 Error status values the **locking** function returns.* *(continued on following page)*

Error Status	Meaning
EDEADLOCK	File cannot be locked after 10 tries
EINVAL	Invalid command specified

*Table 429.2 Error status values the **locking** function returns. (continued from previous page)*

The following program, *locking.c*, changes the program *lockauto.c*, presented in Tip 428, to use the *locking* function to lock the first five bytes of *autoexec.bat*:

```
#include <stdio.h>
#include <io.h>
#include <share.h>
#include <fcntl.h>
#include <sys\locking.h>

void main(void)
{
  int handle;

  if ((handle = sopen("\\AUTOEXEC.BAT", O_RDONLY, SH_DENYNO)) == -1)
    printf("Error opening AUTOEXEC.BAT\n");
  else
  {
    printf("Trying to lock file\n");
    if (locking(handle, LK_LOCK, 5L))
      printf("Error locking file\n");
    else
    {
      printf("File locked--press Enter to continue\n");
      getchar();
      close(handle);
    }
  }
}
```

As before, if you have Windows available, try running the *locking.c* program from within two DOS windows at the same time.

Note: *Before you can use the **locking** function, you must install the DOS SHARE command.*

430 WORKING WITH DOS DIRECTORIES

Within your C programs, you can use the *findfirst* and *findnext* functions to work with files that match a specific wildcard combination (for example, "*.exe"). Because DOS does not treat directories as files, your programs cannot use the DOS services to "open" a directory and read its contents. If you understand how DOS lays out information on a disk, however, your programs can read from the DOS file allocation table and root directory and then read and track the sectors that contain a directory's entries. Disk utility commands (such as UNDELETE) and a directory sort tool perform these low-level disk I/O operations. Several of the following Tips illustrate how your programs can use these directory I/O functions. To simplify the task of reading a directory, some C compilers provide the functions listed in Table 430.

Function	Purpose
closedir	Closes a directory stream
opendir	Opens a directory stream for read operations
readdir	Reads the next entry in a directory stream
rewinddir	Moves the directory stream pointer back to the start of the directory

Table 430 Directory I/O functions and their purposes.

OPENING A DIRECTORY

In Tip 430 you learned that many C compilers provide functions that let you open and read the names of files that reside in a specific directory. To open a directory for read operations, your programs can use the *opendir* function, as shown here:

```
#include <dirent.h>

DIR *opendir(char *directory_name);
```

The *directory_name* parameter is a pointer to a character string that contains the desired directory name. If the directory name is *NULL*, *opendir* opens the current directory. If the *opendir* function succeeds, it returns a pointer to a structure of type *DIR*. If an error occurs, the function returns *NULL*. The following statement, for example, illustrates how you would open the DOS directory for read operations:

```
struct DIR *input_directory;

if ((input_directory = opendir("\\DOS")) == NULL)
  printf("Error opening directory\n");
else
  // Statements
```

After you have performed your directory read operations, you should close the directory stream using the *closedir* function, as shown here:

```
#include <dirent.h>

void closedir(DIR *directory);
```

READING A DIRECTORY ENTRY

In Tip 431, you learned how to use the *opendir* function to open a directory listing. After you open a directory, you can use the *readdir* function to read the name of the next entry in the directory list, as shown here:

```
#include <dirent.h>

struct dirent readdir(DIR *directory_pointer);
```

The *directory_pointer* parameter is the pointer which the *opendir* function returns. If *readdir* successfully reads a directory entry, it will return the entry read. If an error occurs or *readdir* reaches the end of the directory, the function will return *NULL*. The *readdir* function reads all the entries in the directory list, including the "." and ".." entries.

USING DIRECTORY SERVICES TO READ C:\WINDOWS

In Tip 431 you learned how to open and close a directory listing. In Tip 432 you learned how to use the *readdir* function to read the next entry in the directory list. The following program, *showdir.c*, uses the run-time library directory entries to open, read, and then close the directory specified in the command line:

```
#include <stdio.h>
#include <dirent.h>

void main(int argc, char *argv[])
 {
   DIR *directory_pointer;
   struct dirent *entry;

   if ((directory_pointer = opendir(argv[1])) == NULL)
     printf("Error opening %s\n", argv[1]);
   else
     {
       while (entry = readdir(directory_pointer))
         printf("%s\n", entry);
       closedir(directory_pointer);
     }
 }
```

The following command, for example, uses the *showdir.c* program to display the names of the files in the directory *c:\windows*:

```
C:\> SHOWDIR C:\WINDOWS  <ENTER>
```

434 REWINDING A DIRECTORY

In Tip 433 you learned that C provides run-time library functions that let you open and read the names of files in a specified directory. As you read directories, there may be times when you want to start reading files at the start of the directory list for a second time. One way to perform this operation is to close and then reopen the directory list. Alternately, your programs can use the *rewinddir* function, as shown here:

```
#include <dirent.h>

void rewinddir(DIR *directory_pointer);
```

The *directory_pointer* parameter is the pointer to the directory list that you want to reset. If you experiment with the *rewinddir* function, you will find that it is much faster to use than closing and reopening the directory list.

435 READING A DISK'S FILES RECURSIVELY

In Tip 433 you used the *showdir.c* program to display the files in a directory list. The following program, *allfiles.c*, uses the run-time library functions to display the names of every file on your disk. To do so, the program uses the recursive function *show_directory* to display filenames, as shown here:

```
#include <stdio.h>
#include <dirent.h>
#include <dos.h>
#include <io.h>
#include <direct.h>
#include <string.h>
void show_directory(char *directory_name)
  {
    DIR *directory_pointer;
    struct dirent *entry;
    unsigned attributes;

    if ((directory_pointer = opendir(directory_name)) == NULL)
      printf("Error opening %s\n", directory_name);
    else
    {
      chdir(directory_name);
      while (entry = readdir(directory_pointer))
        {
          attributes = _chmod(entry, 0);
            // Check if entry is for a subdirectory and is not "." or ".."
          if ((attributes & FA_DIREC) &&
            (strncmp(entry, ".", 1) != 0))
          {
            printf("\n\n----%s----\n", entry);
            show_directory(entry);
          }
          else
            printf("%s\n", entry);
        }
      closedir(directory_pointer);
      chdir("..");
    }
  }

void main(void)
  {
    char buffer[MAXPATH];
```

```
    // Save current directory so you can restore it later
    getcwd(buffer, sizeof(buffer));
    show_directory("\\");
    chdir(buffer);
}
```

DETERMINING THE CURRENT FILE POSITION

C436

You have learned previously how C tracks the current position in files that are open for input or output operations. Depending on your program, there may be times when you must determine the position pointer's value. If you are working with file streams, you can use the *ftell* function to determine the file pointer position. If you are working with file handles, however, your programs can use the *tell* function, as shown here:

```
#include <stdio.h>

long tell(int handle);
```

The *tell* function returns a long value that specifies the byte offset of the current position in the specified file. The following program, *tell.c*, uses the *tell* function to display position pointer information. The program begins by opening the root directory file *config.sys* in read mode. The program then uses *tell* to display the current position. Next, the program reads and displays the file's contents. After the program finds the end of file, the program again uses *tell* to display the current position, as shown here:

```
#include <stdio.h>
#include <io.h>
#include <fcntl.h>

void main(void)
 {
   int handle;
   char buffer[512];
   int bytes_read;

   if ((handle = open("\\CONFIG.SYS", O_RDONLY)) == -1)
     printf("Error opening \\CONFIG.SYS\n");
   else
     {
        printf("Current file position %ld\n", tell(handle));
        while (bytes_read = read(handle, buffer, sizeof(buffer)))
          write(1, buffer, bytes_read);
        printf("Current file position %ld\n", tell(handle));
        close(handle);
     }
 }
```

OPENING A SHARED FILE STREAM

C437

Several Tips in this section present ways to share and lock files using file handles. If you usually work with file streams, your programs can use the *_fsopen* function, as shown here:

```
#include <stdio.h>
#include <share.h>

FILE * _fsopen(const char *filename, const *access_mode, int share_flag);
```

The *filename* and *access_mode* parameters contain character-string pointers to the desired filename and access mode that you would normally use with *fopen*. The *share_flag* specifies the sharing mode. If the function succeeds, it will return a file pointer. If an error occurs, the function will return *NULL*. Table 437 lists the valid values you can assign to *share_flag*.

Share Flag	Sharing Allowed
SH_COMPAT	Allows compatible sharing
SH_DENYRW	Prevents read and write access

*Table 437 Valid values for the **access_mode** parameter. (continued on following page)*

Share Flag	Sharing Allowed
SH_DENYWR	Prevents write access
SH_DENYRD	Prevents read access
SH_DENYNONE	Allows all access (read and write)
SH_DENYNO	Allows all access (read and write)

*Table 437 Valid values for the **access_mode** parameter. (continued from previous page)*

The following statements, for example, open the root directory file *autoexec.bat* for shared read operations:

```
if ((fp = _fsopen("\\AUTOEXEC.BAT", "r", SH_DENYWR)) == NULL)
    printf("Error opening \\AUTOEXEC.BAT\n");
else
    // Statements
```

438 CREATING A UNIQUE FILE IN A SPECIFIC DIRECTORY

Several Tips in this section show ways that your programs can create temporary files. If you usually work with file handles, you can use the function *creattemp*, which returns a handle, as shown here:

```
#include <dos.h>

int creattemp(char *path, int attribute);
```

The *path* parameter specifies the name of the directory within which you want to create the file. The name must end with two backslash characters ('\\'). The *creattemp* function will append the filename to the string to produce a complete pathname. The *attribute* parameter specifies the desired file attributes (or 0 for none). Table 438 lists the valid settings for the *attribute* parameter.

Constant	Description
FA_RDONLY	Read-only file
FA_HIDDEN	Hidden file
FA_SYSTEM	System file

*Table 438 The valid settings for the **attribute** parameter.*

If the function succeeds, it will return a file handle. If an error occurs, the function will return –1. The following program, *creattmp.c*, uses the *creattemp* function to create a unique file in the TEMP directory:

```
#include <stdio.h>
#include <dos.h>
#include <io.h>

void main(void)
  {
    char path[64] = "C:\\TEMP\\";
    int handle;

    if ((handle = creattemp(path, 0)) == -1)
      printf("Error creating file\n");
    else
      {
        printf("Complete path: %s\n", path);
        close(handle);
      }
  }
```

439 CREATING A NEW FILE

Several Tips in this section show ways to create files. In many cases, if you try to create a file and the name specified in the function already exists, the function will truncate the file's contents. However, you often might only want to create a file if a file with the same name does not already exist. For such cases, your programs can use the *creatnew* function, as shown here:

```
#include <dos.h>

int creatnew(const char *pathname, int attribute);
```

The *pathname* parameter specifies the complete path of the file you want to create. The *attribute* parameter specifies the desired file attributes (or 0 for none). Table 439.1 lists the possible settings for the *attribute* parameter.

Attribute	Meaning
FA_RDONLY	Read-only file
FA_HIDDEN	Hidden file
FA_SYSTEM	System file

*Table 439.1 The possible settings for the **attribute** parameter of the **creatnew** function.*

If *createnew* succeeds, it will return a file handle. If an error occurs, the function will return the value −1 and set the global variable *errno* to one of the values listed in Table 439.2.

Error	Meaning
EXISTS	File already exists
ENOENT	Path not found
EMFILE	Too many open files
EACCES	Access violation

*Table 439.2 The error return values for **creatnew**.*

The following program, *creatnew.c*, uses the *creatnew* function to create a file named *new.dat* in the current directory. Experiment with this program and try to create the file more than once, as shown here:

```
#include <stdio.h>
#include <dos.h>
#include <io.h>

void main(void)
 {
   int handle;

   if ((handle = creatnew("NEW.DAT", 0)) == -1)
     printf("Error creating NEW.DAT\n");
   else
    {
      printf("File successfully created\n");
      close(handle);
    }
 }
```

USING THE DOS SERVICES TO ACCESS A FILE 440

As you have learned, when your programs must access more than 20 files, you might want to use the DOS services, which will let you bypass the C run-time library routines. The following program, *copydos.c*, uses the DOS services to copy the contents of the first file specified in the command line to the second:

```
#include <stdio.h>
#include <dos.h>

void main(int argc, char **argv)
  {
    union REGS inregs, outregs;
    struct SREGS segs;
    char buffer[256];
    unsigned source_handle, target_handle;
```

```
   if (*argv[1] && *argv[2])
     {
        // Open the file to copy
        inregs.h.ah = 0x3D;
        inregs.h.al = 0;         // Open for read access
        inregs.x.dx = (unsigned) argv[1];
        segread (&segs);
        intdosx(&inregs, &outregs, &segs);
        if (outregs.x.cflag)
          printf ("Error opening source file %s\n", argv[1]);
        else
          {
             source_handle = outregs.x.ax;
             // Create the target file, truncating an
             // existing file with the same name
             inregs.h.ah = 0x3C;
             inregs.x.cx = 0;        // Open with normal attribute
             inregs.x.dx = (unsigned) argv[2];
             intdosx (&inregs, &outregs, &segs);
             if (outregs.x.cflag)
               printf ("Error creating target file %s\n", argv[2]);
             else
               {
                  target_handle = outregs.x.ax;
                  do {
                     // Read the source data
                     inregs.h.ah = 0x3F;
                     inregs.x.bx = source_handle;
                     inregs.x.cx = sizeof(buffer);
                     inregs.x.dx = (unsigned) buffer;
                     intdosx (&inregs, &outregs, &segs);
                     if (outregs.x.cflag)
                       {
                          printf ("Error reading source file\n");
                          break;
                       }
                     else if (outregs.x.ax)  // Not end of file
                       {
                          // Write the data
                          inregs.h.ah = 0x40;
                          inregs.x.bx = target_handle;
                          inregs.x.cx = outregs.x.ax;
                          inregs.x.dx = (unsigned) buffer;
                          intdosx (&inregs, &outregs, &segs);
                          if (outregs.x.cflag)
                            {
                               printf ("Error writing target file\n");
                               break;
                            }
                       }
                  } while (outregs.x.ax != 0);
                  // Close the files
                  inregs.h.ah = 0x3E;
                  inregs.x.bx = source_handle;
                  intdos (&inregs, &outregs);
                  inregs.x.bx = target_handle;
                  intdos (&inregs, &outregs);
               }
          }
     }
   else
     printf ("Specify source and target filenames\n");
}
```

Note: *As you have learned, you will generally use the Windows API to perform DOS-service-equivalent activities in Windows. Tip 1471 explains how to copy files using the Windows API.*

FORCING A BINARY OR TEXT FILE OPEN 441

You have learned previously that many C compilers use the global variable _fmode_ to determine whether the program has opened files in text or binary mode. When you use the _fopen_ function, you can control which mode _fopen_ uses by placing the letter _t_ or _b_ immediately after the desired mode, as shown in Table 441.

Access Specifier	Access Mode
ab	Append access binary mode
at	Append access text mode
rb	Read access binary mode
rt	Read access text mode
wb	Write access binary mode
wt	Write access text mode

Table 441 _File mode specifiers for_ **fopen**.

The following _fopen_ statement, for example, opens the file _filename.ext_ for read access in binary mode:

```
if ((fp = fopen("FILENAME.EXT", "rb")))
```

READING LINES OF TEXT 442

When your programs read text files, they will usually do so one line at a time. To read a line from a file, your programs can use the _fgets_ function, whose format is shown here:

```
#include <stdio.h>

char *fgets(char string, int limit, FILE *stream);
```

The _string_ parameter is the character buffer into which _fgets_ reads the file data. Usually your programs will declare an array of 128 or 256 bytes to hold the data. The _limit_ parameter specifies the number of characters the buffer can hold. When _fgets_ reads characters from the file, _fgets_ will read up to _limit_–1 (_limit_ minus one) or to the first _newline_ character (\n), whichever comes first. The function will then place a _NULL_ character in the buffer to indicate the end of the string.

Many programs will use the _sizeof_ function to specify the buffer size, such as _sizeof_(_string_). Finally, the _stream_ parameter specifies the file from which _fgets_ must read the string. You must have previously opened the stream using _fopen_ or used a predefined handle, such as _stdin_. If _fgets_ successfully reads information from the file, _fgets_ will return a pointer to the string. If an error occurs or if it reaches the end of file, _fgets_ will return _NULL_.

WRITING LINES OF TEXT 443

You learned in Tip 442 that your programs will typically read from a file one line at a time. When writing to a file, your programs will typically write one line at a time. To write a string to a file, your programs can use the _fputs_ function, as shown here:

```
#include <stdio.h>

int fputs(const char *string, FILE *stream);
```

The _fputs_ function writes the characters in a specified string up to the _NULL_ termination character. If _fputs_ successfully writes the string, it will return a positive value to the calling function. If an error occurs, _fputs_ will return the constant _EOF_.

PUTTING FGETS AND FPUTS TO USE 444

In Tips 442 and 443 you learned that your programs can use the functions _fgets_ and _fputs_ to read and write file data. The following program, _textcopy.c_, uses _fgets_ and _fputs_ to copy the contents of the first file specified in the command line to the second file specified in the command line:

```
#include <stdio.h>

void main(int argc, char **argv)
  {
    FILE *input, *output;
    char string[256];

    if ((input = fopen(argv[1], "r")) == NULL)
      printf("Error opening %s\n", argv[1]);
    else if ((output = fopen(argv[2], "w")) == NULL)
      {
        printf("Error opening %s\n", argv[2]);
        fclose(input);
      }
    else
      {
        while (fgets(string, sizeof(string), input))
          fputs(string, output);
        fclose(input);
        fclose(output);
      }
  }
```

As you can see, the program opens an input file and output file and then reads and writes text until the *fgets* function encounters the end of file (*fgets* returns *NULL*). To copy the contents of the file *test.dat* to *test.sav*, for example, you would use the *textcopy.c* program as follows:

```
C:\> TEXTCOPY TEST.DAT TEST.SAV   <ENTER>
```

445 FORCING BINARY FILE TRANSLATION

As you have learned, many compilers use the global variable *_fmode* to determine text or binary file access. In text mode, the C run-time library functions translate linefeed characters into carriage return linefeed combinations and vice versa. As you learned, by setting the *_fmode* variable to *O_TEXT* or *O_BINARY*, you can control the access mode. In addition, by placing a *t* or *b* within the access mode specified in *fopen*, you can set the access mode for text or binary mode access. The following *fopen* function call, for example, opens the file *filename.ext* for read access in binary mode:

```
if ((fp = fopen("FILENAME.EXT", "rb")) == NULL)
```

446 UNDERSTANDING WHY TEXTCOPY CANNOT COPY BINARY FILES

Tip 444 presented the program *textcopy.c*, which copied the contents of the first file specified in the command line to the second file. If you try to use *textcopy* to copy a binary file, such as an *exe* file, the copy operation will fail. When the *fgets* function reads a text file, *fgets* considers the CTRL+Z character (the ASCII character 26) as the end of the file. Because a binary file is likely to contain one or more occurrences of the value 26, *fgets* will end its copy operation at the first occurrence. If you want to copy an executable or other binary file, you must use C's low-level I/O routines.

447 TESTING FOR END OF FILE

As you have learned, when the *fgets* function encounters the end of a file, it returns *NULL*. Likewise, when *fgetc* reaches the end of a file, it returns EOF. There may be times when your programs must determine if a file pointer is at the end of the file before it performs a specific operation. In such cases, your programs can call the *feof* function, as shown here:

```
#include <stdio.h>

int feof(FILE *stream);
```

If the file pointer specified is at the end of the file, *feof* will return a non-zero value (true). If it has not yet reached the end of the file, the *feof* will return 0 (false). The following loop reads and displays the characters from the file that corresponds to the file pointer *input*:

```
while (! feof(input))
  fputc(fgetc(input), stdout);
```

Note: *After a function, such as **fgetc**, sets the end-of-file indicator for a file, it remains set until the program closes the file or calls the **rewind** function.*

UNGETTING A CHARACTER 448

Many programs, such as a compiler, for example, often read characters from a file one at a time until they find a specific character (a delimiter or token). After the program finds the character, the program performs specific processing. After the program completes the processing, it continues to read from the file. Depending on the structure of the file your program is reading, there may be times when you want the program to "unread" a character. In such cases, the program can use the *ungetc* function, whose format is shown here:

```
#include <stdio.h>

int ungetc(int character, FILE *stream);
```

The *ungetc* function places the character specified back into the file buffer. You can only "unget" one character. If you call *ungetc* two times in succession, the second character will overwrite the first character that you unget. The *ungetc* function places the specified character in the *FILE* structure *hold* member. In turn, the next file read operation will include the character.

READING FORMATTED FILE DATA 449

You have learned how to use the *fprintf* function to write formatted output to a file. In a similar way, the *fscanf* function lets you read formatted file data, just as the *scanf* function that you have learned about previously lets you read formatted data from the keyboard. The format of the *fscanf* function is as follows:

```
#include <stdio.h>

int fscanf(FILE *stream, const char *format[, variable_address, ...]);
```

The *stream* parameter is a pointer to the file from which you want *fscanf* to read. The *format* parameter specifies the data format—using the same control character as *scanf*. Finally, the *variable_address* parameter specifies an address into which you want the data read. The ellipsis (...) that follows the *variable_address* parameter indicates that you can have multiple addresses separated by commas.

When it completes, *fscanf* returns the number of fields it read. If *fscanf* encounters the end of file, it returns the constant *EOF*. The following program, *fscanf.c*, opens the file *data.dat* for output, writes formatted output to the file using *fprintf*, closes the file, and then reopens it for input, reading its contents with *fscanf*:

```
#include <stdio.h>

void main(void)
 {
   FILE *fp;

   int age;
   float salary;
   char name[64];
   if ((fp = fopen("DATA.DAT", "w")) == NULL)
     printf("Error opening DATA.DAT for output\n");
   else
     {
        fprintf(fp, "33 35000.0 Kris");
        fclose(fp);

        if ((fp = fopen("DATA.DAT", "r")) == NULL)
          printf("Error opening DATA.DAT for input\n");
        else
```

```
    {
        fscanf(fp, "%d %f %s", &age, &salary, name);
        printf("Age %d Salary %f Name %s\n", age, salary, name);
        fclose(fp);
    }
}
}
```

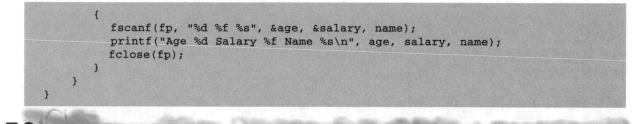

450 POSITIONING OF THE FILE POINTER BASED ON ITS CURRENT LOCATION

You have learned that the file pointer contains a position pointer to track your current position within the file. When you know the format of your file, there may be times when you want to advance the position pointer to a specific location before you start reading the file. For example, the first 256 bytes of your file can contain header information that you do not want to read. In such cases, your programs can use the *fseek* function to position the file pointer, as shown here:

```
#include <stdio.h>
int fseek(FILE *stream, long offset, int relative_to);
```

The *stream* parameter specifies the file pointer you want to position. The *offset* and *relative_to* parameters combine to specify the desired position. The *offset* contains the byte offset into the file. The *relative_to* parameter specifies the location in the file from which *fseek* should apply the offset. Table 450 specifies the values you can use for the *relative_to* parameter.

Constant	Meaning
SEEK_CUR	From current file position
SEEK_SET	From the beginning of the file
SEEK_END	From the end of the file

Table 450 *File positions from which **fseek** can apply an offset.*

To position the file pointer immediately after the first 256 bytes of header information in a file, you would use *fseek*, as follows:

```
fseek(fp, 256, SEEK_SET);   // Offset 0 is the start
```

If successful, *fseek* will return the value 0. If an error occurs, *fseek* will return a non-zero value.

451 GETTING FILE HANDLE INFORMATION

When you work with a file handle, there may be times when you must know specifics about the corresponding file, such as the disk drive that stores the file. In such cases, your programs can use the *fstat* function, which has the following format:

```
#include <sys\stat.h>
int fstat(int handle, struct stat *buffer);
```

The function assigns specifics about the file to a structure of type *stat* defined within the *include* file *stat.h*, as shown here:

```
struct stat
  {
    short st_dev;       // Drive number of disk
    short st_ino;       // Not used by DOS
    short st_mode;      // File open mode
    short st_nlink;     // Always 1
    short st_uid;       // User id--Not used
    short st_gid;       // Group id--Not used
    short st_rdev;      // Same as st_dev
    long st_size;       // File size in bytes
    long st_atime;      // Time file was last opened
```

```
    long st_mtime;     // Same as st_atime
    long st_ctime;     // Same as st_atime
};
```

If *fstat* succeeds, it returns the value 0. If an error occurs, *fstat* returns the value –1 and sets the global variable *errno* to *EBADF* (for a bad file handle). The following program, *autoinfo.c*, uses the *fstat* function to display the date and time of the *autoexec.bat* file's last modification, as well as its size:

```
#include <stdio.h>
#include <io.h>
#include <fcntl.h>
#include <sys\stat.h>
#include <time.h>

void main(void)
  {
    int handle;
    struct stat buffer;

    if ((handle = open("\\AUTOEXEC.BAT", O_RDONLY)) == -1)
      printf("Error opening \\AUTOEXEC.BAT\n");
    else
      {
        if (fstat(handle, &buffer))
          printf("Error getting file information\n");
        else
          printf("AUTOEXEC.BAT is %ld bytes Last used %s\n",
             buffer.st_size, ctime(&buffer.st_atime));
        close(handle);
      }
  }
```

Note: *Tip 1465 details how you can obtain a file's date and time stamp from within Windows.*

REOPENING A FILE STREAM   452

As your programs work with files, at times you may want to override an open file pointer. For example, DOS does not provide a way to redirect the output of the *stderr* file handle from the command line. However, from within your program, you can override the destination of the *stderr* file pointer by reopening it using the *freopen* function:

```
#include <stdio.h>

FILE *freopen(const char *filename, const char, access_mode, FILE *stream);
```

The *freopen* function is similar to *fopen*, except that you pass to the function a file pointer whose value you want to overwrite. If the function succeeds, it returns a pointer to the original file stream. If an error occurs, *freopen* returns *NULL*. The following program, *nostderr.c*, for example, redirects *stderr* functions to the file *standard.err*, as opposed to the screen:

```
#include <stdio.h>

void main(void)
  {
    if (freopen("STANDARD.ERR", "w", stderr))
      fputs("stderr has been redirected", stderr);
    else
      printf("Error in reopen\n");
  }
```

UNDERSTANDING ARRAYS   453

As you have learned, a type describes the set of values a variable can hold and the set of operations that your programs can perform on the variable. Except for character strings, all the types you have examined so far can hold only one value. As your programs begin to perform more useful work, there will be times when you want a variable to hold many values. For example, the variable *scores* might keep track of 100 students' test scores. Likewise, the variable *salaries* might keep track of each company employee's salary. An *array* is a data structure that can store multiple values of the same type. For example, you can create an array that can hold 100 values of type *int* and a second array that can hold 25 values of type *float*.

Every value you assign to an array must be of the same type as the array's type. In this section you will learn how to create and work with arrays in your programs. After you work with one or two arrays, you will find that arrays are easy to understand. If you already feel comfortable with strings, you will soon feel just as comfortable working with arrays. Remember, a character string is simply an array of characters.

454 DECLARING AN ARRAY

In Tip 453 you learned that an *array* is a variable that can store multiple values of the same type. To declare an array, you must specify the desired type (such as *int*, *float*, or *double*), as well as the array size. To specify an array size, you place the number of values the array can store within brackets that follow the array name. The following declaration, for example, creates an array named *scores* that can store 100 test scores of type *int*:

```
int scores[100];
```

In a similar way, the following declaration creates an array of type *float* that contains 50 salaries:

```
float salaries[50];
```

When you declare an array, C allocates enough memory to hold all the elements. The first entry is at location 0. For example, in the arrays *scores* and *salaries*, the following statements assign the values 80 and 35,000 to the first array elements:

```
scores[0] = 80;
salaries[0] = 35000.0;
```

Because the first array element begins at offset 0, the array's last element occurs one location before the array's size. Given the previous arrays, *scores* and *salaries*, the following statements assign values to the last element of each array:

```
scores[99] = 75;

salaries[49] = 24000.0;
```

455 VISUALIZING AN ARRAY

As you have learned, an array is a variable that can store multiple values of the same type. To help you better understand how an array stores information, consider the following array declarations:

```
char string[64];
float salaries[50];
int scores[100];
long planets[13];
```

After you assign values to each array, the arrays will reside in memory in a manner similar to that shown in Figure 455.

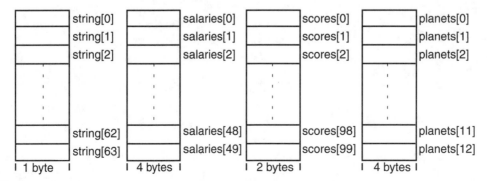

Figure 455 Storing values in arrays.

As you can see, each array's first value resides at offset 0. In the "Getting Started with C" section of this book, you learned that a variable is a name you assign to one or more memory locations. In an array, you may have a large number of memory locations that correspond to a single array.

UNDERSTANDING AN ARRAY'S STORAGE REQUIREMENTS 456

As you have learned, an array is a named collection of values of the same type. When you declare an array, the C compiler allocates enough memory to hold the number of values you specify. The actual amount of memory the compiler allocates depends on the array type. For example, an array of 100 elements of type *int* will usually require 100 * 2 or 200 bytes of memory. An array of 100 elements of type *float*, on the other hand, will require 100 * 4 bytes or 400 bytes. The following program, *arraysiz.c*, uses C's *sizeof* operator to display the amount of memory different array types require:

```
#include <stdio.h>

void main(void)
  {
    int scores[100];
    float salaries[100];
    char string[100];

    printf("Bytes used to hold int scores[100] is %d bytes\n", sizeof(scores));
    printf("Bytes used to hold int salaries[100] is %d bytes\n",
      sizeof(salaries));
    printf("Bytes used to hold char string[100] is %d bytes\n", sizeof(string));
  }
```

When you compile and execute the *arraysiz.c* program, your screen will display the following output:

```
Bytes used to hold int scores[100] is 200 bytes
Bytes used to hold float salaries[100] is 400 bytes
Bytes used to hold char string[100] is 100 bytes
C:\>
```

INITIALIZING AN ARRAY 457

Throughout this book, many of the programs have initialized character strings as follows:

```
char title[] = "Jamsa\'s C/C++ Programmer\'s Bible";
char section[64] = "Arrays";
```

In the first case, the C compiler will allocate 24 bytes to hold the string. In the second case, the compiler will allocate an array of 64 bytes, initializing the first seven characters to the letters "Arrays" and the *NULL* character. Most compilers will also initialize the remaining byte locations to *NULL*. When you declare arrays of other types, you can initialize the arrays in the same way. For example, the following statement initializes the integer array *scores* to the values 80, 70, 90, 85, and 80:

```
int scores[5] = {80, 70, 90, 85, 80};
```

When you assign initial values to an array, you must enclose the values within right and left braces ({}). In the previous case, the array size matches the number of values assigned to the array. The following statement, however, assigns four *floating-point* values to an array that can store 64 values:

```
float salaries[64] = {25000.0, 32000.0, 44000.0, 23000.0};
```

Depending on your compiler, it may assign 0 to the elements to which your program does not assign explicit values. However, as a rule, you should not assume that the compiler will initialize the other elements. Moreover, if you do not specify an array size, the compiler will allocate enough memory to hold only the values you specify. The following array declaration, for example, creates an array large enough to hold three values of type *long*:

```
long planets[] = {1234567L, 654321L, 1221311L};
```

458 ACCESSING ARRAY ELEMENTS

The values stored in an array are called *array elements*. To access an array element, you specify the array name and the element you want. The following program, *elements.c*, initializes the array *scores* and then uses *printf* to display the element values:

```c
#include <stdio.h>

void main(void)
  {
    int scores[5] = {80, 70, 90, 85, 80};

    printf("Array Values\n");
    printf("scores[0] %d\n", scores[0]);
    printf("scores[1] %d\n", scores[1]);
    printf("scores[2] %d\n", scores[2]);
    printf("scores[3] %d\n", scores[3]);
    printf("scores[4] %d\n", scores[4]);
  }
```

When you compile and execute the *elements.c* program, your screen will display the following output:

```
Array Values
scores[0] = 80
scores[1] = 70
scores[2] = 90
scores[3] = 85
scores[4] = 80
C:\>
```

As you can see, to access a specific array element, you specify the element number you want within the left and right brackets that follow the array name.

459 LOOPING THROUGH ARRAY ELEMENTS

In Tip 458 you used the values 0 through 4 to display the elements of the array *scores*. When you reference many array elements, specifying numbers for each array element individually can become time consuming. As an alternative, your programs can use a variable to reference array elements. For example, assuming the variable *i* contains the value 2, the following statement would assign *array[2]* the value 80:

```c
i = 2;

array[i] = 80;
```

The following program, *showarra.c*, uses the variable *i* and a *for* loop to display the elements of the array *scores*:

```c
#include <stdio.h>

void main(void)
  {
    int scores[5] = {80, 70, 90, 85, 80};
    int i;

    printf("Array Values\n");
    for (i = 0; i < 5; i++)
      printf("scores[%d] %d\n", i, scores[i]);
  }
```

460 USING CONSTANTS TO DEFINE ARRAYS

As you have learned, when your programs work with arrays, you must specify the array size. For example, the following program, *5_values.c*, declares an array of five values and then uses a *for* loop to display the array's values:

```
#include <stdio.h>

void main(void)
  {
    int values[5] = {80, 70, 90, 85, 80};
    int i;

    for (i = 0; i < 5; i++)
      printf("values[%d] %d\n", i, values[i]);
  }
```

Assume, for example, that you later want to change the *5_values.c* program so that it supports 10 values. You must then change not only the array declaration, but also the *for* loop. The more changes you must make to a program, the greater your chance of error. As an alternative, your programs should declare arrays using constants. The following program, *5_const.c*, declares an array based on the constant *ARRAY_SIZE*. As you can see, the program not only uses the constant to declare the array, but also uses the constant as the ending condition for the *for* loop:

```
#include <stdio.h>

#define ARRAY_SIZE 5

void main(void)
  {
    int values[ARRAY_SIZE] = {80, 70, 90, 85, 80};
    int i;

    for (i = 0; i < ARRAY_SIZE; i++)
      printf("values[%d] %d\n", i, values[i]);
  }
```

If you must later change the array size, you can change the value assigned to the *ARRAY_SIZE* constant so that the program automatically updates the loops that control the array and the array size.

PASSING AN ARRAY TO A FUNCTION 461

As you have learned, an array is a variable that can store multiple values of the same type. Like all variables, your programs can pass arrays to functions. When you declare a function that works with an array parameter, you must tell the compiler. For example, the following program, *arrfunct.c*, uses the function *show_array* to display the values in an array. As you can see, the program passes to the function both the array and the number of elements the array contains, as shown here:

```
#include <stdio.h>

void show_array(int values[], int number_of_elements)
  {
    int i;

    for (i = 0; i < number_of_elements; i++)
     printf("%d\n", values[i]);
  }

void main(void)
  {
    int scores[5] = {70, 80, 90, 100, 90};

    show_array(scores, 5);
  }
```

When a function receives an array as a parameter, your program does not have to specify the array size in the parameter declaration. In the case of the function *show_values*, the brackets that follow the variable name *value* inform the compiler that the parameter is an array. Other than knowing that the parameter is an array, the compiler does not care about the size of the array your program passes to the function.

REVISITING ARRAYS AS FUNCTIONS 462

In Tip 461 you learned that when you declare the formal parameter for an array, you do not need to declare an array size. Instead, you can specify only the left and right brackets. The following program, *arrparam.c*, passes three different arrays (of different sizes) to the function *show_values*:

```
#include <stdio.h>
void show_array(int values[], int number_of_elements)
  {
    int i;
    printf("About to display %d values\n", number_of_elements);
    for (i = 0; i < number_of_elements; i++)
     printf("%d\n", values[i]);
  }
void main(void)
  {
    int scores[5] = {70, 80, 90, 100, 90};
    int count[10] = {1, 2, 3, 4, 5, 6, 7, 8, 9, 10};
    int small[2] = {-33, -44};

    show_array(scores, 5);
    show_array(count, 10);
    show_array(small, 2);
  }
```

When you compile and execute the *arrparam.c* program, your screen will display each array's values. As you have learned, the function does not care about the array size. However, note that the arrays the *arrparam.c* program passes to the function are all type *int*. If you tried to pass an array of type *float* to the function, the compiler would generate an error.

463 UNDERSTANDING HOW STRING ARRAYS DIFFER

Many Tips presented throughout this book have passed strings to functions. In most cases, the functions did not specify the string size. For example, the following statement uses the *strupr* function to convert a string to uppercase:

```
char title[64] = "Jamsa\'s C/C++ Programmer\'s Bible";

strupr(title);
```

As you have learned, in C, the *NULL* character represents the end of a character string. Therefore, functions can search the array elements for the *NULL* to determine where the array ends. Arrays of other types, such as *int*, *float*, or *long*, however, do not have an equivalent "ending" character. Therefore, you usually must pass to functions that work with arrays the number of elements the array contains.

464 PASSING ARRAYS ON THE STACK

Several previous Tips have discussed passing arrays as parameters to functions. When you pass an array to a function, C only places the address of the array's first element on the stack. Figure 464, for example, illustrates the array *scores* and a function call to *show_array* using *scores*.

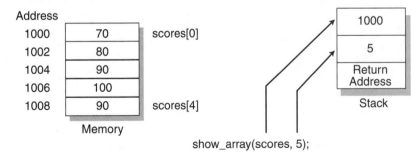

Figure 464 *When you pass an array parameter, C places the array's starting address on the stack.*

As you can see, C places only the array's starting address on the stack. Also, notice that the function receives no information from C regarding the size of the array.

DETERMINING HOW MANY ELEMENTS AN ARRAY CAN HOLD 465

As you have learned, depending on an array's type, the actual amount of memory an array can consume will differ. If you are working in the DOS environment, the amount of memory your arrays can consume will depend on the current memory model. In general, an array cannot consume more than 64Kb of space. The following program, *too_big.c*, for example, may fail to compile because the arrays consume too much memory:

```
void main(void)
 {
   char string[66000L];      // 66,000 bytes
   int values[33000L];       // 33,000 * 2 = 66,000 bytes
   float numbers[17000];     // 17,000 * 4 = 68,000 bytes
 }
```

Note: *Because Windows uses the virtual memory model to manage memory, it does not place limits on array size to the extent that a DOS C program does. For example, you can declare strings (character arrays) in Windows as large as INT_MAX (2,147,483,647) characters in length. If, however, you try to declare an oversized variable within a DOS window, you will cause a stack fault and Windows will close the window.*

USING THE HUGE MEMORY MODEL FOR BIG ARRAYS 466

If the amount of memory an array consumes exceeds 64Kb, you can direct many DOS-based compilers to use the *huge memory model* by treating the array as a pointer and including the word *huge* within the declaration, as shown here:

```
float huge values[17000];
```

The following program, *huge_flt.c*, creates a huge floating-point array:

```
#include <stdio.h>
#include <malloc.h>

void main (void)
  {
    int i;
    float huge *values;

    if ((values = (float huge *) halloc (17000, sizeof(float))) == NULL)
      printf ("Error allocating huge array\n");
    else
      {
        printf("Filling the array\n");
        for (i = 0; i < 17000; i++)
          values[i] = i * 1.0;
        for (i = 0; i < 17000; i++)
          printf ("%8.1f ", values[i]);
        hfree(values);
      }
  }
```

Note: *Because Windows uses the virtual memory model to manage memory, it does not place limits on array size to the extent that a DOS C program does. For example, you can declare an **unsigned char** array in Windows as large as INT_MAX (2,147,483,647) without using the **huge** keyword. If, however, you try to declare an oversized variable within a DOS window without the **huge** keyword, you will cause a stack fault and Windows will close the window.*

THE TRADEOFF BETWEEN ARRAYS AND DYNAMIC MEMORY 467

As you become more comfortable with C and how to use pointers within C, you may start to use arrays less often and instead allocate memory dynamically as you need it. There are several tradeoffs you must consider as you determine whether to use dynamic memory or an array. To begin, many users find arrays simpler to understand and use. As a result, your program itself might be easier for other programmers to follow. Second, because the compiler allocates space for arrays, your programs do not experience the run-time overhead associated with dynamic memory allocation. As a result, an array-based program might execute slightly faster.

As you have learned, however, when you declare an array, you must specify the array size. If you do not know the size you will need, you might have a tendency to allocate a larger array than necessary. As a result, you might waste memory. On the other hand, if the array size is too small, you must edit your program, change the array sizes, and recompile your program.

When you declare an array within your programs, keep in mind that you can perform identical processing by allocating memory dynamically. As you will learn in the Pointer section of this book, you can reference dynamically allocated memory using array indexes and eliminate the pointer confusion that often frustrates new C programmers. Because most operating systems let programs allocate memory very quickly, you might prefer the flexibility and improved memory management opportunities that dynamic memory allocation provides over arrays, despite the slight system overhead it incurs.

468 UNDERSTANDING MULTIDIMENSIONAL ARRAYS

As you have learned, an array is a variable that can store multiple values of the same type. In all the examples presented so far, the arrays have consisted of a single row of data. However, C also supports two-, three-, and multidimensional arrays. The best way to visualize a two-dimensional array is as a table with rows and columns. If an array contains three dimensions, visualize the array as several pages, each of which contains a two-dimensional table, as shown in Figure 468.

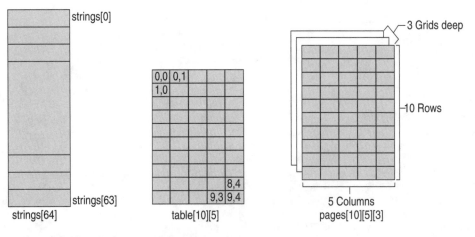

Figure 468 Logical model of multidimensional arrays.

The following array declarations create the arrays shown in Figure 468:

```
char strings[64];
int table[10][5];
float pages[10][5][3];
```

469 UNDERSTANDING ROWS AND COLUMNS

As you have learned, C supports multidimensional arrays that are similar to tables of values. When you work with a two-dimensional array, think of the array as a table of rows and columns. The table's rows go from left to right while the columns go up and down the page, as shown in Figure 469.

Row 0

Row 1

Row 2

Column 0   Column 1   Column 2

Figure 469 *Rows and columns in a two-dimensional array.*

When you declare a two-dimensional array, the first value you specify states the number of rows and the second value the number of columns:

```
int table [2][3];
```

ACCESSING ELEMENTS IN A TWO-DIMENSIONAL ARRAY   470

As you have learned, you can best visualize a two-dimensional array as a table containing rows and columns. To reference a specific array element, you must specify the corresponding row and column position. Figure 470 illustrates statements that access specific elements within the array *table*.

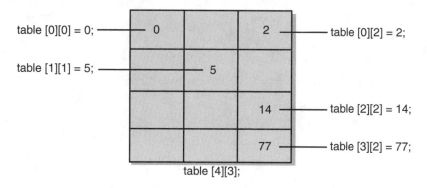

table [0][0] = 0;   0   2   table [0][2] = 2;

table [1][1] = 5;   5

14   table [2][2] = 14;

77   table [3][2] = 77;

table [4][3];

Figure 470 *To access elements in a two-dimensional array, you must specify the element's row and column position..*

As you can see, when you access a two-dimensional array, the row and column offsets begin at 0.

INITIALIZING ELEMENTS IN A TWO-DIMENSIONAL ARRAY   471

In Tip 457 you learned that, to initialize array elements, you can place the element values within left and right braces after the array declaration. The following statement uses the same technique to initialize a two-dimensional array. However, in this case, the statement specifies the values for each array row within their own braces:

```
int table[2][3] = {{1, 2, 3},
                   {4, 5, 6}};
```

The C compiler will initialize the array elements as shown in Figure 471.

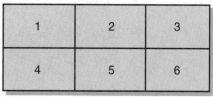

| 1 | 2 | 3 |
| 4 | 5 | 6 |

table [2][3];

Figure 471 *Initializing the elements of a two-dimensional array.*

In a similar manner, the following statement initializes the elements of a larger array:

```
int sales[4][5] {{1, 2, 3, 4, 5},
                 {6, 7, 8, 9, 10},
                 {11, 12, 13, 14, 15},
                 {16, 17, 18, 19, 20}};
```

472 DETERMINING A MULTIDIMENSIONAL ARRAY'S MEMORY CONSUMPTION

In Tip 456 you learned that your programs can determine the amount of memory an array consumes by multiplying the number of elements in the array by the number of bytes required to represent the array's type (such as 2 for *int*, 4 for *float*, and so on). To determine the memory a multidimensional array consumes, you can perform the same calculation. To determine the number of elements in a multidimensional array, simply multiply the number of rows by the number of columns. The following expressions illustrate the memory amount different array declarations consume:

```
int a[5][10];         // 2 * 5 * 10 == 100 bytes
float b[5][8];        // 4 * 5 * 8 == 160 bytes
int c[3][4][5];       // 2 * 3 * 4 * 5 = 120 bytes
```

The following program, *md_size.c*, uses the *sizeof* operator to determine the number of bytes different array declarations consume:

```c
#include <stdio.h>

void main(void)
 {
    int box[3][3];
    float year_sales[52][5];
    char pages[40][60][20];

    printf("Bytes to hold int box[3][3] %d bytes\n", sizeof(box));
    printf("Bytes to hold float year_sales[52][5] %d bytes\n"
           sizeof(year_sales));
    printf("Bytes to hold char pages[40][60][20] %ld bytes\n", sizeof(pages));
 }
```

When you compile and execute the *md_size.c* program, your screen will display the following:

```
Bytes to hold int box[3][3] 18 bytes
Bytes to hold float year_sales[52][5] 1040 bytes
Bytes to hold char pages[40][60][20] 48000 bytes
C:\>
```

473 LOOPING THROUGH A TWO-DIMENSIONAL ARRAY

In Tip 458 you learned how to use a variable to access elements in an array. When your programs work with two-dimensional arrays, you will normally use two variables to access array elements. The following program, *show_2d.c*, uses the variables *row* and *column* to display the values contained within the array *table*:

```c
#include <stdio.h>

void main(void)
 {
    int row, column;
    float table[3][5] = {{1.0, 2.0, 3.0, 4.0, 5.0},
                         {6.0, 7.0, 8.0, 9.0, 10.0},
                         {11.0, 12.0, 13.0, 14.0, 15.0}};

    for (row = 0; row < 3; row++)
      for (column = 0; column < 5; column++)
        printf("table[%d][%d] = %f\n", row, column, table[row][column]);
 }
```

By nesting the *for* loops as shown, the program will display the elements contained in the array's first row (1.0 through 5.0). Next, the program will move to the second row and then the third row, displaying each element within each row in turn.

Traversing a Three-Dimensional Array C474

In Tip 473 you learned how to traverse a two-dimensional array using two variables named *row* and *column*. The following program, *show_3d.c*, uses the variables *row*, *column*, and *table* to traverse a three-dimensional array:

```c
#include <stdio.h>

void main(void)
 {
   int row, column, table;
   float values[2][3][5] = {
                             {{1.0, 2.0, 3.0, 4.0, 5.0},
                              {6.0, 7.0, 8.0, 9.0, 10.0},
                              {11.0, 12.0, 13.0, 14.0, 15.0}},

                             {{16.0, 17.0, 18.0, 19.0, 20.0},
                              {21.0, 22.0, 23.0, 24.0, 25.0},
                              {26.0, 27.0, 28.0, 29.0, 30.0}}
                            };

   for (row = 0; row < 2; row++)
     for (column = 0; column < 3; column++)
       for (table = 0; table < 5; table++)
         printf("values[%d][%d][%d] = %f\n", row, column, table,
                 values[row][column][table]);
 }
```

Initializing Multidimensional Arrays C475

In Tip 474 you learned how to display the contents of a three-dimensional array using three variables: *row, column*, and *table*. The *show_3d.c* program, presented in Tip 474, initialized the three-dimensional array values, as shown here:

```c
   float values[2][3][5] = {
                             {{1.0, 2.0, 3.0, 4.0, 5.0},
                              {6.0, 7.0, 8.0, 9.0, 10.0},
                              {11.0, 12.0, 13.0, 14.0, 15.0}},

                             {{16.0, 17.0, 18.0, 19.0, 20.0},
                              {21.0, 22.0, 23.0, 24.0, 25.0},
                              {26.0, 27.0, 28.0, 29.0, 30.0}}
                            };
```

At first glance, initializing a multidimensional array can seem confusing. To better understand how to initialize such arrays, this Tip presents several sample initializations. As you examine the initializations, perform the initializations from right to left:

```c
int a[1][2][3] =    {
                     { {1, 2, 3}, {4, 5, 6} }
                    };  // Array braces
int b[2][3][4] =    {
                     { {1, 2, 3, 4}, {5, 6, 7, 8}, {9, 10, 11, 12} },
                     { {13, 14, 15, 16}, {17, 18, 19, 20}, {21, 22, 23, 24} }
                    };  // Array braces
int c[3][2][4] =    {
                     { {1, 2, 3, 4}, {5, 6, 7, 8} },
                     { {9, 10, 11, 12}, {13, 14, 15, 16}},
                     { {17, 18, 19, 20}, {21, 22, 23, 24}}
                    };  // Array braces
int d[1][2][3][4] = {
                     {{{1, 2, 3, 4}, {5, 6, 7, 8}, {9, 10, 11, 12}},
                      {{13, 14, 15, 16}, {17, 18, 19, 20}, {21, 22, 23, 24}}}
                    }; // Array braces
```

Each array initialization gets a set of outer braces. Within the outer braces, you then define the different array elements within additional braces.

476 PASSING A TWO-DIMENSIONAL ARRAY TO A FUNCTION

As your programs work with multidimensional arrays, there will be times when you must write functions that work with the arrays. In Tip 461, you learned that when you pass arrays to a function, you do not need to specify the number of array elements. When you work with two-dimensional arrays, you do not need to specify the number of rows in the array, but you must specify the number of columns. The following program, *funct_2d.c*, uses the function *show_2d_array* to display the contents of several two-dimensional arrays:

```c
#include <stdio.h>

void show_2d_array(int array[][10], int rows)
  {
    int i, j;

    for (i = 0; i < rows; i++)
      for (j = 0; j < 10; j++)
        printf("array[%d][%d] = %d\n", i, j, array[i][j]);
  }

void main(void)
  {
    int a[1][10] = {{1, 2, 3, 4, 5, 6, 7, 8, 9, 10}};
    int b[2][10] = {{1, 2, 3, 4, 5, 6, 7, 8, 9, 10},
                    {11, 12, 13, 14, 15, 16, 17, 18, 19, 20}};
    int c[3][10] = {{1, 2, 3, 4, 5, 6, 7, 8, 9, 10},
                    {11, 12, 13, 14, 15, 16, 17, 18, 19, 20},
                    {21, 22, 23, 24, 25, 26, 27, 28, 29, 30}};

    show_2d_array(a, 1);
    show_2d_array(b, 2);
    show_2d_array(c, 3);
  }
```

477 TREATING MULTIDIMENSIONAL ARRAYS AS ONE DIMENSIONAL

In Tip 476 you learned that when you pass a two-dimensional array to a function and you want to access the array's row and column positions, you must specify the number of columns, as shown here:

```c
void show_2d_array(int array[][10], int rows)
```

If you want to work with the elements of a multidimensional array, but you do not need to access the elements in their row or column positions, your functions can treat the multidimensional array as if it were one-dimensional. The following program, *sum_2d.c*, returns the sum of the values in a two-dimensional array:

```c
#include <stdio.h>

long sum_array(int array[], int elements)
  {
    long sum = 0;
    int i;

    for (i = 0; i < elements; i++)
      sum += array[i];
    return(sum);
  }

void main(void)
  {
    int a[10] = {1, 2, 3, 4, 5, 6, 7, 8, 9, 10};
    int b[2][10] = {{1, 2, 3, 4, 5, 6, 7, 8, 9, 10},
                    {11, 12, 13, 14, 15, 16, 17, 18, 19, 20}};
    int c[3][10] = {{1, 2, 3, 4, 5, 6, 7, 8, 9, 10},
                    {11, 12, 13, 14, 15, 16, 17, 18, 19, 20},
                    {21, 22, 23, 24, 25, 26, 27, 28, 29, 30}};
```

```
    printf("Sum of first array elements %d\n", sum_array(a, 10));
    printf("Sum of second array elements %d\n", sum_array(b, 20));
    printf("Sum of third array elements %d\n", sum_array(c, 30));
}
```

As you can see, the function *sum_array* supports one-, two-, or multidimensional arrays. To understand how *sum_array* works, you must first understand how C stores multidimensional arrays in memory. Tip 478 discusses how C stores multidimensional arrays in detail.

UNDERSTANDING HOW C STORES MULTIDIMENSIONAL ARRAYS 478

In Tip 454 you learned that when you declare an array, such as *int scores[100]*, C allocates enough memory to hold each array element. When you allocate a multidimensional array, the same is true. Although multidimensional arrays conceptually consist of rows, columns, and pages, to the compiler a multidimensional array is one long byte range. For example, assume that your program declares the following array:

```
int   table[3][5];
```

Figure 478 illustrates the array's conceptual appearance and actual memory use.

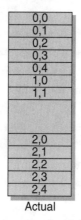

Figure 478 Mapping a multidimensional array to memory.

In Tip 477 you created a function that treated a multidimensional array as one-dimensional to add the values the array contained. Because the C compiler actually maps the multidimensional array to a one-dimensional memory range, treating the array as one-dimensional is valid.

UNDERSTANDING ROW-MAJOR VERSUS COLUMN-MAJOR ORDER 479

In Tip 478 you learned that the C compiler maps multidimensional arrays to one-dimensional memory. When the compiler maps a multidimensional array to memory, the compiler has two options. As shown in Figure 479, the compiler can place the array's row elements in memory before the column values, or the compiler can place the column elements first.

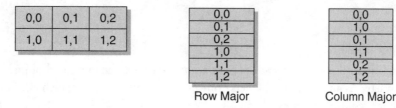

Figure 479 Mapping array elements to memory.

When the compiler places the array's row elements in memory before the column elements, the compiler is performing *row-major ordering*. Likewise, when the compiler places the column elements first, the compiler performs *column-major ordering*. C compilers store multidimensional arrays in row-major order.

480 ARRAYS OF STRUCTURES OF ARRAYS

Arrays and structures let you group related information. As you have learned, C lets you create arrays of structures or use arrays as structure members. In general, C does not place a limit on the depth to which your programs can go with respect to nested data structures. For example, the following declaration creates an array of 100 employee structures. Within each structure is an array of *Date* structures that correspond to the employee's hire date, first review, and last review:

```
struct Employee
  {
    char name[64];
    int age;
    char ssan[11];    // Social security number
    int pay_grade;
    float salary;
    unsigned employee_number;
    struct Date
      {
        int month;
        int day;
        int year;
      } emp_dates[3];
} staff[100];
```

To access members and array elements, you simply work from left to right, starting from the outside and working inward. For example, the following statements assign an employee's hire date:

```
staff[10].emp_dates[0].month = 7;
staff[10].emp_dates[0].day = 7;
staff[10].emp_dates[0].year = 7;
```

Although nesting structures and arrays in this way can be very convenient, keep in mind that the deeper your programs nest such data structures, the more difficult the structure will become for other programmers to understand.

481 UNDERSTANDING UNIONS

As you have learned, structures let your programs store related information. Depending on your program's purpose, the may be time when the information you store in a structure will be only one of two values. For example, assume that your program tracks two special date values for each employee. For current employees, the program tracks the number of days the employee has worked. For an employee who no longer works for the company, the program tracks the employee's last employment date. One way to track such information is to use a structure, as shown here:

```
struct EmpDates
  {
    int days_worked;
    struct LastDate
      {
        int month;
        int day;
        int year;
      } last_day;
};
```

Because the program will either use the *days_worked* or *last_day* members, the memory holding the unused value for each employee goes to waste. As an alternative, C lets your programs use a *union*, which allocates only the memory the union's largest member requires, as shown here:

```
union EmpDates
  {
    int days_worked;
```

```
   struct LastDate
    {
      int month;
      int day;
      int year;
    } last_day;
  };
```

To access the union members, you use the *dot* operator just as you would with a structure. Unlike the structure, however, the union can only store one member's value. Figure 481 illustrates how C allocates memory for the structure and member.

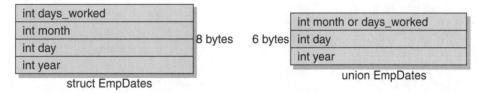

Figure 481 *Allocating memory for a similar structure and union.*

As you will learn, using unions not only saves memory, but also provides your programs with the ability to interpret memory values differently.

SAVING MEMORY WITH UNIONS C482

In Tip 481 you learned that C lets you store information within a *union*. When you use a union, C allocates the amount of memory required to hold the union's largest member. The following program, *unionsiz.c*, uses the *sizeof* operator to display the amount of memory different unions consume:

```
#include <stdio.h>

void main(void)
 {
   union EmployeeDates
    {
      int days_worked;
      struct Date
       {
         int month;
         int day;
         int year;
       } last_day;
    } emp_info;

   union Numbers
    {
      int a;
      float b;
      long c;
      double d;   // Largest--requires 8 bytes
    } value;

   printf("Size of EmployeeDates %d bytes\n", sizeof(emp_info));
   printf("Size of Numbers %d bytes\n", sizeof(value));
 }
```

When you compile and execute the *unionsiz.c* program, your screen will display the following output:

```
Size of EmployeeDates 6 bytes
Size of Numbers 8 bytes
C:\>
```

483 USING REGS—A CLASSIC UNION

As you have learned, unions let your programs reduce their memory requirements and view information in different ways. In the DOS & BIOS section of this book, you will learn that to access the DOS and BIOS services, your programs usually assign parameters (at the assembly language level) to specific PC registers. To make the DOS and BIOS services available to your C programs, most C compilers provide access through run-time library routines that use a union of type *REGS*:

```
struct WORDREGS
  {
    unsigned int ax, bx, cx, dx, si, di, cflag, flags;
  };
struct BYTEREGS
  {
    unsigned char al, ah, bl, ah, cl, ch, dl, dh;
  };
union REGS
  {
    struct WORDREGS x;
    struct BYTEREGS h;
  };
```

When your programs access one of the PC's general purpose registers (AX, BX, CX, and DX), the PC lets you refer to the register in a 16-bit (word) format. Alternatively, you can refer to the register's high and low bytes (AL, AH, BL, BH, CL, CH, DL, and DH). Because both methods refer to the same register, you have two ways of accessing the same storage location. Using a union, your programs have two ways to access the general purpose registers. Figure 483 illustrates how C stores variables of the *REGS* union in memory.

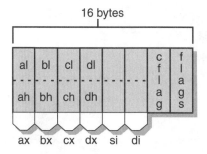

Figure 483 *How C stores variables of the union REGS.*

484 PUTTING THE REGS UNION TO USE

In Tip 483 you learned that one of the most frequently used unions in DOS-based programs is the *REGS* union. The following program, *get_verx.c*, uses the *REGS* union to display the current DOS version, accessing the general purpose registers in their word form:

```
#include <stdio.h>
#include <dos.h>

void main(void)
  {
    union REGS inregs, outregs;

    inregs.x.ax = 0x3000;
    intdos(&inregs, &outregs);
    printf("Current version %d.%d\n", outregs.x.ax & 0xFF, outregs.x.ax >> 8);
  }
```

The following program, *get_verh.c*, uses the union's byte registers to display the current DOS version:

```
#include <stdio.h>
#include <dos.h>

void main(void)
  {
    union REGS inregs, outregs;

    inregs.h.ah = 0x30;
    inregs.h.al = 0;
    intdos(&inregs, &outregs);
    printf("Current version %d.%d\n", outregs.h.al, outregs.h.ah);
  }
```

UNDERSTANDING BIT-FIELD STRUCTURES 485

Many functions in this book reduce the number of variables (and hence the amount of allocated memory) your programs must use by returning values whose bits have specific meanings. When a value's bits have specific meanings, your programs can use C's bitwise operators to extract the values (the specific bits). Assume, for example, that your program must track 100,000 dates. You can create a structure of type *Date* to track the dates, as shown here:

```
struct Date
  {
    int month; // 1 through 12
    int day;   // 1 through 31
    int year;  // last two digits
  };
```

As an alternative, your programs can use specific bits within an *unsigned int* value to hold the date fields, as shown in Figure 485.

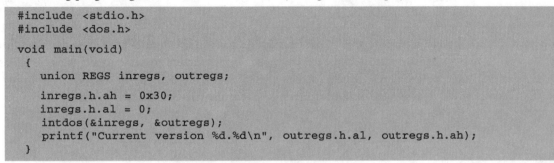

Figure 485 *Using bits to represent a date.*

Then, each time your program must assign a date, it can perform the correct bitwise operations, as shown here:

```
unsigned date;

date = month;
date = date | (day << 4);
date = date | (year << 9);

printf("Month %d Day %d Year %d\n", date & 0xF, (date >> 4) & 0x1F, (date >> 9));
```

However, to make your programs easier to understand, C lets you create a *bit-field structure*. When you declare a bit-field structure, you define a structure that specifies the meaning of the corresponding bits:

```
struct Date
  {
    unsigned month:4;
    unsigned day:5;
    unsigned year:7;
  } date;
```

Your programs will then reference the bit-fields individually, as shown here:

```
date.month = 12;
date.day = 31;
date.year = 94;

printf("Month %d Day %d Year %d\n", date.month, date.day, date.year);
```

Note: *When you declare a bit-field structure, the structure's members must each be **unsigned int** values.*

486 VISUALIZING A BIT-FIELD STRUCTURE

In Tip 485 you learned that C lets you represent bits within a value using a bit-field structure. When you declare a bit-field structure, C allocates enough bytes of memory to hold the structure's bits. If the structure does not use all the bits in the last byte, most C compilers will initialize the bits to 0. To help you better visualize how C stores a bit-field structure, Figure 486 illustrates how the C compiler will represent the bit-field structure, *Date*, as shown in the following code:

```
struct Date
  {
    unsigned month:4;
    unsigned day:5;
    unsigned year:7;
  } date;
```

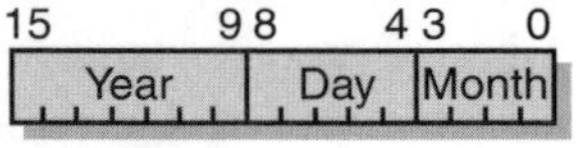

Figure 486 How C represents the Date bit-field structure.

487 UNDERSTANDING A BITWISE STRUCTURE'S RANGE OF VALUES

In Tip 486 you learned that C lets you represent bits within a value using a bit-field structure. When you create a bit-field structure, you must allocate enough bits to hold each member's desired value. To help you determine the number of bits you require, Table 487 specifies the range of values that a given number of bits can represent.

Size of Field	Range of Values
1	0–1
2	0–3
3	0–7
4	0–15
5	0–31
6	0–63
7	0–127
8	0–255
9	0–511
10	0–1023
11	0–2047
12	0–4095
13	0–8191
14	0–16383
15	0–32767
16	0–65535

Table 487 The range of values your programs can represent with a given number of bits.

488 SEARCHING AN ARRAY FOR A SPECIFIC VALUE

As you have learned, arrays let you store related values of the same type. At times, you may want to search an array for a specific value. There are two common ways to search an array: a *sequential search* and a *binary search*. To perform a sequential search, your program starts at the array's first element and searches one element at a time until the program finds the desired value or the until the program reaches the last element in the array. For example, the following *while* loop illustrates how your programs might search an array for the value 1,500:

```
found = 0;
i = 0;

while ((i < ARRAY_ELEMENTS) && (! found))
  if (array[i] == 1500)
    found = true;
  else
    i++;

if (i < ARRAY_ELEMENTS)
  printf("Value found at element %d\n", i);
else
  printf("Value not found\n");
```

If you have previously sorted the values in an array from lowest to highest, your programs can perform a binary search, which you will learn more about in Tip 489.

Understanding a Binary Search 489

As you have learned, one way of locating a value within an array is to search through every array element. Although such a sequential search is acceptable when your array size is small, looping through a large array can be time consuming. If your program has already sorted the values in the array from lowest to highest, it can use a *binary search* to locate the value. This type of search is called a binary search because with each operation the search divides the number of values it must examine by two.

The best way to conceptualize the binary search is to think of how you look up a word in the dictionary. Assume you want to find the word "Dalmatian." To begin, you may open the dictionary to the middle and examine the words on the page. Assuming that you open to the letter M, you know that "Dalmatian" appears before the current page, so you have just eliminated more than half the words in the dictionary. If you turn to the middle of the remaining pages, you will very likely find words that begin with the letter F. Again, you can discard half the possible choices, and continue your search in the pages that precede the current page. This time when you turn to the middle page, you will probably turn to the letter C. The word "Dalmatian" appears somewhere in the pages between C and F. When you select the middle page, you will likely be in the D words. By repeatedly discarding pages and selecting the middle page, you can quickly close in on the page containing the word "Dalmatian."

Note: *To perform a binary search, your program must sort the values in the array either from lowest to highest or from highest to lowest before you try the search.*

Using a Binary Search 490

As you learned in Tip 489, a binary search provides a quick way to search a sorted array for a specific value. The following program, *binary.c*, uses a binary search to search for several values in the array *count*, which contains the values 1 to 100. To help you better understand the processing the binary search performs, the function *binary_search* will print out messages that describe its processing:

```
#include <stdio.h>

int binary_search(int array[], int value, int size)
  {
    int found = 0;
    int high = size, low = 0, mid;

    mid = (high + low) / 2;
    printf("\n\nLooking for %d\n", value);
    while ((! found) && (high >= low))
      {
        printf("Low %d Mid %d High %d\n", low, mid, high);
        if (value == array[mid])
          found = 1;
        else if (value < array[mid])
          high = mid - 1;
```

```
          else
             low = mid + 1;
          mid = (high + low) / 2;
       }
    return((found) ? mid: -1);
  }

void main(void)
  {
     int array[100], i;

     for (i = 0; i < 100; i++)
       array[i] = i;
     printf("Result of search %d\n", binary_search(array, 33, 100));
     printf("Result of search %d\n", binary_search(array, 75, 100));
     printf("Result of search %d\n", binary_search(array, 1, 100));
     printf("Result of search %d\n", binary_search(array, 1001, 100));
  }
```

Compile and execute the *binary.c* program and observe the number of operations the search must perform to find each value. The program uses the variables *high*, *mid*, and *low* to keep track of the range of values it is currently searching.

491 SORTING AN ARRAY

As you have learned, arrays let you store related values of the same type. As your programs work with arrays, there will be times when your programs must sort an array's values, either from lowest to highest (ascending order) or from highest to lowest (descending order). Your programs can use several different sorting algorithms to sort arrays, including the *bubble sort*, the *selection sort*, the *Shell sort*, and the *quick sort*. Several Tips that follow discuss each of these sorting methods.

492 UNDERSTANDING THE BUBBLE SORT

The *bubble sort* algorithm is a simple array-sorting technique that is usually the first method most programmers learn. Because of its simplicity, the bubble sort is not very efficient and will consume more processor time than other sorting techniques. However, if you are sorting small arrays with 30 or fewer elements, using the bubble sort is fine. Assuming that you sort values from lowest to highest, the bubble sort loops through the values in an array, comparing and moving the largest array value to the top of the array (like a bubble in water rises to the surface). Figure 492 illustrates four iterations of a bubble sort.

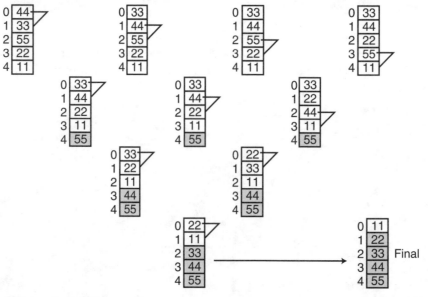

Figure 492 Four iterations of a bubble sort.

The first iteration moves the array's largest value to the top of the array. The second iteration moves the array's second largest value to the second-to-the-top position. The third iteration moves the third-largest value, and so on.

PUTTING A BUBBLE SORT TO USE 493

Tip 492 briefly illustrated how the bubble sort functions. The following program, *bubble.c*, uses the bubble sort to sort an array containing 30 random values:

```c
#include <stdio.h>
#include <stdlib.h>
void bubble_sort(int array[], int size)
 {
   int temp, i, j;

   for (i = 0; i < size; i++)
    for (j = 0; j < size; j++)
      if (array[i] < array[j])
        {
          temp = array[i];
          array[i] = array[j];
          array[j] = temp;
        }
 }
void main(void)
 {
   int values[30], i;

   for (i = 0; i < 30; i++)
     values[i] = rand() % 100;
   bubble_sort(values, 30);
   for (i = 0; i < 30; i++)
     printf("%d ", values[i]);
 }
```

*Note: The **bubble_sort** function sorts values from lowest to highest. To reverse the sort order, simply change the comparison to if (array[i] > array[j]).*

UNDERSTANDING THE SELECTION SORT 494

The *selection sort* is a simple sorting algorithm similar to the bubble sort Tip 492 presented. Like the bubble sort, your programs should only use the selection sort to sort small arrays (30 elements or fewer). The selection sort begins by selecting an array element (such as the first element). The sort then searches the entire array until it finds the minimum value. The sort places the minimum value in the element, selects the second element, and searches for the second smallest element. Figure 494 illustrates two iterations of the selection sort on an array of values.

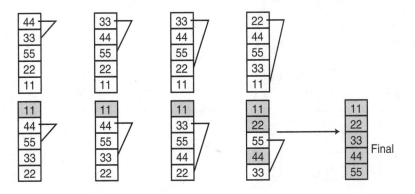

Figure 494 Sorting values with the selection sort.

495 PUTTING A SELECTION SORT TO USE

Tip 494 briefly illustrated the selection sort's functioning. The following program, *select.c*, uses the selection sort to sort an array containing 30 random values:

```c
#include <stdio.h>
#include <stdlib.h>

void selection_sort(int array[], int size)
 {
   int temp, current, j;

   for (current = 0; current < size; current++)
    for (j = current + 1; j < size; j++)
      if (array[current] > array[j])
        {
           temp = array[current];
           array[current] = array[j];
           array[j] = temp;
        }
 }

void main(void)
 {
   int values[30], i;

   for (i = 0; i < 30; i++)
     values[i] = rand() % 100;
   selection_sort(values, 30);
   for (i = 0; i < 30; i++)
     printf("%d ", values[i]);
 }
```

Note: The **selection_sort** function sorts values from lowest to highest. To reverse the sort order, simply change the comparison to *if (array[current] < array[j])*.

496 UNDERSTANDING THE SHELL SORT

The *Shell sort* is named after its creator, Donald Shell. The Shell sort technique compares array elements separated by a specific distance (known as a *gap*) until the elements it compares with the current gap are in order. The Shell sort then divides the gap by two, and the process continues. When the gap is finally one and no changes occur, the Shell sort has completed its processing. Figure 496 illustrates how the Shell sort might sort an array.

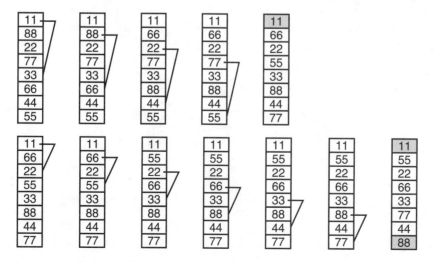

Figure 496 *Sorting an array with the Shell sort. (continued on following page)*

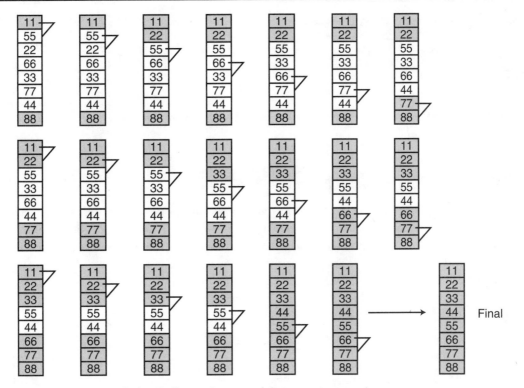

Figure 496 *Sorting an array with the Shell sort. (continued from previous page)*

PUTTING A SHELL SORT TO USE 497

Tip 496 briefly illustrated the Shell sort's functioning. The following program, *shell.c*, uses the Shell sort to sort an array containing 50 random values:

```c
#include <stdio.h>
#include <stdlib.h>

void shell_sort(int array[], int size)
  {
    int temp, gap, i, exchange_occurred;

    gap = size / 2;
    do
      {
        do
          {
            exchange_occurred = 0;
            for (i = 0; i < size - gap; i++)
              if (array[i] > array[i + gap])
                {
                  temp = array[i];
                  array[i] = array[i + gap];
                  array[i + gap] = temp;
                  exchange_occurred = 1;
                }
          }
        while (exchange_occurred);
      }
    while (gap = gap / 2);
  }

void main(void)
  {
    int values[50], i;
```

```
    for (i = 0; i < 50; i++)
      values[i] = rand() % 100;
    shell_sort(values, 50);
    for (i = 0; i < 50; i++)
      printf("%d ", values[i]);
}
```

Note: *The shell_sort function sorts values from lowest to highest. To reverse the sort order, simply change the comparison to if (array[i] < array[i + gap]).*

498 UNDERSTANDING THE QUICK SORT

As the number of elements in your array increases, the *quick sort* becomes one of the fastest sorting techniques your programs can use. The quick sort considers your array as a list of values. When the sort begins, it selects the list's middle value as the *list separator*. The sort then divides the list into two lists, one with values that are less than the list separator and a second list whose values are greater than or equal to the list separator. The sort then recursively invokes itself with both lists. Each time the sort invokes itself, it further divides the elements into smaller lists. Figure 498 illustrates how the quick sort might sort an array of 10 values.

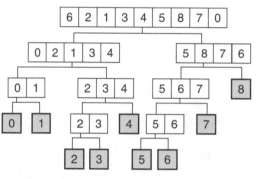

Figure 498 Sorting values with the quick sort.

499 PUTTING A QUICK SORT TO USE

Tip 498 briefly illustrated how the quick sort functions. The following program, *quick.c*, uses the quick sort to sort an array containing 100 random values:

```
#include <stdio.h>
#include <stdlib.h>

void quick_sort(int array[], int first, int last)
 {
   int temp, low, high, list_separator;

   low = first;
   high = last;
   list_separator = array[(first + last) / 2];
   do
    {
      while (array[low] < list_separator)
        low++;
      while (array[high] > list_separator)
        high--;
      if (low <= high)
       {
         temp = array[low];
         array[low++] = array[high];
         array[high--] = temp;
       }
    }
```

```
      while (low <= high);
   if (first < high)
      quick_sort(array, first, high);
   if (low < last)
      quick_sort(array, low, last);
}

void main(void)
{
   int values[100], i;

   for (i = 0; i < 100; i++)
      values[i] = rand() % 100;
   quick_sort(values, 0, 99);
   for (i = 0; i < 100; i++)
      printf("%d ", values[i]);
}
```

Note: The **quick_sort** function sorts values from lowest to highest. To reverse the sort order, change the comparisons in the two **while** statements, as shown here:

```
while (array[low] > list_separator)
   low++;

while (array[high] < list_separator)
   high++;
```

PROBLEMS WITH PREVIOUS SORTING SOLUTIONS  500

Several previous Tips have shown different sorting techniques your programs can use to sort arrays. However, each of the Tips presented worked with arrays of type *int*. If your programs need to sort a different array type, you must create new functions. For example, to sort an array of type *float*, your programs must change the *quick_sort* function's header and variable declarations, as shown here:

```
void quick_sort(float array[], int first, int last)
{
   float temp, list_separator;
   int low, high;
```

If you want to sort an array of *long* values later, you must create a different function. As you will learn, however, your programs can use the C run-time library *qsort* function to sort different array types. The *qsort* function uses memory indirection to sort values of all types.

SORTING AN ARRAY OF CHARACTER STRINGS 501

As you have learned, C lets you create an array of character strings, as shown here:

```
char *days[] = {"Monday", "Tuesday", "Wednesday" };
```

Just as there may be times when your programs must sort arrays of other types, the same is true for sorting character-string arrays. The following program, *str_sort.c*, uses a bubble sort to sort an array of character strings:

```
#include <stdio.h>
#include <stdlib.h>
#include <string.h>

void bubble_sort(char *array[], int size)
{
   char *temp;
   int i, j;

   for (i = 0; i < size; i++)
    for (j = 0; j < size; j++)
      if (strcmp(array[i], array[j]) < 0)
        {
```

```
          temp = array[i];
          array[i] = array[j];
          array[j] = temp;
        }
  }
}

void main(void)
  {
    char *values[] = {"AAA", "CCC", "BBB", "EEE", "DDD"};
    int i;

    bubble_sort(values, 5);
    for (i = 0; i < 5; i++)
      printf("%s ", values[i]);
  }
```

When the function sorts the array of character strings, the function does not change the string contents to rearrange the array; rather, it arranges the character string pointers so the character strings are in order.

502 SEARCHING AN ARRAY WITH LFIND

As you have learned, a sequential search operation searches the elements of an array in order until it finds a specific value. To help your programs search arrays of any type, the C run-time library provides the *lfind* function:

```
#include <stdlib.h>

void *lfind(const void *element, void *base, size_t *number_of_entries,
            size_t element_width, int (*compare)(const void *, const void *));
```

As you can see, the function makes tremendous use of pointers. The *element* parameter is a pointer to the desired value. The *base* parameter is a pointer to the start of the array. The *number_of_entries* parameter is a pointer to the number of elements in the array. The *element_width* parameter specifies the number of bytes required for each array element. Finally, the *compare* parameter is a pointer to a second function that compares two array elements. Unlike the functions previously shown, which returned an array index to the desired value, the *lfind* function returns a pointer to the desired value or the value 0 if *lfind* did not find the element. The following program, *lfind.c*, uses the *lfind* function to search for a value of type *int* and a value of type *float*:

```
#include <stdlib.h>
#include <stdio.h>

int compare_int(int *a, int *b)
  {
    return(*a - *b);
  }

int compare_float(float *a, float *b)
  {
    return((*a == *b) ? 0: 1);
  }

void main(void)
  {
    int int_values[] = {1, 3, 2, 4, 5};
    float float_values[] = {1.1, 3.3, 2.2, 4.4, 5.5};
    int *int_ptr, int_value = 2, elements = 5;
    float *float_ptr, float_value = 33.3;

    int_ptr = lfind(&int_value, int_values, &elements, sizeof(int),
                    (int (*) (const void *, const void *)) compare_int);
    if (*int_ptr)
      printf("Value %d found\n", int_value);
    else
      printf("Value %d not found\n", int_value);
    float_ptr = lfind(&float_value, float_values, &elements, sizeof(float),
                    (int (*) (const void *, const void *)) compare_float);
    if (*float_ptr)
      printf("Value %3.1f found\n", float_value);
```